50th Birthday Edition

Can this be School?

Fifty years of Democracy at ALPHA

Fifty years of alternative schooling

As a boy I attended a village school where the bairns chatted and were happy. I trace my love of freedom to my free life there.

A. S. Neill

Strange it would be, indeed, if intelligent and serious attention to what the child now needs and is capable of in the way of a rich, valuable, and expanded life should somehow conflict with the needs and possibilities of later, adult life.

John Dewey

ALPHA Alternative School was founded in 1972 in Toronto—a self-governing democratic school, run by parents, teachers and the children themselves. Some called it a "free school". It was part of a wave of educational exploration that arose in the 1960s, but two things make ALPHA stand out: it was established and funded by the Toronto School Board, and it has lasted fifty years. In Toronto's public school system, there are now over 40 alternatives—a rare situation that offers educational choice to families who can't pay private school fees. ALPHA, which has operated continuously since 1972, is the only elementary school that still tries to teach and self-govern democratically. Deb O'Rourke, drawing on personal experience and extensive research, presents ALPHA School as a case study of the challenges, obstacles and successes in sustaining different visions and methods in public systems. She argues for the democratizing influence and innovative possibilities of local vision and control in a diverse education system.

Can this be School?

Fifty years of democracy at ALPHA

Deb O'Rourke

Artword Press

Can this be School?
Fifty years of democracy at ALPHA

By Deb O'Rourke

First published in 2022 by
Artword Press
166 Prospect Street South, Hamilton Ontario.
Editor: Ronald Weihs

For information, contact Artword Press, 166 Prospect Street South, Hamilton Ontario, Canada, L8M 2Z4. Phone 905-543-8512
Email: rweihs@artword.net

Cover photo: Ron Austin
Author photo: Michael Barker

ISBN 978-0-9920096-6-3
9 780992 009663 >

To ALPHA, with Love

ALPHA Alternative School, a democratic community school that has existed for a half-century in a large public education system, could not have grown anywhere except in Toronto, Canada. For millennia, this beautiful forested location on the shore of Lake Ontario has been a place of hunting and gathering, fishing, agriculture, respite, spiritual and festive congregation, and of the creativity, cultural exchange and conflict that arise when diverse peoples are attracted to its bounty. It was to this refuge for original thinkers from all over that I was drawn in 1977. I thank the Anishinaabe, Wendat and Haudenosaunee people for sharing this land with all of the risk-takers, hostages and refugees from far away, and for giving desperate migrants, like my ancestors and myself, a chance for life. I commit to fulfill my obligations to share and care for this land under the Dish with One Spoon Treaty. I am especially grateful for the little corner of life and love that is ALPHA.

TABLE OF CONTENTS

Table of Contents

Table of Contents

ACKNOWLEDGEMENTS

In my lifelong struggle to live democratically and responsibly, ALPHA Alternative School has been my great challenge and my teacher. Above all, I thank those who started this school, and the successive waves of teachers, parents, students, (and a few administrators), who helped it to survive through the decades.

I thank all who previously documented democratic and free schools. Their books, brimming with stories, life, humor, and insight into the lives and needs of children, inspired this one. I quote at length the anonymous authors of Toronto's *The Free School Handbook* (circa 1972). This pioneering work, accomplished in their teens, is still a valuable resource. As Greta Thunberg demonstrates, the young are capable people.

I'm also deeply indebted to Murray and Beverly Shukyn's 1973 history of Toronto's first alternative school SEED, which documents foundational alternative school struggles. Through the York University library and the bookstore of the Alternative Education Resource Organization (AERO), I accessed rare books and publications from the free school movement, as well as accounts of still-surviving schools and contemporary education critiques. Many of the authors I found are quoted in these pages.

After a flurry in the 1970s, little was published about Canadian alternatives except for Esther Sokolov Fine's work on Downtown Alternative School (DAS). In 2012, ALPHA alumni Michael Barker and Ariel Fielding began to document ALPHA and other alternative schools in *Notes from the Field*, an online resource that can be seen at michaelbarker.ca. In 2017, Esther Fine and Malcolm Levin edited the collection *Alternative Schools and Student Engagement: Canadian Stories of Democracy within Bureaucracy*. In 2019, Sharon Berg, in consultation with Elder Pauline Shirt, released a history of Toronto's indigenous school, *The Name Unspoken: Wandering Spirit Survival School.*

I'm grateful to Artword Press for allowing me the opportunity to add ALPHA's story to what I hope is a growing literature about alternative education in Canada. Ronald Weihs, artistic director of Artword Theatre and publisher of Artword Press, brought to this project a playwright's knack and an understanding of a history whose earliest stages he witnessed in real time.

This book is no longer an academic thesis, but it started as one. I offer my deepest thanks to York University and my thesis committee consisting of professors Don Dippo, Penny Stewart and Susan Dion. Special blessings go to my thesis advisor, Professor Emeritus Harry Smaller, who not only co-founded several alternative schools, but also challenges the Hidden Curriculum through his writings, his international support work and his involvements in urban education. This book stretches its commentary far beyond the thesis these academics approved, but it abides by the ethical protocols that governed the research phase.

Also at York, the late Dr. Alison Griffith's discussions of Dorothy Smith's *Institutional Ethnography* helped me with my most difficult task—to understand bureaucracy. Ryan Slashinsky, fellow MEd and ALPHA teacher from 2003–2012, set the available school archives in order and provided technical support.

Early ALPHA parent Andre LeRoux entrusted me with a precious box of ALPHA's earliest records, which became the documentary foundation of this research. Former ALPHA parent Lisa Freeman supplied the records of the "Report Card Fight" that are quoted in Chapter 17.

This book includes a brief account of a struggle to solve a problem that had long been identified in many elementary alternative schools—their unintentional Whiteness. I deeply thank ALPHA's 2006 Admissions Committee—former parents Jody Nyasha Warner, Brenda Joy Lem and Nadya Burton—for the effort they made to revisit this difficult time and to share recollections and analysis that allowed their hard-won but successful innovation to be included in this history.

The story of ALPHA couldn't have been told without the recollections of fifteen former students, parents and teachers, who participated in oral history focus groups from three different time periods, ending at the turn of the century. Academic protocols protect the anonymity of research participants; consequently, I've given them some generic designations: "parent", "student" and "co-founder".

One research participant is named, with her consent. I agree with the parents and teachers who worked with Susan Garrard that she was the rock of the school during its first 25 years. It would be misleading to simply call her "a teacher." I name her as a pioneering democratic school educator, like the Albany Free School's Mary Leue and Helen Hughes of Vancouver's Windsor House.

Belle Auld, a writer friend who was with me in this movement in our teens, gave editorial feedback. Jerry Mintz, a pioneering school creator of the 1960s free school movement and founder of the Alternative Schools Resource Organization (AERO), read a draft and responded with suggestions and corrections.

My deepest thanks and love go to John Williams, my dear husband, whose personal library and memories of the political milieu that gave rise to Toronto's alternative schools were often helpful. He also financially supported the research and the book.

ABOUT THE AUTHOR

> *Let us acknowledge that the objective or disinterested researcher is always on the side that pays best.*
>
> Wendell Berry

I am not a disinterested researcher. Like the American teacher Kristan Morrison, I am a refugee from "the deep, underlying paradoxes"[1] of a system that I initially believed and excelled in.

I still remember the relaxed sociability with which I settled into my first morning at kindergarten, in 1958. It was to be the last time I would feel like that. A few hours later, I was shocked into complete docility. The technique was gentle and positive, and would have been admired for its effectiveness and civility in any school in the land.

There were no warnings or instructions as we settled into the bright room and played with plasticene. There was no admonishment that our friendly chatter as we created and fantasized was disruptive. But at the end of the morning, the teacher placed gold stars on the foreheads of children who had been quiet, the shy ones. The mothers who picked us up expressed their disappointment to those of us who emerged with bare foreheads. This was a gentle tactic for the time, but my spontaneity, trust and self-confidence instantly crashed and burned. Aware that I was constantly watched and judged, I could afterward barely speak in front of adults, and avoided children who might lure me into illicit behaviours—like friendly sociability.

Award-winning American teacher John Taylor Gatto claims that teachers don't teach subjects, they always "teach school"—with seven lessons that, whatever content they are purportedly trying to transmit to students during any particular era or fad, "constitute a national curriculum".[2]

In a single morning, my kindergarten teacher had transmitted lessons 4 to 7. Through "stars and red checks . . . prizes, honors, and disgraces" this gentle teacher taught me *emotional and intellectual dependency*, the surrender of my will "to the predestined chain of command" (Lessons 4 and 5). Most effective was Lesson 6, *provisional self-esteem*, through being "constantly evaluated and judged". This was enforced by Lesson 7, the awareness that *one can't hide* from the judgmental gaze.

I was a quick study. Timid and attentive, I quickly learned to read, and developed a taste for the quiet, bookish life that kept me out of trouble. I did well academically, and tried hard to face the rigors that education put me through: the hours of silence and boredom, lining up, marching, struggling to keep up with faster children, watching "naughty" students spanked with rulers and straps. In my own experience it wasn't the playground bullies who were most often strapped. It was small people, usually boys, whose itchy bodies couldn't stop moving, or who couldn't understand group instruction and were accused of being willfully inattentive and disruptive.

As I got older, my elders began to criticize me for not being social enough, for being too studious, for reading too much. I started to wonder what they wanted from me. When I first became aware of the youth counterculture that was forming as I entered my teens in 1966, I still accepted social control of youth as necessary for our betterment. But I was confused when adults who preached to me about freedom of thought, speech and action became upset about young men and women who grew their hair long and said what they thought. I began to wake up.

My first reaction to this betrayal of the "democracy" I had been recruited into was deep disorientation and depression. As my compliance went down, so did my marks. I lost my former peer group, the social conservatives on the honour role, but followed my interests into the school newspaper, where students only a year or two older showed me the ropes.

My eighteen-year-old editor sent me to look into a radical student organization called Educational Youth Enterprises

(EYE), an organization of students from various high schools who came together weekly. I stayed with the school newspaper until it was closed—in response to an article that I wrote about student rights with respect to physically abusive teachers. And I stuck with EYE. Thus, I fell out of the mainstream, and found myself, at sixteen, belonging to a creative, intelligent and caring youth counterculture.

Community organizers from a federal program, the Company of Young Canadians, had initially helped with EYE, but its savvy students formed a self-sustaining group of dozens of youths, aged 14 to 19, who met weekly in the Unitarian Church in Calgary, Alberta. They introduced me to the writings of John Holt, Paul Goodman and A. S. Neill. I cried during a film showing of *Summerhill*. My own mental state and verbal abilities were so far below the confidence of the mucky, articulate little kids who attended Neill's free school. I resolved that, if I ever had a child, I would send them to a free school.

I found among my peers the support and mentorship I had been missing in the education system. I couldn't escape the school situation that directly depressed and oppressed me, but in the communal self-governance I shared every week at EYE, I experienced freedom and responsibility. For the first time, I felt at home, and at ease with myself and others. *Summerhill*, A. S. Neill's book about the free school he founded, became my escape literature. Through the free school movement, I began to live a life of hope and agency.

Operating independently of any adult control, the teenagers of EYE were living proof of the veracity of the authors whose work we embraced. We ran a weekly dance and drop-in center, and, inspired by correspondence with the students of Project SEED in Toronto, organized a *free school* in the summer of 1969. The caretaker of the Unitarian church organized encounter group sessions where we learned about the circle format of communication, each person in turn speaking from the heart. Each of us had roles in EYE and roles we took on in our own schools. We pitched in on each other's projects, spending every

Saturday and much of the summer together. My primary roles were as a high school journalist and, at the drop-in center, breaking up fights and cleaning up at the end of the dance.

Our group empowered women as leaders, and supported boys in resisting the cult of masculinity. We knew that males in security roles would be seen by fighters as challengers. In those days, boys didn't hit girls (in public, anyway), so we used female security to de-escalate violent situations. On one of these occasions, as we herded out some fighters, one of them swung a knife. To dodge it, the target had to fling himself backwards down the stairs. My buddy and I locked arms to catch him, preventing his skull from hitting the concrete.

Based on our encounter group experience, my whole group, male and female, then spontaneously performed peer conflict resolution with the local young "biker" club. They were just rebellious teens, perhaps somewhat relieved we'd stopped them from damaging each other. We found common ground as we talked about having found a home within our respective peer groups, and reached an agreement that enabled them to enjoy our dances but kept their violence out. As we grew older, some of us rebuilt a half-demolished house and operated it as a home and "free school". Our final act as an organization was to run a youth candidate for mayor.

As I moved into adult life and traveled, I made friends with an Anishinaabe person who changed forever the way I look at my own culture. I feared, and was revolted by, many aspects of that culture, from the relentless enforcement of conformity to the nuclear and ecological threats. The revelation that Indigenous people knew of deeply different ways to be in the world strengthened my hope and faith in life.

After traveling through Canada and the USA, I went to art school and began that lifelong struggle to live a creative, ethical life. Serendipitously, when my child turned four in 1985, the school nearest to the garment factory where I worked happened to be ALPHA Alternative School. The influence of Summerhill was apparent in ALPHA during this period, so I always thought of it as a *free school.*

Summerhill freed its kids even from their parents, but ALPHA needed the help of parents to operate. For four years I chaired a seminar on science (my other passion) with 4 to 8 year-olds, in the format of a Dinosaur Club. Examining dinosaur skeletons, playing dinosaur games, and reading dinosaur books led to discussions of the structure of the earth and solar system, comparative anatomy and classification, ecology, evolution, time, the age and size of the universe, and God. (I stayed silent on that last subject!) When the kids moved on to other interests, I fell into supporting students with special needs. I also became more active in the political life of the school.

In 2004, as part of the volatile employment pattern that characterizes the life of an artist, I joined ALPHA's staff. Working as a lunchroom supervisor and as a volunteer coordinator, a community role that was created in the school's second year, I put myself through graduate school at York University. At York, I did the research at the heart of this book, earning a master's degree in education in 2010.

I never tried to earn a teaching qualification. For a person so interested in education, my difficult art career was almost the easy way out. I knew I couldn't "manage" a class of twenty to thirty students, or more. I've worked with students only in creative and non-oppressive ways, in partnership with consenting pupils and other educators.

During six years as a professional arts educator, I toured art projects based on nature to over twenty public schools. The artist/teacher partnership and classroom volunteers created manageable adult/child ratios. I sought out varied experiences—from crowded classrooms in the Toronto Catholic District School Board, to a small hospital-run school for emotionally disturbed children, where very small classes were staffed by a teacher and a therapist.

I've spent time in two rural schools, real community schools that are the same size as ALPHA. I made repeated visits as an

Ontario Arts Council artist/educator to Eagle River School (now closed) in Northern Ontario, and spent six weeks collaborating with a village school in Trinidad on a sculpture project, sponsored by the Canada Council.

In nearly all the schools I've worked in, I partnered with dedicated teachers who strove to maximize their pupils' enjoyment of learning. Some of these fine public schools made me wonder whether ALPHA was worth the immense effort needed to keep it alive. But after working in them for a week, I was usually depressed by what goes on in even the most collegial classes in the public system at large.

Tensions are incredible in a room of twenty to thirty-plus children who, though trying hard to please their well-meaning, talented teachers, cannot stop themselves from moving and dreaming, feeling and forgetting. In one beautiful public school, I engaged a lively boy to use his vast energy to fetch me tools and be my helper. I'd learned that if I didn't quickly find things for the most excited kids to do, they would often be sent to the office, losing their opportunity to work on my art project. This child was a great problem solver and had strong aesthetics. Building a landscape in which to display the animals the students had made, we worked well and efficiently together. When I pointed out his accomplishment to the teacher, she was happy for him.

"I'm so glad he had a chance to shine," beamed this creative, caring teacher. Then she whispered, "He's slow." Active kids like this boy grow up to use their strength, energy and talent to solve problems, and often to build places where people live. If he wanted to leave his beautiful town, he could excel in design, possibly even go into engineering. (Yes, strong math often shows up in these kids, later on). But first, he'd have to survive years of being labeled "slow". By good people. In authority.

As a kid, I remember hiding my head in my hands as tiny kids in my class—boys—were strapped and spanked. Today, active, social boys and girls get labeled and medicated. But at ALPHA, they socialize, play and build. Lacking sufficient support in our public-system school, sometimes we can't keep up with their disruption and mischief, but they are valued for their energy and verve.

I can testify that ALPHA is no stranger to compromise, conflict and even coercion. But it usually manages to shield its students from the worst aspects of the huge, dehumanized school system in which it exists. As a participant in the free-school movement that influenced ALPHA, I feel that, in some form, this school has nearly always been a part of my identity. I am a former parent, a retired employee, and always a student of ALPHA.

INTRODUCTION:

CHALLENGING MASS COERCIVE EDUCATION

There is nothing more human than learning. As many parents discover to their awe, the drive to learn comes from children themselves. When babies struggle to reach, to roll over, to crawl, to walk and climb, to talk to us, they are *learning*. When toddlers follow us and imitate us as we wash dishes, watch TV, scroll our phones, play ball, garden—they are learning. As children explore, try things out and ply us with questions, they are learning—in the same ways that our inventive ancestors learned how to thrive on every continent on the planet.

Our children show us that we all start out with curious, skeptical minds. Children who ask *why?* are practicing critical thinking. It's just as well that critical thinking hardly needs to be taught, because no one really knows how to teach it. Many educators try to encourage it, and it has been added to long lists of curriculum requirements. But no one can say whether critical thinking can recover after it has been smothered by having to follow commands and schedules unquestioningly day after day. This, essentially, is what mainstream school systems all over the world make children do, year after year.

I characterize this mainstream approach as *mass coercive education*. The requirements that fill children's days—the curriculum documents, the schooling structures that jump from dictated subject to subject to subject, the insistence on quiet and obedience (now even from 4 year-olds)—form what many critics call education's *hidden curriculum*, one that is absorbed and never leaves us. (More on that later in this book.) This mass coercive education agenda has taken ownership of the word *learning*.

In George Orwell's book *1984*, about a totalitarian technocratic takeover of the earth, everyone speaks one language, *Newspeak*. In Newspeak, most words, in all the world's languages, have been dropped. The meanings of the remaining words are rigidly defined and shrunken, their shadings and histories stripped. This has happened to the word *learning* in our time.

Education officials have been calling their offerings, during the COVID-19 pandemic that began in 2020, not *on-line school* or *on-line education*, but *online learning*. As though watching the news and witnessing science happening in real time, with scientists debating about the virus they are fighting, is not learning. As though hearing arguments about next steps, talking things through with family and friends, trying to make informed decisions, is not learning. As though children and youth are not learning when they struggle through this pandemic with their caregivers, cook with them, and take walks in the blossoming world. As if, without curriculum experts, families in lockdown can't help their children by sharing skills and knowledge they themselves possess—not only reading and household math, but family history and stories, heritage languages, arts, life skills.

One effect of equating "learning" with whatever is being offered by school is to make families desperate and anxious that their children will "fall behind" and fail at life if they can't access the standardized product and succeed within the designated timelines. This is an unnecessary fear, created and promoted by the education system itself.

Since the 1990s, as schooling sank deeper into rating, grading and a universal curriculum, it also deepened its reach into children's lives. Starting school at age four, and with homework from early grades on, children have never been worked harder. Psychologist Peter Gray has long sounded the alarm that youth mental health is at risk. Gray correlates "the decline of play and the rise of psychopathology in young people over the past several decades" as they are confined "for ever more hours in settings where they are more or less continually directed and evaluated by adults, settings almost designed to produce anxiety and depression".[3]

Education isn't an esoteric discipline, to be governed only by experts according to formulas incomprehensible to the rest of us. Though it has profound consequences for societies, education is a human and accessible art. Since our origins, that fine art was practiced by caring relatives and thoughtful communities who couldn't take personal and cultural survival for granted.

Community-based schools such as ALPHA Alternative School follow this time-honored tradition. Much effort, research, collaboration, planning and thought goes into keeping up with children's needs, and helping them to become skilled and aware of the world. A scaffold of experience, culture and ethics maintains the rich and safe community environment that is the foundation of individual and group well-being.

On the other hand, in mass coercive education, factory models are applied to this vital and caring art. In 1900, prominent American educator John Dewey raised concerns about the "mechanical massing of children" in crowded classes under the care of a single stressed adult.[4] Those concerns were never resolved in public systems.

Every decade brings yet another moral panic about literacy. Each generation hears the same litany of public system insufficiencies: failure to support boys' learning, girls' learning, the learning of children with challenges and disabilities, lively children, those from immigrant and oppressed communities, the low-income, the precarious, the "at-risk" children. Together, arguably, these make up the majority of youth.

In 1971, Ivan Illich, a theologian and Catholic pastor working in international literacy, described the unchanging structure that marginalizes most students as a *hidden curriculum*. He declared that it "leads inevitably to physical pollution, social polarization and psychological impotence".[5] In 1992, John Taylor Gatto described how this hidden curriculum works on the front line in a classroom. In his thirty years as a school teacher, wrote Gatto, he didn't teach academics or literacy: "I teach school".

He laid out the seven lessons "universally taught from Harlem to the Hollywood Hills":

1. Confusion: "*Everything* I teach is out of context."

2. Class Position: "My job is to make them like being locked together with kids with numbers [age, test scores] like their own. Or at least to endure it like good sports."

3. Indifference: "Nothing is so important that it cannot be dropped at the sound of a bell."

4. Emotional Dependency: "By stars and red checks, smiles and frowns, prizes, honors, and disgraces, I teach kids to surrender their will to the predestined chain of command."

5. Intellectual Dependency: "Good students wait for a teacher to tell them what to do."

6. Provisional Self-Esteem: "I teach that a kid's self-respect should depend on an expert opinion. My kids are constantly evaluated and judged."

7. One Can't Hide: "There are no private spaces for children; there is no private time."[6]

"All of these lessons," wrote Gatto, "are prime training for permanent underclasses, people deprived forever from finding the center of their own special genius." In 1991, the third time Gatto was hailed as the New York City Teacher of the Year, he quit, quite spectacularly. In an op-ed published in the Wall Street Journal, he wrote, "I can't teach this way any longer."

In this third millennium, education is seldom discussed except in terms of success and failure—of students, teachers and schools—within an education model that itself is rarely challenged. However, discussions about education weren't always this restricted. In the past, some critics looked at the mass institutionalization of children as a human-rights issue, including the renowned educator Maria Montessori, who lamented: "No social problem is as universal as the oppression of the child".

She wrote:

> Never were the rights of man so disregarded as in the case of the child. No worker has had to blindly follow orders as must the child. . . . No one has ever had to work like the child, who must submit to an adult who imposes hours of work and hours of play according to a rigid and arbitrary set of rules.[7]

During the foundation years of Toronto's alternative schools, campaigns to defend human rights were strong, in education as elsewhere. Some see the roots of alternative schools in the 1960s as reason to dismiss them—relics of a time when people ate too much granola and dressed badly.

Fashion and culinary errors certainly happened. But there was much more to what Toronto sociologist Dorothy Smith described as the "great democratic impulse of the movements of the sixties and seventies".[8] Debates about education were hot, as educators and families all over the world tried out ways of schooling that would embody the postwar global struggle for human rights.

Loris Malaguzzi expressed the aims of this period when he reflected on building the famed Reggio Emelia schools in an Italian district that had been razed by Mussolini's fascists during World War II:

> The first philosophy learned . . . in the wake of such a war, was to give human, dignified, civil meaning to existence, to be able to make choices with clarity of mind and purpose, and to yearn for the future of mankind.[9]

After two world wars and a genocidal Holocaust, and during an arms race that threatened all of life on earth, radical and progressive education critics argued that schools should promote democracy and equity, meet children's developmental needs, and foster happy childhoods.

Critique isn't enough, as bell hooks explains:

> When we only name the problem, when we state complaint without a constructive focus or resolution, we take hope away. In this way critique can become merely an expression of profound cynicism, which then works to sustain dominator culture.[10]

The international free school movement of the 1960s and 1970s was committed to trying out possible solutions. Students, parents and teachers, networking long before the Internet, generated thousands of grassroots schools. Some survive today, and more are started every year by parents and educators whose students can't wait for systemic change.

The Alternative Education Resource Organization (AERO) lists hundreds of alternative schools worldwide. These include well-known models such as Montessori, Waldorf, holistic and forest schools. Many are small democracies, inspired by the 1960 publication of A. S. Neill's book about his private boarding school, Summerhill. With thousands of alumni and half a century of experience, these schools are no longer experiments. They are what Neill and Dewey called *demonstration schools*,[11] showcasing diverse ways that responsive, humane schools can work.

By 1970, Toronto, Canada was already known as a locus of the movement for independent, self-created *free schools*, a place where many educators, parents and students used personal and community resources to try out grassroots solutions. Wanting to make alternatives sustainable and available to families of all incomes, school creators in Toronto lobbied for their school board to host what US educator Mario Fantini called "public schools of choice".[12]

Toronto's unique contribution, as described by administrator Dale Shuttleworth, would be to ensure "the universal right of parents, students and teachers to initiate alternative programs which are cooperatively governed and supported in response to local needs".[13] There are now forty alternatives in Toronto's system, including ALPHA Alternative School, the main subject of this book. Such schools are not only sanctuaries for the families who want and need them, they are also resources for public education innovation.

Most of the attempts at democratic, humane education that still survive are small grassroots schools, outside public systems. Except in rare jurisdictions such as Finland and Reggio Emelia, Italy, progressive educators of the 20th century couldn't maintain the influence necessary to secure public systems that would foster egalitarianism, literacy, enquiry, self-reliance and critical thinking. Despite the best efforts of many educators, public education has failed to be the democratic counterforce identified by Dewey as necessary to empower citizens and to balance the hegemonic tilt of big business and the State.

As I write, during the second year of the COVID-19 pandemic, anxious students are being called back to schools that have been defunded since the 1990s—dirty and over-populated, yet jammed with confusing expectations. More than ever, they are *zombie schools in a zombie system*, a system that crashed in 2020 as surely as did the cruise ship and airline industries. Industrial models of caring were revealed as killers in our long-term care sector. In schools, classes of from twenty to thirty-five students—never optimum and always the greatest threat to the least privileged—now place families at physical risk.

As schools closed, families felt deeply the loss of the vital role of schools in childcare, family support, respite, and the social lives of the children. More than ever in an age of social, economic and climate change, families need a public school system based on the authentic needs of children and youth, focused on the well-being of students and employees. All ages need to help themselves, and one another, to learn, cooperate, thrive and contribute.

When (and if) this pandemic is beaten, the challenges won't cease. Today's youth face social, environmental, health, ethical and economic challenges—threats to their well-being and their very lives. Powerful forces strategize to divide them, just as their elders were divided. Simply to live an ethical life that allows everyone to be watered, fed, housed, and protected from violence and exploitation, today's youth will have to resist economic and military might. They need to be thoughtful, strong and caring, as well as flexible problem-solvers. They need the solid support of the older generations.

This book documents a lost history of parents and educators who continued to educate in a kindly and democratic spirit, through decades of neo-conservative attack. It's about making real changes in public education systems, both immediately and gradually, both locally and systemically, with the consent of the children, parents and teachers involved.

I hope this book will be useful to parents and educators who may have differing ideas about pedagogy, but who agree that school can and should be a happier, more nurturing place for all of our kids. I hope that it will help many varieties of alternative schools to survive, and that it can inspire parents and teachers to operate many of their local public schools as responsive, supportive community schools.

Finally, I hope this book will help public school administrators to see that their working lives need not be spent as paper shufflers and enforcers, but as vital creative and supportive links within a community of community schools.

1:

A DEMOCRATIC SCHOOL

> *I never wanted to leave.*
>
> *The best thing that ever happened to me.*
>
> *I was lucky I went to ALPHA.*

These are quotes from alumni of a small alternative primary school in Toronto, Canada: ALPHA Alternative School.

How many children say such things about their schools? Aside from needing to get out of the house and to be with other young people, how many children are eager to go to school?

Other alumni, who had moved on from ALPHA to attend various alternative and mainstream secondary schools, offered these comments about what ALPHA did for them:

> *ALPHA gave me time to figure out who I was.*
>
> *ALPHA recognized everyone as an individual.*
>
> *You're not reduced to statistics and awards.*
>
> *I am achieving the same as other students but because I know what I am capable of, I know I haven't reached my potential yet.*
>
> *Basically, you are a number in the regular system. I am the one who wants to speak up and learn.*
>
> *ALPHA helped me make my own decisions—made me feel like I had power. It was a good experience.*
>
> *They gave us social skills—I'm doing fine. It was easy to pick up the facts when I left.*

How can a school accomplish this? In good part, that's what this book is about. But from one of the alumni, here it is in a nutshell:

> *They let us run wild with our imaginations. They gave us the building blocks.*

What kinds of "building blocks" make possible such valuable, but ineffable, things as freedom, validation as an individual, habits of decision-making, courage to speak up, desire and confidence to learn, and the social skills that can also be helpful in other, less free places? As we prepare children for the unknown future, how can we give them good childhoods? This history may provide some clues.

ALPHA Alternative School's first home was a single large room at a YMCA, complete with that staple of the era, a homemade geodesic dome. In the fall of 1972, a hundred kids, three teachers and a motley crew of parents all piled in and tried to figure out how to help kids learn and grow without bossing, intimidating, scaring or judging them.

No one, in this new school, knew how to do that. Except for one teacher who had previously taught at a small free school in another province, even the professionals were attempting something few people had tried before. The first year, press and parents agreed, was *chaos*.

The student/teacher ratio in the public system at the time was over 30:1, with order enforced by punishments, including being hit with a strap or ruler. To try to meet a ratio that had been recommended by John Dewey, about 10:1, ALPHA parents had committed to do much of the teaching and care of the children. And not just their own kids—in their role as community educators, parents had to learn to help any interested kid. To do this was even harder than the founding parents thought it would be.

Did I mention it was chaos?

But everybody learned. Everybody is still learning. That's why, to this day, ALPHA's motto is *Sharing Education*. ALPHA is now fifty years old. And counting.

ALPHA Alternative School has been called a lot of things. *Alternative* only means that a school differs from the mainstream. ALPHA's earliest documents passionately identify it as a *community school*, operated by its community of parents, teachers and students. ALPHA certainly is both an alternative school and a community school.

Committed to democratic self-governance, ALPHA is often called a *democratic school*. *Democratic* may be the term I use most; however, like democratic nations, democratic schools sometimes settle for process—elections, committees—without allowing citizens much liberty or control over their lives, or even over what's on the agenda.

Free schools, modeled on British educator A. S. Neill's Summerhill, place their democratic meetings at the centre of the school experience. But equally vital is the child's freedom to play and to choose. Free school educators see such personal liberty as a necessary foundation for mental health and social skills, and as essential to liberate intellect, curiosity, confidence and critical thinking. Free schools try to offer as much freedom as can be permitted to children, given the child's need for care and community, and the necessity that the rights of others be respected. Neill expresses this vital ethic as *freedom, not license*.

Though they now vary considerably, Toronto's forty alternative schools began with the activism of the *free school movement* of the 1960s and 1970s. Started by parents in 1972, ALPHA wasn't the first, but it is Toronto's oldest surviving elementary alternative school. Successive parent communities have passed along a culture that is both cooperative and combative: working together to support all the kids, arguing about freedom and pedagogy, and struggling when necessary to defend the school.

ALPHA's teachers work as a team to meet the needs of the eighty students, ages 4-12. Some volunteer parents work in the school, in shifts of about four hours per week. One of the first things ALPHA's parents and teachers had to learn was how to work with children in multi-age groups. ALPHA's first students, milling about their space at an old YMCA, chose their work and playmates according to a developmental watershed that seems to occur at about age nine. When ALPHA moved in 1977 to the old brick school building that it still shares with another alternative school, these cohorts were settled on different floors. Until the isolation measures required by the Covid-19 pandemic, they still met on the playground, at lunch, at parties and gatherings, for visits, and at their all-school meetings. They will again.

On their floor, the 4 to 9 year-olds (*littlekids*) flit about like minnows, slipping off to play and create in any space they can find in a cramped school in a public system that provides only a modest amount of space for each student. Four rooms are allotted to art, play, science, basic literacy/numeracy, daycare and a library. The 9 to 12 year-olds (*bigkids*) on the other floor share two classrooms, a kitchen and various small rooms that are assigned to functions such as computers, special education and music.

ALPHA's littlekids aren't locked into a set curriculum, but are offered a range of activities and resources in a literacy-rich environment. Their teachers support their curiosity about life and nature. There's time and space for children to ask questions—the basis of all science. Children's relentless *whys* aren't suppressed, but respected as the *critical thinking* that we want them to keep throughout their lives. By means of this *emergent curriculum*—exploration based on their interests—students build a base of interconnected general knowledge over their time at ALPHA, while gaining literacy and numeracy skills.

Because learning at ALPHA is social and cooperative (like most workplaces!), students share their discoveries and often help one another. Of all ALPHA's ways, social, cooperative, non-judgmental learning is the easiest to understand. It's also the cheapest and most easily shared with the system at large. Eliminating judgment and competition to create a school milieu in which all children can help and be helped would free families of unnecessary anxieties, and allow schools to concentrate on student well-being, awareness of the world and (in their time) literacy and numeracy. It would cost nothing.

Reading and writing rule at ALPHA. The detailed, sequential, atomized public school curriculum is set aside, but as adults share their knowledge and the children's questions are explored, a more relevant, holistic curriculum constructs itself each year. Adults hold classes and workshops in which they share knowledge and skills. While building, making, playing, and investigating, young children also work on these skills on their own.

ALPHA is committed to ensure that each child can read and write by school-leaving age at grade 6. Sharing stories, interests and meaningful words—such as kids' names, beloved animals, and communicative signage—are ways to teach written language as naturally as oral language is absorbed. Sylvia Ashton Warner and others called this approach *organic*. In a process that ALPHA founding teacher Susan Garrard called "fishing", the staff draw into lessons those who have avoided numbers and letters for too long.

How long is "too long"? The answer is different for each kid. In its rich environment, many ALPHA students achieve basic literacy and numeracy during their early years with little formal teaching. In mainstream schools, there are significant numbers of students (often boys) who don't begin to read before grade 3 or 4; ALPHA has a similar finding within its informal system. This fact has been the foundation of many literacy panics in the culture at large, but there are plenty of reasons to see it as developmental—and not in itself a problem.

When fundamental needs, such as emotional and social contact and spoken language, are neglected during a child's infancy and toddlerhood, the consequences are catastrophic and can be permanent. However, this concept of a vital "sensitive period" doesn't apply to cultural add-ons such as reading and math. These can be, and are, learned at any age. Free school educators find that kids who read later are not "slow" or deficient, but if forced too early, they may come to believe that they are. Once kids calm down, or start to spend more time out of their childhood dream-state, experienced teachers often find that reading takes only months to learn, not years.

I think of the transitional age of 8 to 9 as a golden age for an alphakid (or Alphibian, as some call themselves). If they haven't yet achieved basic numeracy and literacy, it's a time when that problem can usually be wrestled to the ground, when their nervous systems tend to be settling down. At ALPHA, kids who read later are observed to be busy, curious, bright people. They are often talented builders, three-dimensional thinkers, and real world problem-solvers, with high sociability and passionate interests. Barring cognitive challenges or early schooling trauma, every ALPHA kid learns to read.

ALPHA doesn't grade or rate children. It offers patience and help, not judgment, to foster literacy and numeracy—the vital, foundational tasks of schooling.

A Nonjudgmental School

Adult expectations—curriculum requirements, exams, marks, family fears and ambitions, teachers' assumptions—can undermine the confidence of a child who is inclined to read later, or who just needs more help than the frantic, over-stuffed curriculum allows time for.

Often, kids are moving too fast for the system. Sheer liveliness, which used to be seen as the sign of a healthy child, can be a factor leading to later literacy. There's a significant gender aspect to this, and time usually resolves the difficulty. We are used to differences in children's developmental timetables for basics like walking, talking and puberty (though parents also worry about these). Is it reasonable to expect kids to master all the layers of learning at identical ages?

As they mature, ALPHA students spend more of their school time in lessons. This is controversial. At the private free schools Summerhill, Sudbury Valley and the Albany Free School, children are never forced to attend lessons. They often do, but it is by choice.

These independent schools have a high adult/pupil ratio. Their model for child care is the community and the family, not the factory, as it is in the public system. So, when a child has a question, or decides to take on a project, mentors are available. In their woods and meadows, or in the city block that the Albany school's playgrounds and gardens sprawl through, a free kid can roam and learn experientially, just as all kids did before industrialization and urbanization. Boredom and chaos are not the problems that they can be at ALPHA, a public school in which kids are confined to a building in a traffic-choked neighborhood, and where a teacher is responsible for twenty or more kids at a time.

ALPHA teachers are even more vulnerable to pressure from the opposite direction: concern that to allow a young child to spend time dreaming, playing, creating, socializing will damage the child's chances in life. The staff are well aware that much learning happens in these pursuits. But they worry that, as at any public school, there aren't enough adults to respond to the four-year-old who wants to learn math—now! Or to assist the six-year-old who needs help with a project, and the eight-year-old who has noticed anxiously that friends are reading and needs support to make that leap.

Children soon become aware of society's general expectations, and can begin to fear that something is wrong with them. To spare them that barrier, and to ensure that a genuine disability is spotted, ALPHA staff coerce a little. They make sure that, as the students grow, they regularly sit down to do some developmentally appropriate schoolwork.

When ALPHA students grow into bigkids, at about the age of nine, they wrestle with math, French and writing on a daily basis. Over the years, ALPHA's alumni reported difficulty in middle school with math and French. So now the grade 5-6 students, like other public school students, spend hours per week daydreaming in, and disrupting, the friendly, informal math and

French classes their teachers create for them. I feel sorry for them, and for their teachers.

Summerhill's A. S. Neill called ages 10-12 the "gangster age" because, in his day, those were the games the children spent their time playing. His former student Albert Lamb noted that, while "young kids at Summerhill almost always go to lessons eagerly" and older kids also took an interest in their studies, "kids between ten and twelve at Summerhill spend very little time in lessons. At this particular age they seem to have a great need to get out from under the weight of adult expectations."[14]

As an understaffed and restricted public school, ALPHA can't even offer daylong access to the schoolyard; certainly, its kids can't spend their rowdy years roaring about the woods, as they do at Summerhill. Teacher Susan Hess developed strategies to draw in the students of this resistant age and reduce their acting-out from the boredom of their confinement to a school-building (which alas could often consist of socially torturing one another). Integrated arts-based teaching was the core of Hess's approach, which she shared with her successors. Doing projects and creating books, scrolls, dramas, and model villages, they do research in social studies and science, and build English and math competencies.

At ALPHA, *life-long learning* is a way of being, for all ages. The teachers constantly research and try out best practices in student-centered education. Parents struggle to understand, and often contribute their expertise. The arbitrary curriculum is set aside to respond to students' questions and interests, allowing them to follow meaningful, relevant paths toward knowledge of the world.

In this century, teacher Emily Chan introduced to ALPHA the practice of programming within an *anti-oppression* framework. In an article she wrote for her union magazine about a year-long Black History initiative, Chan described her approach:

> In my social justice framework for teaching, it's vital that I listen to students' big questions, provide space for them to challenge ideas on their own terms and

> respond with meaningful, hands-on curriculum. I work hard to develop connections outside the classroom and collaborate with local community members to nurture students' personal relationships and spark deep learning. . . . Challenging bias in curriculum about the history of Black peoples in Canada not only confronts dominant norms of racial privilege, it goes further by dismantling this legacy of colonization. This serves in the interest of both white students and students of colour; everyone gains when we broaden the lens through which we see ourselves.[15]

There is much direct teaching at ALPHA—as there is in most free schools. Lessons can be effective and satisfying as long as they are focused where the child is, instead of speeding past them or boring them silly. There's time during school hours for physical activity, social life, and the pursuit of individual interests. Music is a common student-generated activity, helped by talented parents and teachers. Often, there is a rock and roll band or two at the school.

People who meet ALPHA students and alumni often note that they're articulate and display remarkable general knowledge. Other distinguishing traits tend to be self-assertion and people skills. These qualities are attained through a school atmosphere that is open, cooperative and social, a democracy that is participatory, and a justice system, called *Committee*, that is child-focused and restorative.

Children are taught to deal with conflict verbally, to express their needs, to listen and negotiate. Repeated behavioral problems will be taken before a rotating Committee of five students, balanced for age, gender and experience. When a child has impactful emotional problems that can't be resolved at Committee, families are asked to help to work on them. The principal isn't called upon to be a disciplinarian, but may be asked to help access social workers and psychological supports for children with serious emotional and/or developmental issues.

At least once during the week, ALPHA students and staff, as well as any parents who are in the school, meet as a whole to discuss issues of concern. All ages participate in meetings and Committee; a tiny kid's first speech at a meeting, or turn at chairing or on Committee, is a special moment. Some students aged seven to nine (*midkids*) have both the interest and the experience to help make these institutions work, and a few bigkids become true elders. But it takes a strong group of midkids to hold up against sardonic 10 to 12 year-olds, so ALPHA's democracy is a struggle.

But then, democracy is *always* a struggle. Those who teach at ALPHA, and who send their kids to ALPHA, constantly ask themselves, "Is this democratic? Are we respecting the children? Are we respecting the workers? Are we respecting the families? Are we patient enough? Are we inclusive enough? Are we courageous enough to confront with respect, when necessary? Do we have the stamina to meet the challenges presented by a public education bureaucracy whose employees are well-intentioned, but whose regulations conflict with alternative schooling methods?"

Staff and parents struggle to support children who, according to ALPHA's constitution, are seen as "unique and of non-comparable, non-measurable worth". The adults weren't trained to work as part of a direct democracy, and the extra meetings, responsibilities and complexities can be exhausting for all. There are obstacles, misunderstandings, arguments, tensions, mistakes—and sometimes a crisis. Adults constantly learn as the kids do: experientially, holistically, through looking, listening, absorbing, making mistakes.

But it must be said, and said here: ALPHA is also fun, relaxed, caring and natural-feeling, like a village. One ALPHA former student summed it up: "The most important lesson of ALPHA was love."[16]

As in the family or the village, relaxation and affection don't mean that everyone gets what they want. Some parents and teachers seek out free schools to fulfill their own desires and needs. This has, at times, created difficult problems. But schools are for the children and youth of their time. Adults must take their responsibilities seriously, and work out their issues elsewhere. To address the confusion that can arise when parents are invited—nay, begged—to share the work in meaningful ways, ALPHA drafted a handbook, and adopted a unique and informative Code of Conduct.

Not all families would want to engage as intensely in their children's school as many ALPHA parents do. Nor do all schools need to be so democratic, in order to benefit from the existence of ALPHA's ongoing democracy. But all of our children resist coercion and reach out for life. It is their birthright, and the rights of these most precious, vulnerable people need to be discussed and defended in the public schools where they spend most of their childhood.

This is a story of some defenders of democracy who set about to create and sustain schools that would treat their students as feeling and thinking individuals, deserving of good lives as children. Together, they worked on a school where, as another founding student described it, "Students of all ages are invited and expected to be compassionate, thinking, engaged members of a community."[17] Their story begins many decades ago, here and on the other side of the world. The struggle for democratic education parallels the growth of democracy itself.

2:

EDUCATING DEMOCRATICALLY

Freedom for children is too often seen as a simple absence of adult control and authority, and a free or progressive school as something arbitrary, whimsical and indulgent—an easy, or a lazy person's, way out. This is a destructive myth.

Progressive and radical concepts in education closely follow research and experience on how children actually learn and thrive. Their histories parallel the history of public schooling and of the eternally attacked and frequently undermined institution of democracy. ALPHA developed in context with other schools that sought to "free the children" from oppressive schooling practices.

Indigenous Education

The *free school movement* arose in Canada in the 1960s and 70s, at a time when Indigenous people had only recently acquired the right to retain legal counsel, to vote and to be off-reservation without passes. They immediately set out on the decades-long struggle to free their children from the Indian Residential School system and to get access to quality public and secondary education. Even after local public schools began to accept Indigenous students in the 1960s, racism and ostracism were the norm. From Alcatraz to Akwesasne, Indigenous communities in the 1960s and 1970s began to reclaim culture through education.

Jerry Mintz, a school creator in the 1960s free school movement, who later founded the Alternative Education Resource Organization (AERO), took students from his Shaker Mountain School to visit Mohawk people in Akwesasne who were occupying the bridge that crossed the border from Cornwall to the US. They would continue to visit, and Mintz credits "the Iroquois Confederacy, especially the Mohawk tribe as a lifelong influence for their teachings on democratic process."[18] He is not alone. Arguments are gaining ground maintaining that encounters with Indigenous democracies in the Americas, most notably the Haudenosaunee, inspired European and American democratic revolutions. Mintz describes how he was able to reciprocate:

> In 1971 I got an urgent call from Ann Jock at one o'clock in the morning. She told me that seventy Mohawk children had been kicked out of the public high school because they wanted to learn their own language and culture . . . Ann asked if we could come to the reservation the next day, bring some of our students, bring slides, talk about our school and tell them how they could go about starting a school.[19]

Mintz recalls that Jock's idea for an Indian Way School was taken up in the Mohawk border communities of Akwesasne and Kanawake. The American Indian Movement (AIM) was active in Toronto, as elsewhere, and Indian Way Schools, also called *Survival Schools*, were also starting in Minneapolis and in Saskatchewan. As with Black-run Freedom Schools, which had existed since the end of slavery and were having a resurgence during the 1960s, families and educators in Indigenous Survival Schools were striving to give their kids solid educations, immerse them in their culture and history, and prepare them for the challenges they face.

In 1970 and 1971, Wilfrid Pelletier from Wikwemikong opened a rare window into traditional education among Anishinaabe people, whose territory includes the Great Lakes area and Toronto. In *This Magazine is About Schools* Pelletier wrote that "being educated in white schools was a painful experience for me like for most Indian kids. I have therefore given a lot of thought to the Indian way of learning."

> I grew up in a community where kids were allowed to discover everything for themselves, by personal observation rather than formal instruction. . . . We made the same discoveries that other people had made centuries before us, but they belonged to us, they didn't belong to some despot or expert, someone who tells you, I've got the answers, so you quit being curious, quit exploring. That didn't happen to me until I went to school.[20]

Interestingly, student activists of the 1960s, who were unaware of what was happening to Indigenous youth, and whose own experience didn't approach that depth of oppression, would independently note that they also felt that genuine learning ended with entry into the authoritarian arena of schooling.

Pelletier confronted the cultural bias in generalizations and judgments that were often made about Indigenous students, such as the frequent complaint that "Indian kids have difficulty with abstractions":

> It is hard for us Indians to make sense of the segmented approach to learning taught in the schools to study "chemistry" or "math" or "French" without relating them to each other and to some larger whole. We Indians approach things the opposite way. We start with the whole and examine every part in relationship to the whole.[21]

The traditional education Pelletier describes takes a *holistic* approach. To treat the student as a whole person is fundamental to all of what I might call developmentally appropriate education, including the work of Dewey, Montessori, free schools, and the Reggio Emelia schools. As described by Ron Miller, holistic education embodies "a worldview that honors the spiritual, ecological, and existential dimensions of life and does not subsume human existence under a consuming economic materialism".[22]

In contrast to the coercion and corporal punishment that ruled the day in public schools, and that was killing children in Indian Residential schools, Pelletier described the Indigenous *principle of non-interference*.

> One of the practiced ethics of the community was non-interference. No one interfered with us, and this way of living still exists today. . . . [The children] will sit and listen to people talk, and when they get the opportunity they will speak, but they won't cut you off or interfere. . . . The whole background of the educational system was that of observing and feeling. This is how they learned.[23]

Pelletier describes how traditional Indigenous education is holistically entwined with the student's total well-being. Young children are treated as thinking individuals linked within culture and community. These precepts aren't just about education, but about governance and about democracy itself.

There is no direct evidence that the founders of ALPHA were aware of Indigenous human rights, or of how Indigenous thought influenced the democratic values they struggled for. However, Pelletier's work was published twice in *This Magazine is About Schools*, which was regularly read by ALPHA's creators—and by me as a sixteen-year-old in faraway Calgary. Only nine years after his people were allowed to leave their reserves without Indian Agent permission, his writing was likely the first that I read by an Indigenous person. Pelletier also operated the Institute for Indian Studies at Rochdale College.[24] We can only guess how influential he may have been.

As Indigenous activists all over the continent rose to defend their children and reclaim their cultures, Toronto witnessed the beginnings of Wandering Spirit Survival School. Pauline Shirt and Vern Harper's children resisted going to the local school, where they were racially targeted. Risking the intervention of Children's Aid,[25] Shirt began to teach them and a few other children at home, and then with volunteers at the Native Canadian

Centre. In a pamphlet from the charitable organization Indspire, Shirt recalled:

> I started a school in 1976 with other parents. If we are going to make our way of life fertile, we have to know our own history; so we asked ourselves, how did our people teach our kids? We sat and listened to our elders. So we did that [at WSSS]. We started each day in a big circle with a smudging ceremony; we taught in Ojibwe and in Cree; we hired an Indigenous teacher, and we developed our own curriculum.[26]

In 1977, Shirt and Harper successfully lobbied for the inclusion of Wandering Spirit Survival School as an alternative school in Toronto's system. After decades of struggle to survive and to carry out authentically Indigenous programming in a resistant system, Wandering Spirit is now a complete JK-grade 12 school with its own building.

John Dewey and Progressive Education

In the United States, at the turn of the twentieth century, John Dewey became the pre-eminent thinker on progressive education, a scholar whose books have been on teacher education reading lists for a century. Dewey was a professor of philosophy, psychology and linguistics at the University of Chicago, where he founded his *Laboratory School* in 1896. In 1900, as mass public schooling gained ground in North America, he wrote:

> What the best and wisest parent wants for his own child, that must the community want for all of its children. Any other ideal for our schools is narrow and unlovely; acted upon, it destroys our democracy.[27]

Dewey's writings show that the economic preoccupations and urgencies of our time were powerful a full century ago. He wrote of "the growth of a world-wide market", and of "vast manufacturing centers to supply this market, of cheap and rapid means of communication and distribution between all its parts".[28]

He expressed optimism that public schooling could be a democratizing force. But this hope was tempered by an uneasy sense that the forces of mass industrialization could overpower this vision.

In 1900, Dewey unhappily described

> schoolrooms, with their set desks . . . arranged for handling as large numbers of children as possible; for dealing with children *en masse*, as an aggregate of units; involving, again, that they be treated passively.[29]

Dewey saw learning as active, dependent on experience, making the most of children's drive to join adults in their work and gain competence and knowledge of how and why things are made. Dewey scholar Philip Jackson describes the kinds of activities that formed the basic curriculum of the laboratory school:

> broad-scale and open-ended group projects that involved activities such as carpentry, weaving, cooking, and candlemaking . . . planting, building, nature walks, and neighbourhood excursions . . .
>
> He supported the necessity of acquiring quite a lot of factual knowledge. . . . But what he did insist upon was that many of these traditional goals could be better achieved if treated secondarily, which meant being subsumed under a broadened vision of what education was all about.[30]

Dewey's holistic vision paid homage to the human relationship with the cosmos, proclaiming the earth as man's "continual shelter and protection".[31] He accepted handicraft and concrete learning as work that "engages the full spontaneous interest and attention of children . . . keeping them alert and active, instead of passive and receptive".[32] He argued against regarding crafts as mere preparation for practical trades. In Dewey's view, these activities were intellectual engagements, "methods of living and learning . . . agencies for bringing home to the child some of the primal necessities of community life". They were "instrumentalities through which the school itself shall be made a genuine form of active community life, instead of a place set apart in which to learn lessons".[33] (This language would be echoed in Ontario's *Hall-Dennis* report, sixty years later.)

Dewey realized in his later years that the democratic ideal he had worked for all his life was being marginalized by powerful interests. Noam Chomsky quotes an aging Dewey as saying: "politics is the shadow cast on society by big business. . . . Power today resides in control of the means of production exchange, publicity, transportation and communication. Whoever owns them rules the life of the country".[34]

A. S. Neill and Summerhill

Andrew Sutherland Neill was the son of a schoolmaster. He began his own career as a schoolmaster at seventeen and later acquired a degree in English at Edinburgh University.[35] After a few years of teaching, he threw his "tawse" (the belt used to punish students in Scotland) in the fire and created his own school.[36] It opened in 1921 and within a few years settled into its current location in Leiston, England. Neill's school, Summerhill, is the "oldest self-governing school offering non-compulsory lessons in the world".[37] A century old, it is now watched over by the son of the daughter of that son of a schoolmaster, Henry Readhead—together with his mother, Zoe Readhead.

At Summerhill there is a schedule to the day, built around mealtimes, tea, lessons and bedtime. Lessons are in the morning, with arts and craft facilities open in the afternoons and activities often offered during the evenings. On its rural property, free play and adventure of all sorts can be indulged. Pupils are not pampered; there is freedom not to show up to what's on offer, but there is no personal educational valet service.

"No pupil is compelled to attend lessons," writes Neill. "But if Jimmy comes to English on Monday and does not make an appearance again until Friday of the following week, the others quite rightly object that he is holding back the work, and they may throw him out for impeding progress."[38] This doesn't doom

Jimmy to eternal ignorance. He just has to wait until the next time those skills are being worked on, or to convince someone to tutor him.

Neill was an outlier in education, but his theories found support in the emerging psychoanalytic profession. He underwent psychoanalysis, conducted first by the American Homer Lane, whose self-governing institutions for "delinquent" kids were the model for Summerhill, and later on by Wilhelm Reich, formerly a student of Sigmund Freud, whose book *The Mass Psychology of Fascism* Neill admired.

Freud pioneered the idea, now generally accepted, that early childhood experiences can generate lifelong suffering and influence adult thought and behavior. Until Freud, people said that "children forget". Neill and his friend Reich believed that the long-term effects of emotional and sexual repression showed themselves not only in child behaviour but in adult submission, scapegoating and violence, finding mass expression in war and fascism.

Before World War II, as fascism rose in Europe, German Jewish Wilhelm Reich sought refuge in the United States. The two friends were permanently separated, but in their long correspondence Neill dropped his tough, salty tone and revealed his vulnerability and despair.

The British government's initial appeasement of the Nazis led some to fear that Britain might also embrace fascism politically. In 1938 Neill wrote to Reich:

> Everything points to England's going Fascist now, and I fear that soon freedom of the press will go. Then there will be no country worth living in.[39]

In 1935, John Dewey had also looked uneasily at the political situation in Europe:

> Three of the great nations of Europe have summarily suppressed the civil liberties for which liberalism valiantly strove, and in few countries of the Continent are they maintained with vigor.[40]

During World War II, the army expropriated Summerhill's Leiston location. Writing to Reich from temporary digs in Wales, Neill detailed the hardships of keeping the school going while England was under attack:

> I spend hours digging to produce food, and so do the children. . . . They are grand and clever and lovable, and I know that this system is the only one of any value in the world. They don't seem to need therapy of any kind, and that is the ideal education—to educate children in such a way that they won't need therapy later on.[41]

Yet Neill was not optimistic about the future of his work in education:

> Of course, the uncertainty of the future makes it all so difficult. We are moving to State control of everything, and after the war the middle class may not be able to send their children to private schools. All the schools will be State ones, and I can't see myself in a State school with control from above. It is queer that only under Capitalism have I been able to be a pioneer in education. I know what Nazism would have done with me, but what would a Communist State do with me? I couldn't make children sing the Red Flag or study Marx. No, Reich, the future is dark for my work, but I carry it on and will do so as long as I'm allowed to.[42]

After the war finally ended in 1945, it took years to repair the damage done to the school by the British army. In the nineteen fifties, Summerhill nearly fell victim to a conservative education resurgence. It had only twenty-five students when Neill was approached by a publisher who wanted to assemble a collection of his articles in a book for the American market.[43] Published in 1960, *Summerhill: a radical approach to child rearing* distilled forty years of educational practice, in which Neill recorded some of his experiences with students in a storytelling format.

Under such headings as Self-Government, Work, Play, The Free Child, Rewards and Punishment, Noise, Moral Instruction, The Road to Happiness and Spoiling the Child, *Summerhill* laid out Neill's alternative methods. Confronting a nearly universal culture of child control and discipline, it became an unlikely best-seller.

A close look at Summerhill shows that it was, and is, an anti-fascist institution that prevailed in defiance of toxic puritanism, a brutalizing British education system, rising fascism, and war. In 1964, in a spirited dialogue with Italian educator and Montessori heir Mario Montessori, Neill made his priorities clear:

> It's beyond me because you're talking about education, the three R's and science, and I'm thinking about the dynamics of life, the dynamic in a child, how we're going to prevent that child from becoming a Gestapo, or becoming a color hater and all these things. The sickness of the world. I'm interested in what we're going to do for children to stop them from being haters, to stop them from being anti-life.[44]

However, Neill seldom discussed politics. Allen Graubard noted that "Neill avoided dealing with problems of social change, partly on principle and partly from prudence. He was afraid the society would close him down if he gave them a good excuse."[45] The "principle" Graubard refers to is Neill's unqualified opposition to imposing any kind of politics or ideology on the young.

> The only hope for the world is the abolition of "character-molding", of that authority in the home and school that gives children a slave mentality for life. A nation of molded children produced Hitler. History and geography are forgotten when one leaves school, but the emotional molding lives on.[46]

Neill had a long view of cultural and social change: "the way of rebellion against paternalism is not violence; it is the slower way of practical work for freedom . . . to let the kids be themselves, and in a few generations the world will become healthy and happy." He insisted that "there is no shortcut to this end".[47]

Ever practical, he focused on helping the children under his care, and on sustaining Summerhill long enough to prove that his vision of schooling works. Neill carefully chose his battles, expressing to Reich that "to fight too many battles is to lose the lot".[48]

Summerhill promised no "advanced" teaching methods. The heart of Neill's method was freedom: both personal liberty and the practice of self-governance.

> Summerhill is a self-governing school, democratic in form. Everything connected with social, or group, life, including punishment for social offenses, is settled by vote at the Saturday night General School Meeting.
>
> Each member of the teaching staff and each child, regardless of his age, has one vote. My vote carries the same weight as that of a seven year old.
>
> Summerhill self-government has no bureaucracy. There is a different chairman at each meeting, appointed by the previous chairman, and the secretary's job is voluntary. Bedtime officers are seldom in office for more than a few weeks.[49]

First published in 1960, Neill's book disseminated his ideas to an eager international audience:

> It was an instant hit in the USA rising to the number one non-fictional best seller nationally. It was soon published in UK and many other countries and things began to take a turn for the better at Summerhill. Pupil numbers went up, many from the USA; interest in the school bloomed bringing in many visitors, to the dismay of the kids. At times there were coach loads.[50]

Exposing the Hidden Curriculum

Neill's book *Summerhill* hit the USA at a time when both conservative and progressive education critics had declared a "crisis in the classroom" and educational critique had gone mainstream. Some of that critique would be familiar today. Bestselling books like Rudolf Flesch's *Why Johnny Can't Read—And What You Can Do About It* addressed eternal concerns about literacy. But many writers questioned the very structure of schooling and the effect it had on children.

Radical and *liberal* are words whose meanings have changed in recent years. John Dewey's liberalism was based on faith that modernist progress will improve the quality of human life. Progressives like Dewey work to improve what they see as an essentially brilliant and democratizing society.

In our time, radicalism is often equated with violent extremism. This isn't how education writers use the word. The political meaning of *radical* is based on its mathematical meaning, which is "root". Radical critique examines structures, to detect the sources of stubborn problems. It considers structural solutions, that challenge entrenched priorities and methods. It has nothing to do with violence, but can be uncomfortable for vested interests. Graubard explained this perspective in education:

> To see that schools need radical reform depends on a perception of deep and pervasive harm that can be ascribed to the dominant structures, values and techniques of the existing schools.[51]

Radical critics of the time, in varied ways, communicated the insight that Charles Silberman described in *Crisis in the Classroom*:

> What educators must realize, moreover, is that how they teach and how they act may be more important than what they teach. The way we do things, that is to say, shapes values more directly and effectively than the way we talk about them. . . . And children are taught a host of lessons about values, ethics, morality, character and conduct every day of the

> week, less by the content of the curriculum than by the way schools are organized, the ways teachers and parents behave, the way they talk to children and to each other, the kinds of behavior they approve or reward and the kinds they disapprove or punish. These lessons are far more powerful than the verbalizations that accompany them and that they frequently controvert.[52]

Graubard and Silberman identified structure, not content, as the most powerful influence in schooling. This concept originated with "anthropologists studying education in the early fifties" and was named the *hidden curriculum* by Philip Jackson in 1968.[53] It's an illuminating idea, described by Illich, Gatto, and many education critics through the years. Dozens of popular books in the 1960s and 1970s explored *radical education critique* and free schooling. In *How Children Fail*, teacher John Holt looked at how school pressures drive children into fear-based strategies that interfere with learning. Holt's influential work became part of a critical literature created largely by working teachers.

When any scenario lasts through apparent failures, it makes sense then to ask, "what does it succeed in doing?" Therein, one might find its *hidden curriculum*, its underlying purpose. In 1972, Graubard recalled French sociologist Charles Durkheim's perspective:

> Education, far from having as its unique or principal project the individual and his interests, is above all the means by which society perpetually recreates the conditions of its very existence . . . a systematic socialization of the young generation.[54]

Graubard pointed out that "looking at the schools and functions described, one might consider that apparent failures might be quite functional to the status quo social structure".[55] In his 2005 introduction to Gatto's *Dumbing Us Down*, David Albert suggested that "failure is not failure at all, only a continuing round in the socialized enforcement of intellectual and emotional dependency".[56]

Decades later, Toronto academics Carl James and Julia Samaroo would note the impact of the hidden curriculum on minoritized students:

> Not only did the Eurocentric curriculum content not reflect the lived experiences of minoritized students, but the hidden curriculum implied that the problem was within the students themselves.[57]

Like Pauline Shirt trying to carry out Indigenous pedagogies at Wandering Spirit Survival School, James and Samaroo would note the struggle of staff at the Africentric School

> to grapple with implementing Africentric pedagogy and curriculum within the very type of Eurocentric, Western framework, and structures of a school board that that have been failing Black students in Ontario for decades.[58]

Since the hidden curriculum is embedded in school structures, it survives whether a progressive or authoritarian vogue is ascendant at any given era. As many children fail to thrive in this structure under either ideology, each can point to the failures of the other—and the cycle continues, without fundamental change.

3:

THE FREE SCHOOL MOVEMENT

Free school is a term with several historical roots. Educators in that movement often acknowledge the school that Leo Tolstoy, Russian author of *War and Peace*, held in his home from 1859 to 1862. Sylvia Ashton-Warner described Tolstoy's school in this way:

> He began by discarding all existing traditions and by refusing to follow any method of teaching already in use. First he must fathom the mind of the peasant child, and by doing away with punishments, let his pupils teach him the art of teaching. . . .
>
> These free Tolstoy schools, without programmes, without punishments, without rules, without forcing the will of the child, were remarkably successful. The children spent entire days at their studies and were reluctant to leave the schoolhouse.[59]

In many parts of the world, including Ontario, the term *free school* was used in movements for literacy and public education, where it meant providing education free to people of all classes. Paul Avrich used the term *free school* to describe the Modern Schools inspired by Spanish anarchist Francisco Ferrer, deeply democratic school communities that existed in the USA and internationally from about 1910 until 1960.[60] In the United States, schools that African-Americans created for their children after emancipation from slavery, and later during the Civil Rights struggles of the 1960s, were called *freedom schools* or *free schools*.

Samuel Yanes credits Harvey Haber, founder of the *New Schools Exchange* (an early alternative school network) with first applying the term *free school* as it was used by the free school movement of the 1960s and 1970s.[61]

Fertile Ground

The oldest still-existing Summerhill-influenced school in North America is Play Mountain Place, founded in Los Angeles in 1949. But the North American *free school movement* essentially began with the publication of *Summerhill* in 1960. To understand why the seeds of Summerhill fell on fertile ground, one has to be aware of the contradictory decade in which this and so many other seeds of freedom were sown.

Ironically, the optimism of this era in North America was rooted in prosperity that grew out of a war-based economy. World War II had ended a decade-long economic depression. American self-confidence was further fed by the destruction of Europe, which left the United States as the great world power. There was relief and hope at the defeat of Nazi forces in World War II, a feeling of starting anew that led to the creation of the United Nations, and a body of international law to keep the peace and to protect human rights.

At the same time, the nuclear weapons that were used at war's end gave humanity another set of worries. Optimism co-existed with an atmosphere of extreme anti-communism and nuclear fear, the Cold War era, within which the brilliant modern world was portrayed as under constant threat. The American former student activist Todd Gitlin said of the 1960s, "This generation was formed in the jaws of an extreme and wrenching tension between the assumption of affluence and its opposite, a terror of loss, destruction and failure."[62]

Nowadays, the critics and dropouts of this period are often dismissed as extreme and impractical, but the mainstream *zeitgeist* of the time was arguably even wackier than that of the counter-culture fringe. The mainstream ethic saw technology as a snake oil to cure all of society's ills. Answering the anxieties of those who feared that ever-increasing mechanization would create boring, dehumanizing jobs and unemployment, the promise was that computerization and automation would bring about some kind of workers Utopia. The greater productivity achieved by automation would bring all employees into a new leisure class.

Writing for *Fortune Magazine* in 1955, David Sarnoff, chairman of the Radio Corporation of America (RCA), set the tone with glowing prose about the technological miracles that would bring "new grace to life":

> The material triumphs now at our disposal and the greater ones to come must be translated into a happier life for mankind everywhere. We must give a clear right-of-way to the things that are good, beautiful and enriching. . . . Leisure, of course, will be greatly extended. A much shorter work week will no doubt prevail in 1980. . . . Not labor but leisure will be the great problem in the decades ahead . . . We have reason to foresee a fantastic rise in the demand for and appreciation of the better, and perhaps the best, in art, music and letters.[63]

This was the promise of gleaming modernity: to free humanity from the centuries-old working-class experience of exhausting labour and escapist release. That humanity should not, and would not, have to spend all its energy on the task of survival wasn't just the wild idea of a few bohemians. The *Hall-Dennis Report* of 1968 articulated a position that was common across the political spectrum: that education would have to address the "problem of leisure".

> Automation dictates an orchestration of new job requirements and a flexibility heretofore unrealized; added to this, leisure time is growing in importance. . . . We are also beginning to recognize that preparing oneself to cope with leisure time is as important as preparing oneself to cope with a job.[64]

The benefits touted for North American democracy had been delayed for many of its citizens by two world wars, an economic depression, and generations of hard-scrabble immigration. In the wake of the defeat of fascism, there was a widespread expectation that the fortunate postwar generation should be able to live out the democratic promise.

Charles Silberman described the "revolution of rising expectations," in which

> improvements themselves . . . generated expectations for further improvements—improvements of a sort and at a rate that society was unable, or unwilling, to fulfill.[65]

There were vital economic issues underlying the personal and public conflicts of the post-war decades: what should be done with postwar prosperity, and how this related to peace and war. In this strange new era that promised either unimaginable wonders or global destruction, all issues had a link to education.

In 1957, a Soviet technological success threw the USA into a panic-driven attempt to force its children to become brilliant technocrats like the communist competition. The trigger was the first man-made object in space, a tiny Soviet satellite named Sputnik. The public school system was blamed for the USA's apparent technological lag, particularly those elements that leaned toward progressivism. Phyllis Fleishman, the founder of Play Mountain Place, described the influence of this event on the American schoolroom:

> With Sputnik, public school curriculum was just shoved downward bodily. Even decent nursery school training places just started making nursery-aged children behave the way they were going to have to behave in public school. That was directly opposed to the way we were all trained—starting where a child is and going at his speed, letting him live this year as the best preparation for the next year. They said: "He'll just have to start practicing what he'll have to do in public school." It's shocking.[66]

Influence of Summerhill in America

The publication of *Summerhill* had provided a starting point for people who wanted to be a part of a solution and were willing to help create it. Some not only started schools, they also wrote about them. Herb Snitzer visited Summerhill in 1962 to take photographs for a book he called *Summerhill: A Loving World*. In 1963, he started his own rural boarding school at Lewis-Wadhams in New York State, and in 1972 he published a book about it, *Today is for Children: Numbers Can Wait*. Inside its cover was a hand-drawn map of a school, an idyllic site bordered by forest, its lawn dotted with gardens. The classic farm structures were supplemented by six specimens of what became a staple of American counterculture, the geodesic dome.

Although Snitzer's rural school was visibly modeled on Summerhill, A. S. Neill wrote in his introduction to Snitzer's book that Snitzer was "no slavish follower. . . . We all go through stages of discipleship, but . . . a wise man does not label himself Montessorian, Steinerite, Deweyite, Summerhillian; to do so is to look backward".[67]

All the same, they could still learn from one another. AERO's Jerry Mintz taught at Lewis-Wadhams before starting Shaker Mountain, and he recalled that Neill's daughter Zoe had helped Snitzer with his school. Carrying on such work into the present, Mintz has mentored the creation of hundreds of schools.

Many who adapted A. S. Neill's ideas in North America retained the aspect of the small rural private boarding school. In this context, a frequent criticism of free schools has been that they predominantly serve the White upper middle class. Neill lamented this reality in Summerhill:

> When we opened the school, the difficulties were especially grave. We could only take children from the upper and middle classes because we had to make ends meet. . . . we have never been able to take the children of the very poor. That is a pity, for we have had to confine our study to only the children of the middle class. And sometimes it is difficult to see

> child nature when it is hidden behind too much money and expensive clothes.[68]

Yet the roots of Neill's thought lay in the American Homer Lane's work in creating self-governing residential institutions for "delinquent" boys and girls, highly oppressed children from often destitute families. Neill knew Lane's work on the Little Commonwealth in England, but Lane had first tried his ideas on self-governance in Detroit.

> His belief that coercion breeds delinquency, whereas freedom can lead to responsibility, was based on observations in the Detroit playgrounds. His unconventional methods and beliefs forced him to resign his position in 1906. After a period of settlement house work, he was invited to serve as superintendent of the newly founded Ford Republic, a residential institution for wayward boys. During his six years as head of the Republic he put his ideas on teaching responsibility through self-government to the test. The boys wrote their own constitution and governed themselves by it.[69]

The work Lane did on juvenile restorative justice and rehabilitation through self-governance has been all but lost. It's ironic that it survived in the middle-class private school Summerhill for half a century before finding its way back to the American inner city.

First Street School

The First Street School, whose story is told in George Dennison's book, *The Lives of Children*, was started in 1964 by Mabel Chrystie, a young teacher who wanted to apply Neill's methods "where they had never been found before, namely, among the urban poor". The pupils at the First Street School were from low-income Manhattan families. Half "had come to us from the public school with severe learning and behavior problems".[70]

Funded by a private two-year grant, the First Street School reached a community that was ill-served by public education, had no access to private schooling, and had never heard of the kind of education these teachers wanted to try out.

Dennison recalled:

> With two exceptions, the parents of the children at First Street were not libertarians. . . . If they persisted in sending us their children, it was not because they agreed with our methods, but because they were desperate. As the months went by, however, and the children who had been truants now attended eagerly, and those who had been failing now began to learn. . . . There was a high morale among them, and great devotion to the school.[71]

The First Street School rented rooms in a YMCA. The teachers all lived nearby, often socialized with the families, and allowed their homes to be treated as adjuncts to the school. The 23 pupils were cared for by three full-time teachers and by Dennison, a "luxurious intimacy" that he pointed out was achieved with the same cost per pupil as in New York City public schools.[72]

Dennison worked in the morning and then used his afternoons to record in a journal "whatever had impressed me that day at school".[73] The result of this methodology is a document that Jonathan Kozol called the "best 300 pages about Free Schools, and one of the most eloquent and stirring books that ever has been written about education".[74]

Dennison primarily described the children in their relationships with each other and with the teachers:

> The children called upon us as persons, and we responded as persons.

Applying the convictions of John Dewey to a demographic that Dewey's Laboratory Schools did not reach, he found that

> school was not a parenthesis inserted within life, but was actually an intensified part of life . . . that was the one source of every good thing that happened.[75]

Reading Dennison's enchanting book, one senses the vast forces arrayed against the school and its students. The insecurity of the school and of the children's lives, and their families' understandable concern that their disadvantaged kids gain the tool of literacy, necessitated different terms of engagement than Summerhill: the teachers were proactive in engaging the children to learn to read. This urgency was warranted, for the First Street School did not outlive the initial philanthropic grant that gave it two intense years of life.

Jonathan Kozol

Boston teacher Jonathan Kozol also confronted the public schools' abandonment of poor and Black students and the "school-fraud" that "doesn't deliver what it promises and advertises, and does deliver something poisonous and vicious that it never mentions on the label".[76]

In March 1966 Kozol, together with his girlfriend and twelve parents of children he had taught in the Boston Public Schools, decided to "begin a little school outside the public system and available for free to kids whose parents had no money".[77] Kozol's account of how this group managed to buy a building and pay teachers the going rates without charging private school fees includes a description of a meeting with a loan shark late at night on a deserted highway. By hook or by crook, their school was operating by September of that year. Most importantly, the New School for Children was "begun and operated under black control".[78]

By 1970, Kozol and the parents with whom he had started the New School were receiving correspondence from community-run schools in California, Seattle, Milwaukee, St. Paul and Minneapolis, Winston-Salem, Santa Fe, Santa Barbara, Toronto, Philadelphia, San Francisco, Cincinnati and St. Louis.

> All in a rush around the winter of 1969 and spring of 1970, each of us began to be aware of one another. We started to sense that we were not out on our

> own, but that we were in fact part of a growing movement.
>
> It was at this point that we began to stop and pause and ask ourselves where we were heading, what we intended, to what kinds of dreams we were accountable and by what values and with what aspirations we were setting forward.[79]

Kozol wrote *Free Schools* to address these questions. He expressed admiration for the larger kind of "public-school-connected, neighbourhood-created and politically controversial operation" that tackled the problems of schooling in poor neighborhoods, and skepticism of the "relatively isolated, politically non-controversial and generally all-white rural Free School". But he didn't devote much space in the book to either. As Kozol explained, *Free Schools* mainly described schools:

> 1) outside the public education apparatus, 2) outside the white man's counter-culture 3) inside the cities 4) in direct contact with the needs and urgencies of those among the poor, the black, the dispossessed, who have been the most clearly victimized by public education, 5) as small, "decentralized" and "localized" as we can manage, 6) as little publicized as possible.[80]

Kozol began his career as a teacher in the poorest schools of Boston. His first book, *Death at an Early Age*, released in 1967, was an indictment of the damage the American school system caused to the children of poor and minority classes.

Kozol saw the rural free schools that some counter-culture people were creating for their children as islands of privilege where people escaped their responsibilities. To Kozol, they were "dangerous and disheartening", "a registered escape-valve for political rebellion" and a "drain on activism and the perfect way to sidetrack ethical men from dangerous behavior".[81]

He argued that the power and privilege that came with a white skin and middle-class background could not be escaped:

> Whether they like it or not, whether they wish to speak of it or not, the beautiful children of the rich and powerful within this nation are going to be condemned to wield that power also.[82]

This is a chilling analysis, with the gap between privilege and poverty starkly laid out. A. S. Neill had written to Wilhelm Reich that "governing is an inferior brand of creation, and the second-rate fellows will want to run our civilization for us as politicians or bureaucrats".[83] In *Free Schools* Kozol argued that to relinquish the small power that one inherits to those "second-rate fellows" is an abdication of responsibility.

> Some of the most conscientious and reflective of the people in the country Free Schools will seek to justify their manner of escape by pointing out that they . . . have, in a sense "retired" from the North American system as a whole, and especially from its agencies of devastation, power and oppression.[84]

Ivan Illich, no slouch as a critic, felt that this resistance through withdrawal had some value. He defended the "hippies and dropouts" who exasperated Kozol and alarmed the general population. Illich argued that these "outsiders" who refused to collaborate with military economies and worked to create their own forms of social organization "threaten the consumer economy, democratic privilege, and the self-image of America".[85]

Two books, brimming with photos of messy, smiling children and geodesic domes—Richard Bull's *Summerhill USA* and Samuel Yanes's *The no more gym shorts, build-it-yourself, self-discovery, free school talkin' blues*—serve as yearbooks or photo albums, sentimental souvenirs of the education counterculture of the late 1960s and early seventies.

Lacking Neill's irony, Dennison's methodology or Kozol's class critique, these dated anthologies by Bull and Yanes indicate what Kozol is driving at in his critique of the frequent self-indulgence found within the free school movement. But beyond the euphoric vision, *Summerhill USA* also calls attention to the time in which these schools grew, a time when students could be "brutalized . . . smacked down . . . hurt, either physically or verbally" in school.[86]

Kozol is still writing, calling his nation to account for what he calls the "savage inequalities" of American education. *Free Schools*, even the earliest edition, is still a priceless reference.

Allen Graubard

Like Kozol in the Boston area, Allen Graubard in Santa Barbara combined writing and teaching with working on the communication and mutual support network among grassroots free schools. His book, *Free the Children*, was described by Kozol as an

> important, serious and comprehensive picture of the Free Schools nationwide, with a much broader focus and somewhat less partisan view than I have been able to present, but with lots of strong subjective viewpoints too.[87]

Free the Children documented an educational phenomenon, the simultaneous creation of hundreds of independent schools:

> The founding during the past few years of several hundred "new schools" sharing various degrees of commitment to libertarian methods, significant student and parent participation in decision-making, and an articulate opposition to the methods and spirit of normal public and private school education is sometimes called a movement, though this word obscures as much as it illuminates.[88]

Free the Children tracked the development of the free school movement, detailing the arguments and tracing different applications of libertarian concepts to their different sources in literature and social life. It examined the difficulties and stumbling blocks with a critical but more forgiving eye than Kozol.

Graubard recorded that in the USA in "1967 and 1968, 20 to 30 new schools were started annually".

> Nineteen sixty-nine saw the beginning of the surge of free school growth with the founding of around 60 or 80. Over 150 were founded in 1970, and the figure for the 1971-1972 school year should be well over 200.[89]

Both Kozol and Graubard's 1972 books ended with lists of the numerous networks, newsletters and publications through which schools and groups shared knowledge and informed one another of the existence of previously unknown free schools.

> The growth of the schools has been accompanied by the development of several regional switchboards and a national New Schools Exchange in Santa Barbara, California, which publishes a bimonthly newsletter. Regional newsletters are distributed, and there have been regional and national conferences and "festivals of alternatives". Most indicative of official recognition, courses on alternative schools have begun to appear at schools of education throughout the country.[90]

In Toronto, much experimentation was taking place. These experiments were documented by a number of periodicals that were devoted to education. Many education activists, including George Martell and Satu Repo, edited and wrote from within the Community Schools movement. Beverley and Murray Shukyn, and Mark Novak wrote books about two early public alternative schools in the Toronto area. Malcolm Levin, a professor at the newly created the Ontario Institute for Studies in Education (OISE), co-founded MAGU, the first public alternative school in Ontario. He would keep a critical eye on how all these activities were received by the mainstream players.

4:

TORONTO: A PLACE TO MAKE A DIFFERENCE

During the nineteen sixties and seventies, people interested in working out different answers to social questions such as education, made the most of the considerable openness that existed in Canada during this time of change and conflict.

Canada proudly celebrated its centennial as a nation in 1967, and there was an invigorating (though somewhat illusory) sense of separation between Canadian and American politics. Several of ALPHA's original families came from the wave of expatriate Americans who, fleeing cities in decay and the Vietnam War, contributed their energy to Canadian causes. One remembered:

> *In my scenario, an important series of events was the fact that I was living in Detroit from 1967 to 1970. So I experienced the incredible chaos of moving into a city where the tanks had left the streets a month after I arrived. Those riots really went on for months afterwards. And through Detroit becoming murder city, the violence becoming greater and greater, the height of the protests about the Vietnam War, the killing of Martin Luther King and the tensions around that. When I was teaching, I used to get my class disrupted all the time by the police coming through and saying there was a bomb scare—we had to clear the building.*

Kozol would describe this era as "a time of torment", a vital reminder that this period was wartime for the draft-age youth of the United States, and a time of intense racial strife. He also mentions the "embattled city" and "siege conditions" in Detroit, Los Angeles, and Philadelphia.[91]

In 1970, in the context of protests against the war in Vietnam, dozens of students were shot by National Guard or police, with four killed at Kent State University and two killed at Jackson State.

While the United States was demonstrating daily that it was a violently divided nation, Canadians functioned in an easier atmosphere. Except for the Quebec self-determination movement, which culminated in the War Measures Act of 1970, Canada was largely free of the violence and fear that afflicted American reform attempts. While anti-war protestors were being shot on American campuses, the Canadian government did little to stem the influx of young Americans fleeing the draft.

The Liberal government of Prime Minister Pierre Trudeau, who had traveled the world for several years in his youth, projected almost the attitude of an amused parent toward the antics of the youth counterculture. Government funds supported hostels for young travelers and buses for stranded hitchhikers.

In this spirit, the Canadian government's ways of dealing with youth unemployment were imaginative and even loving: assisting youth to get to know their country, to learn for the sake of learning, and to create their own opportunities. In the name of job creation, the federally supported Company of Young Canadians (CYC), Opportunities for Youth (OFY) and the Local Incentives Program (LIP) funded young people who created or attached themselves to projects considered to be socially useful. Community organizers employed by the CYC mentored my radical youth group in Calgary and created the Community Schools Workshop in Toronto. Free school movements in Canada were given some support through CYC, OFY and LIP.

At the civic level, reformers ran for Toronto City Council and the Board of Education, achieving short-lived majorities. One ALPHA co-founder recalled:

> *In 1968 or 1969 there was a reform group of trustees that were elected for the first time. . . . They came partly out of working class minority groups organizing the inner city. Most of the reformers came from the inner*

city, concerned about what was happening to those kids. But as well, concerned about schooling generally.

An American expatriate involved in ALPHA described how Canada seemed then:

When I came to Toronto in 1970, I went "Holy shit. This is a different situation altogether. This is a place where people can actually work in relationship through a State authority to make some difference in their lives."

Two ALPHA co-founders named a specific citizen victory for giving impetus to the movement for alternative schools:

The one other thing that really is quite important is the connection in my mind between the Alternative School Movement and the Stop Spadina Movement. . . . In the early nineteen-seventies, they were going to put the Spadina Expressway all the way straight through the city, and I think John Sewell and other folks—Jane Jacobs was involved. It was seen as an extremely successful citizen movement to articulate the needs and aspirations of a local citizenry in relationship to their view of what life in the city should be, compared to what government was imposing.

The alternative school movement in Toronto was also connected to other groups advocating social justice and challenging some of the agendas of change. Change was not driven only by radicals. It was a fact of life, a modernist phenomenon driven by technology and an expanding economy.

Environment, education and neighbourhood activists worked to establish democratic control over such change. They were concerned with maintaining local control over what happened to people and neighbourhoods, and their causes and methods were interrelated.

The relative openness of the federal government, as well as the activism at the civic level, had equivalents in the provincial government. For some visionary trustees, and for the students, parents and educators who wanted to work within the public system, Ontario's *Hall-Dennis Report* of 1968 opened the doors wider than they have been before or since.

During the late 1960s, American free school activists Allen Graubard and Jonathan Kozol noted that Toronto was a centre where notable education critique and free school activity were taking place. It was happening at grassroots, school and Ontario Ministry of Education levels. The province's teacher education and research institute, the Ontario Institute for Studies in Education (OISE) supported such activity, sometimes unwittingly. Several education magazines were published from Toronto. They included *This Magazine is About Schools* and *Community Schools*, produced by activist educators, and, interestingly, radical publications from teachers' organizations and unions, including one with the shaggy name of *Mudpie*.

This Magazine is About Schools

Founded in 1966, Toronto's *This Magazine is About Schools* was described by Jonathan Kozol as the "best in-depth background reading on the Free Schools and the struggle to 'de-school' our imagination and our own ideas about education".[92] It still exists, with a broader mandate and a shorter name, as *This Magazine*.

Founding Editor Robert Davis wrote that *This Magazine is About Schools* was started by a "group of personal friends in Toronto . . . teachers, social workers, and childcare workers" who had a "hunch" that "a radical magazine about schools will strike a chord". With humour to help "survive the outrages of modern schools", the editorial vowed to report on "utopian experiments and pilot projects" as well as document "the established school system".[93]

The first issue, dated April 1966, contained an article by media guru Marshall McLuhan, articles about high school protests and a school for emotionally disturbed children, and a transcript of a lively conversation that took place between A. S. Neill and Mario Montessori (son of Maria Montessori) in London, in 1964. The magazine reported that a Montessori school, possibly the first in Toronto, had been founded in 1961, and predicted that "schools following A. S. Neill's Summerhill, England model will open within a year in Toronto and Winnipeg".[94]

Davis's editorial challenged assumptions that Summerhill, Warrendale and Montessori schools

> work only for special groups—for talented teachers; for bright children, disturbed children, suburban children or slum children; for small classes or well-equipped classes; for country schools or for private schools.

This Magazine is About Schools proposed to prove that such experiments were relevant to public education as a whole.[95] It also aimed to share the work of teachers who were exploring ways to make the public system more welcoming, interesting and relevant for students:

> When you start digging it is remarkable how much experiment you find and how open-minded some authorities are. The founding editorial issued a challenge—"There's lots of freedom there waiting to be used."[96]

Writers for *This Magazine is About Schools* participated in a number of independent free schools. Point Blank School and Superschool are mentioned.[97]

Associated closely with *This Magazine is About Schools* was the independent rural free school Everdale Place, established in 1966. *This Magazine* would document Everdale through the years, publishing its newsletters and progress reports. An organic farm where students boarded during the week and went home on weekends, Everdale had a greenhouse, a kiln, a horse and beehives. Students watched its cow give birth. Everdale lasted until 1974 but, as with many independent free schools, its tuition of $1300 per year proved prohibitive to the class of families who wanted to send their kids. Its legacy and name are carried on by an organic farm that has a substantial education and outreach program.

This Magazine is About Schools had a national and international profile. Far away in Calgary, I had joined a self-governing group of youth called Educational Youth Enterprises (EYE), who were trying to change the education system that controlled our young lives. We eagerly passed around copies as they came out, and followed Everdale's ups and downs. I never saw Everdale, but I wished that I, a high school student at the time, could be part of this kind of "school community".

The magazine also reported on other initiatives across the country. The Summer 1968 issue included a "staple-in" booklet, titled *Some biased information on New Schools in Canada*. The seven schools in Ontario and British Columbia included a Quaker School, a Waldorf School, several free schools, and a school in Vancouver that had split into two—a progressive teacher cooperative and a free school.[98]

In another staple-in booklet, titled *Starting a Free School in Ontario,* John Barber noted that there were "few legal barriers" for those inspired to start independent free schools in Ontario.

> The only definite requirement is that any institution which offers instruction to 50 or more school-age children during school hours must register with the Department of Education by completing an application for registration as a private school.
>
> The government has traditionally exempted children at private schools from the compulsory school attendance law, and, since they have laid down no standards for private schools, it would be almost impossible for them to apply the law to the children at one private school without applying to all since they have no means of measuring the quality of one school against another.[99]

Independent Free Schools: The Free School Handbook

The *Free School Handbook*, first issued in Toronto in the late 1960s, is my favorite publication of the time. The irreverence, informality and goofy illustrations, coupled with an immense sense of social responsibility, express my best memories of the youth movements of the 1960s. It appears to have been compiled by students at a free school called Mother. Like most of the American free schoolers at the time, they rejected involvement with the public school system. According to the *Handbook*,

> Mother was generated as a response to a school board initiated experiment in liberal education in North York. Many students who had worked to bring this program into being were disappointed by the limits placed on it, and their response was to form their own school.[100]

Operating out of a donated space with volunteer "resource people" sharing knowledge, Mother found funding "sparse and virtually unnecessary". Its philosophy was a "perfectly libertarian one. There had to be room in it for any individual to study any subject he chose."

Students at Mother discovered that there was an upper limit to how many people could be involved in a free school and still have it operate as a democratic community. Its biggest curriculum item was the organization of the school itself:

> The business of actually getting the school into operation . . . was foreseen as a process out of which natural community would develop. This assumption proved well-founded. As the school continued to expand however, this community became too large to function under its original principles regarding individual responsibility for the school. Accordingly, a second location was sought and located, and the school divided into Mother I and Mother II. Provisions were made for giving advice and information to other students who wished to become involved in a free school. This led to the formation of a third school, Home.[101]

The student mentorship practiced within Mother expanded into supporting and documenting other schools. This was the free school movement at its best.

As Kozol and Graubard noted, there was a tremendous drive to network, to share ideas and survival strategies, to help one another out. Rochdale College, a controversial experiment in group living and learning that had managed to get a mortgage to construct a modern building in downtown Toronto, let Home operate from its premises.

Like Everdale, independent free schools in Ontario sometimes started, with shoestring budgets, on rural properties that were inexpensive during the urbanizing sixties. One listed in the *Free School Handbook* was Fairchild near Brantford, "founded originally by Mrs. Shaw, the owner of the farm, in order to protect her children from the public school system". Among the resources were a "vast library", musical instruments, a church grant to help with salaries, and resource people from McMaster University. There was also a substantial real-world curriculum in this farm-based boarding free school, with everyone pitching in on chores and cooking. With twelve to fifteen students in Fairchild's first year, the *Free School Handbook* noted seven University applications and seven acceptances. The Handbook noted that Fairchild's "isolation precludes interaction with the surrounding community but cements the relationships within it".[102]

Urban Free Schools

The Free School Handbook portrays urban free schools as the opposite of insular. They survived by making links with the local community, inviting working professionals to become volunteer teachers, trolling for donations, and welcoming anyone and everyone to join in, or create a class. Instead of teachers, free schools sought out "skilled and knowledgeable people who enjoy what they are doing enough to be willing to help other people discover it too".[103]

To differentiate this mentoring role from the top-down curriculum delivery that teachers carried out in public schools, these "teacher-people" were called "resource persons" or "catalysts". Volunteers came from a number of professions and trades, or they could be people with a valuable life experience or hobby to share. Many were professors or teachers who wanted to investigate a different kind of educational relationship.

Often started by high school students, the urban free schools were inventive in the ways they found spaces where their learning communities could meet.

> One of the fundamental requirements for entering a free school is to rid yourself of the misapprehension that you have to have official sanction before you can do anything. You can hold classes in Universities (there are hundreds of empty rooms throughout the day), in libraries, in homes, in restaurants. . . . A class is nothing more than a bunch of people getting together to learn and you don't need permission from Ottawa to do it.[104]

The *Free School Handbook* pointed out that "there is a school in Toronto that uses OISE for almost all its classes, and for its meetings as well . . . all this with nobody knowing or caring . . . what they don't know won't hurt them".[105] One of ALPHA's co-founders recalled "a whole bunch of independent programs that high school kids themselves set up". This person had served as a volunteer speaker or a "catalyst" for some projects that ran informally at OISE.

> *Even though the authorities didn't know anything about it, we knew where the classrooms were. . . . These high school kids would come down, come together; they didn't usually last longer than the original group. They'd go for a few years, gave themselves assignments, worked on projects.*

It's hard to imagine now a period of such excitement about learning that students created informal schools for themselves and took courses without credit. But this was the atmosphere in

Toronto and elsewhere during the late sixties and early seventies. Young people went to self-organized classes on weekends and in the summer, not to gain qualification or do remedial work, but because they wanted to learn.

Of necessity, rural free schools charged tuition, or at least room and board, but most creators of urban free schools wanted their schools to be free financially as well as academically. So they sought out cheap or free space. The authors of the *Free School Handbook* found that, as sites for free schools, public schools were anathema:

> since they are against anything you do that is really innovative almost by definition. They will be particularly worried about protecting the rest of the kids in their school from your influence and are bound to consider themselves to have a say in your program. And they have a direct line to the Department of Education.[106]

It is interesting that churches and YMCAs were frequently willing to host these experiments in education and social living. In Toronto, student-operated free schools Mother I and Mother II operated from YMCAs, and a Y would also be the first site of ALPHA Alternative School in 1972. Historically, such social organizations didn't see their spaces as an income stream, but as resources to share with communities.

Square School, operating out of the home of its principal, anticipated what would become perhaps the most common mandate of alternative schools: to work with alienated, at-risk teens.

> Square School composed itself mainly of "street" kids, i.e., those students sufficiently alienated from Don Mills (or its equivalent) to spend most of their time away from Don Mills, especially in the streets (hence "street") of downtown Toronto.[107]

At that time, "street kids" didn't mean what it does today. These youth engaged in public life together in the streets, parks and wherever they could hang out. But they had homes with their parents, in communal houses shared with other youth, or in "crash pads" where anyone could stay for a few nights. The worried parents associated with the Square School paid tuition to keep their bored truant kids off these increasingly interesting streets. Three full-time staff worked with fifteen students who "found a lot to occupy themselves on a short-term basis ... there was never much consideration given to credits".[108]

Seeing the experience of governing a school as a vital part of a free school curriculum, the authors of the *Free School Handbook* found it problematic that students didn't run the Square School.

> They did make use of it. It was an important event in their lives. They enjoyed the experience and probably benefited from it. But when the school closed after one year because the full-time staff could not continue to subsist on their past salaries the students were unable (or unwilling) to carry on the school themselves.
>
> I think the obvious lesson to be learned (or ignored) from this experience is that it is possible to have a very fine "learning environment", but the power to determine this environment is fundamental to its really teaching you anything.[109]

Although it was adult-driven, Square School was still quite libertarian. Nohant seems to have been its mirror opposite:

> Initiated and governed entirely by its students, it cannot be considered to be less than a free school, yet its patterns are obviously different.

Situated in the "hushed atmosphere of a North York Library", it was "a distinct challenge to the free school movement". Placing "a great deal of emphasis on academic study", Nohant was "the free school most likely to appeal to parents." It pleased "the Department of Education inspector who speaks highly of the school".

> At the very least, Nohant offers a less risky alternative to high school students looking for an out. Saving them from the experience of high school is a

> valuable function in itself. Allowing for freedom and encouragement of academic study is also a valuable gain for students.[110]

Like Jonathan Kozol, the authors of the *Free School Handbook* thought it important to pose the question: "Would students during or after the Nohant experience feel the need or responsibility to alter their society in any way?"

> The most important effect that a free school can have is to undo much of the oppressive socialization which the individual had previously undergone, to free him or her to act in a liberated and responsible manner in relation to the environment in which he finds himself. I don't think this is achieved when you attend a liberal high school, even when you set it up yourself.[111]

The authors of the *Free School Handbook* editorialized:

> free schools are an active protest—by going to a free school, you are stating in action that you do not approve of the manipulative and dehumanizing education system.[112]

Kozol would have agreed, but he would also point out that many low-income and racialized students and families had to prioritize academics, knowing that "without a certain degree of skillful and aggressive adaptation to the real conditions of the system they are fighting, they will simply not survive".[113]

Community Schools

The concern about acquiring tools for survival motivated the activism of the Trefann Court Mothers, who started Laneway in 1969. According to ALPHA's co-founders, neighbours in Trefann Court whose children weren't doing well in the mainstream system "brought a lot of pressure" to the Toronto Board of Education, "really shook them up".

Fighting against the placement of their kids into the dead-end streams called "opportunity" classes, these mothers experienced the class issues that would be described by Kozol, Dennison and Mercogliano. The families were poor, some were Black, and they were aware that their children would need a solid education in order to get by. When they got little support from the Toronto Board for their concerns, they established Laneway School in a local community centre and operated it as an independent alternative for several years. As explained in a news story,

> The Laneway people are most concerned to ensure their children learn to read and write, something they claim they haven't been able to do in the public system. They want a structured, disciplined setting, with a high proportion of adults to pupils.[114]

Created by parents in a low-income neighbourhood, Laneway was a *community school*. Activists in Toronto's community schooling movement worked hard during the 1960s and 1970s to inspire and support community-controlled schooling. *This Magazine is About Schools* followed this movement closely. Soon it had its own magazine called *Community Schools*. Its organizational base was the Community Schools Workshop, described by Toronto activist George Martell as "a group of individuals committed to the promotion of community schools in Metropolitan Toronto through a process of public education and community development".[115]

The Community Schools Workshop advocated for local public school communities, consisting of "teachers, parents, and older students", to organize around creating curricula that taught the basics, building "social sciences programs that relate directly" to the neighborhood, and employing local residents as teachers and resource people.[116] The Workshop's goals were to "improve the educational system through a process of decentralizing decision-making", placing it in the hands of parents, students and teachers, and to foster the "use of the community as a total learning environment".[117] Its publication, *Community Schools*, critiqued the mainstream and took both a critical and supportive interest in educational projects and initiatives, including the new alternative schools.

Hall-Dennis

Living and Learning: The Report of the Provincial Committee on Aims and Objectives of Education in the Schools of Ontario was an example of a type of project that is part of governance in Canada, whereby a group of citizens is appointed to investigate an aspect of Canadian life. The report's common names, *The Hall-Dennis Report* or simply *Hall-Dennis*, came from its co-chairs: Justice of the Supreme Court of Canada Emmett Hall and school principal Lloyd Dennis.

Twenty-four researchers were appointed to "make a careful study of the means whereby modern education can meet the present and future needs of children and society".[118] They were not diverse in terms of race, class, cultural background or gender identity (for example, there were only four women), but they came from a range of professions. Educators were strongly represented, but others were involved with labor, business, manufacturing, law, accountancy, farming and psychology—all with records of public service in education, on school boards and committees. These researchers were not libertarians, but a gathering of solid middle-class folk who believed that an advanced, affluent society could and should meet the needs of all children.

Noting the governmental tradition of commissioning and then ignoring such research, these authors addressed the public, thinking big, in the spirit of the time. Word spread. I and my fellow student activists in faraway Alberta wrote away for free copies of this Ontario report, issued as a glossy soft-cover book teeming with photographs.

The *Hall-Dennis Report* stood on the United Nations *Universal Declaration of Human Rights* and devoted one section to a discussion of democracy. It criticized the common educational approaches in Ontario during its research period of 1965-1968:

> Basically, the school's learning experiences are imposed, involuntary, and structured. The pupil becomes a captive audience from the day of entry. His hours are regulated; his movements in the building and within the classroom are controlled; his right to

> speak out freely is curtailed. He is subject to countless restrictions about the days to attend, hours to fill, when to talk, where to sit, length of teaching periods, and countless other rules. Often the rules of the game can be just as mystifying to the child and his family as the English language to a newly arrived immigrant.[119]

The Report went on to describe students being "stuffed or programmed like a computer at any hour of the school day", a practice that Paulo Freire in 1970 named the *banking* concept of education—and as much in force in 2022 as it was in 1968.

The *Hall-Dennis Report* firmly repudiated the physical punishments that were, in the mid-sixties, still quite widely used in Canadian schools. More challenging was its skepticism about the value of rewards as incentives to learning, noting that "the children who most need the incentive of good marks are least likely to get them, even when given for effort rather than achievement".[120]

Hall-Dennis argued against grading and streaming, seeing them as part of an essentially punitive approach to teaching, in which failure itself was seen as the most brutal and permanent of punishments:

> Failure in our society too often takes on the form of a public stigma and unfortunately the "loser" in the early years of school acquires an image of himself as a failure, which becomes deeply ingrained in his psyche. Children can be helped to cope with the stress of real failure if their differences are understood, if they are loved despite their inabilities, and if they are given the courage to try again.[121]

The report recommended the elimination of "lock-step systems of organizing pupils, such as grades, streams, programs, etc." It advised removing barriers based on age, freeing children to engage any subject on any level where it interested them, "to let the child be one's guide in opening the doors to learning".[122]

The report saw removal of such barriers as addressing not only individual, but also class and gender-based difference. Noting that "girls in the early years are far more successful in our present graded system than boys—in fact, one or two years ahead of boys of the same age", its solution was not to isolate or label students, but to expand the range of opportunities for all children, regarding "difference" as the norm:

> Helping each child develop at his own tempo and point of readiness should avoid such unnecessary failures. . . . It is for this reason that a broad spectrum of opportunities must be provided from which children, of both sexes, can make their choice.[123]

Hall-Dennis called for every gift to have an opportunity for development and every disability to be accommodated "in an atmosphere of self-respect and dignity, and without the stigma of failure".[124]

A startling departure from over a century of public school practice was Recommendation 74:

> Abandon the use of class standing, percentage marks, and letter grades in favor of parent and pupil counseling as a method of reporting individual progress.

Hall-Dennis did hold teachers and schools accountable; they were to be accountable directly to their students' families. The report recommended local control of education, with teachers designing education experiences appropriate for their students. The Ministry of Education would "prepare and present curriculum guides only as broad statements and make the design of detailed curriculum programming the responsibility of the teachers in the schools". (Recommendation 85)

These ideas were deeply radical in the sense that to dismantle systems that placed children into hierarchies based on age and perceived ability was a structural reform that removed the main instrument of the *hidden curriculum*. Such reform would entail substantial re-thinking on the part of every person in the education system—including parents.

The Committee made 258 wide-ranging recommendations regarding major issues, including teacher accreditation, funding, curriculum, grading, roles of various levels of bureaucracy, school-based anti-poverty measures, "Indian control of Indian education", bilingualism, language and ethnic diversity, immigration, students with disabilities and lifelong learning. And in keeping with the rhetoric of the day, it addressed the "problem of leisure" promised by labor efficiencies to be created by automation and computerization.

This inclusive, research-based approach to education policy, expressed by successful, mainstream people, represented a significant consensus. The industrialists, educators, businessmen, union organizers, parents and professionals in this committee didn't behave like representatives of interest groups, but as citizens who pooled their experience to carry out a task in service of the common good. Prioritizing humanism over industrialism, yet friendly to industry, the report amounted to a practical blueprint to apply John Dewey's best principles to Ontario public schools.

There were weaknesses in the *Hall-Dennis Report*. Its concept of local control didn't include any structures for local decision making, but relied on principals and benign authorities in the administration. There may have been problems with the way authorities ensured that the ideas would be applied in schools: in a coercive culture, even schemes for democratization typically are enforced rather than encouraged.

In the wake of the report, many teachers eagerly put into practice reforms they had long awaited. Others, however, who suddenly found themselves, with little preparation or support, trying to team-teach in a noisy "open classroom pod," or who were expected to somehow institute "inquiry methods" in large classes overwhelmed by "integrated" special-needs kids, were quite understandably resentful.

Problems of this kind could have been corrected down the line by caring educators, politicians and bureaucrats, but became instead part of the proposal's eventual undoing.

Finland's much-lauded system, humane and child-focused, yet scoring high on international tests, is similar in many ways to the structure recommended by *Hall-Dennis*. However, rather than being imposed within just a few years as *Hall-Dennis* was, Finland's reforms were instituted during a full decade of consultation with all of the stakeholders.

"Reforming education is a complex and slow process" writes Finnish educator Pasi Sahlberg.

> To rush this process is to ruin it. . . . Steps must be grounded in research and implemented in collaboration by academics, policy makers, principals and teachers.[125]

Hall-Dennis was research-based, and many educators were ready to run with its recommendations. But those who disagreed weren't offered time to adjust, or space to contribute their experience and feedback. This was incredibly divisive.

Despite its flaws, the *Hall-Dennis Report* laid a conceptual and organizational groundwork for educating diverse children in a humane, democratic manner in a large public system. The challenge was embraced by many individual teachers and public schools, and facilitated the creation of new models of schooling inside the public school boards in Ontario. ALPHA's co-founders would report that Neill's Summerhill "was very much talked about in the initial formative stages" of crafting ALPHA's democratic vision, but agreed that "*Hall-Dennis* was just as important as Summerhill, in terms of people thinking about what they wanted for their kids."

5:

ALTERNATIVES IN THE PUBLIC SYSTEM

The Free School Movement consisted largely of independent schools that generally subsisted on tuition, donations, grants and fund-raising. In the USA, and internationally as well, this would persist. In Canada, independent schools flourished for a few years. But Canada's long-lived alternative schools would be created inside public school systems.

The authors of *Public Alternative Schools in Metro Toronto*, looking back from the perspective of 1987, recalled that their movement for local control and children's rights was inspired not only by Summerhill and the radical critics, but also by the struggles of the least privileged people in the Americas:

> Alternative schooling had its origins in the civil rights movements of the late 1960's as part of a wide rejection of authority and established values and as a seeking of new ways of being, particularly among student communities all over the world. The movement was not merely critical of the existing order, but actively attempted to establish workable alternative lifestyles. Naturally, there was widespread interest in changing methods of education since schools implicitly and explicitly reflect and perpetrate social values.[126]

During this era, many people worked without pay to design ways to live low-impact lives, and devoted great effort toward society-changing projects. These included defending and rehabilitating run-down neighbourhoods, as well as creating intentional communities around ecological projects and public services like housing, health, child care, culture and education.

MAGU in North York

The first elementary alternatives in the greater Toronto area were created by parents and teachers in a north end suburb. By 1970, the North York Board of Education had broken ground with AISP and MAGU, "free" schools that shared facilities with existing schools. Daily life at an established urban free school was later described in this passage about MAGU in a 1975 article in *Toronto Life*:

> It's the constant noise of children moving and talking that immediately strikes a visitor to MAGU. It takes a while to sort out the learning activities, but they're going on. In one corner, children are getting their word lists, and two 5 year-olds are building a walkie-talkie out of string and paper cups. When they break into a quarrel a teenager steps in to help them sort it out. There are parents helping kids, kids helping one another and 8-month-old Jonah, who belongs to teachers Mike and Laura Schein, crawling around.
>
> Baby Jonah's what the school is all about. It's a community school where teachers, students and parents share experiences and learn from one another, often outside of classrooms. Some older kids go to York University for music or women's studies, others to Channel 19 for filmmaking. Some are closeted away with a teacher or a parent volunteer for anything from science to art. There are periods for such subjects as math, but kids decide whether or not to take it.[127]

MAGU didn't survive the seventies, but it was influential. In part due to connections within the University of Toronto's Ontario Institute for Studies in Education (OISE), the push for an elementary alternative school spread to the adjacent Toronto Board of Education.

According to one journalist, what it took to start a public school in Toronto in the early seventies was “a duplicating machine, several people who know what they want, and a delegation to a board subcommittee.”

> After that it takes a lot of telephone calls, leg-work, and persuasion. You have to select a compatible teaching staff, get the administrators to go along and the board to approve it, and you have to make sure enough pupils will attend to make the school worthwhile. Fifty will do, 100 is better.[128]

That is what groups of parents, teachers and even high school students did during the late sixties and early seventies. ALPHA parents recall the Toronto of this time as “a hugely exciting place”.

SEED: the Groundbreaker

In the Toronto Board of Education (TBE), the first alternative school developed gradually from a project to keep unemployed students occupied. Project SEED (*Summer of Experience, Exploration and Discovery*) began in 1968 as a summer collaboration between politicians, activists, teachers and students. It was a student-run communications hub as much as a school. Long before social media, its newsletters had a national influence. In 1969, my fellow high school activists in Calgary eagerly read SEED’s communiqués.

Here is an account of SEED’s origins from two of its co-founders, Murray and Beverly Shukyn:

> In the spring of 1968, the newspapers were full of dire forecasts of high student unemployment for the coming summer. Canada Manpower estimated that over 100,000 students would be unemployed in Metro alone. There were very few jobs, or alternatives to jobs, available. There were summer-school programs, but these were generally considered to be simply an extension of the traditional school program.

> Parents were apprehensive about their children doing nothing for two months. News of student riots in the United States did little to quell their anxiety. The impact of these anxieties was felt by trustees of the Toronto Board of Education through telephone calls from their constituents asking what the board was going to do about the situation. As a result Ying Hope, chairman of the board at that time, formed an ad hoc committee to create a new summer program for students.
>
> The committee was a diverse group consisting of Toronto Board of Education employees and representatives of the Toronto Teachers' Federation, the Students' Administrative Council of the University of Toronto, the Canadian Association for Adult Education, the Social Planning Council of Metropolitan Toronto, and other community organizations. . . . The initial target group of SEED was secondary school and university students who were unable to find summer employment.[129]

Shukyn had been drawn into the project by his principal at Dewson School, Les Birmingham. They worked as volunteers all that summer. There was no recipe for what they were doing; everyone pitched in on a program that was to begin within a few weeks, in a space that was empty, pending renovation. Students soon took over much of the work. They distributed posters that had been printed up through school trustee Ying Hope's office, a few ads were placed, and the phones began ringing: "Kids could telephone, state their interests, and be formed into groups very quickly." Subjects requested included "Economics as it Affects the Social Order, Puppetry, Child Care, and Watchmaking".

In conversation with the author, a founding SEED student recalled their participation:

> *"I had read McLuhan's Understanding Media and all the stuff then current about Summerhill and other free form schools and thought, why don't we build a school on a telecommunications network? If the medium in education — a network, rather than a classroom — was the message, what would education look like? I set*

> *myself up with a desk and a phone and started creating connections between potential students calling in and resource people they could use.*

The "only guidance for the program" was a brief statement of philosophy:

> Basically, the idea behind SEED is one of a fresh approach to learning through a voluntary informal program of involvement. In all areas it is intended to be an open-ended type of situation where the program that develops is that which the participants declare to be their need. It is also open-door in nature having activities both in and beyond the school facilities as the needs arise to allow experiences, explorations and discoveries to take place.[130]

A number of teachers worked during their summer vacation as volunteer administrators, counselors and "catalysts". In this experimental atmosphere of sharing knowledge without compulsion or evaluation, students also recruited volunteer resource people who did not necessarily have teaching qualifications, but had some knowledge or expertise that interested them.

Volunteers, noted Shukyn, "were not typing, cleaning up or shepherding kids . . . they were teaching, an activity very different from those usually assigned to volunteers". Board of Education chair Ying Hope held an oriental philosophy class and writer June Callwood led a course on "human emotions". Toronto Board trustee Fiona Nelson held a class on politics.[131]

By the second summer, SEED students were working toward creating a full-time program that they argued would help prevent drop-outs and enable interested students to perform to their potential, as well as provide a model for the public Board of Education: "The SEED program would be a useful stepping stone, keeping in pace with the Board's increasing experiment and reform in education."[132]

In an article she wrote for *Canadian Forum* in 1972, Nelson recalled that the new reform-minded School Board, of which she was a member, "took office in January 1970. They had barely settled in when the SEED students presented a brief requesting a full-time, ungraded, accredited secondary school for 100 pupils".[133]

The school board accepted this concept in principle and established the SEED Subcommittee—thereby, according to the Shukyns, establishing a process through which "community groups could present a concept in its early stages of development and receive the assistance of an entire board of education in ironing out the details".[134]

Blood Relations

Like ALPHA, SEED still survives in the Toronto District School Board (TDSB), though it has gone through changes in location and format. SEED is probably ALPHA's nearest blood relation, an older sibling who broke the ice with their conservative parent, the Toronto Board of Education (TBE). But according to a co-founder, cousin MAGU, in the adjacent municipality of North York, was a greater influence.

> *I think the influence of SEED on ALPHA was simply the notion that we knew that there was some receptivity on the part of the Toronto Board to alternatives, and we knew who the trustees were that were supporting SEED, and whom we should go to, in relationship to getting support for ALPHA. But MAGU was a far bigger influence on ALPHA than SEED was. People went and visited MAGU. I don't know how much of "The ALPHA Experience" was actually cribbed from MAGU's submission to the North York Board, but I'm sure some of it was.*

A copy of MAGU's charter was found in the archives of one of ALPHA's co-founders. The Shukyns' "biography" of SEED showed the importance of another sibling, as the activist parents of Laneway lobbied for public system support for their school. Though they didn't yet exist as public alternative schools, both Laneway and ALPHA would influence SEED's future.

Early Battles

As SEED settled into the public board as a secondary alternative, and ALPHA and Laneway began their relationships with the board, a column in *Community Schools* noted serious problems that would beset those trying to carry out different educational mandates within the Toronto Board of Education.

In a *Report from the Board* subtitled "Who makes decisions?", journalist Ellen Murray warned:

> The power of elected officials is deceptive; the decisions they can make are often very wide in scope, but they are dependent upon a career bureaucracy or civil service to carry them out. If this bureaucracy dislikes the politician's decisions—or even if they just aren't committed to them—they probably won't be executed as the legislators intended. When an unpopular decision comes on the scene, "administrative difficulties" arise, foot-dragging begins, information is withheld or not just mentioned, and although the letter of decision will probably be carried out, the spirit is ignored.[135]

This article detailed a spirited battle between the Toronto Board of Education administration and the largely reform-minded school trustees that took place during the March 23, 1972 trustee meeting. Two of the arguments impacted alternative schools:

> 1) a report on the possibility of some schools having complete control over their budgets, and
>
> 2) a solicitor's report pointing out all the technical illegalities in both [Laneway] and the ALPHA project.[136]

Murray reported that trustee Fiona Nelson called both reports "hatchet jobs." With respect to the first report, Nelson claimed that board administrators found the idea of schools controlling their own budgets "so threatening that they didn't want it to happen".

> Several principals and at least one group of parents, teachers and a principal had indicated interest in the idea, and Director of Education Ronald Jones was supposed to explore its feasibility with four principals representative of various areas of the city.
>
> The principals consulted included at least one who had been quite committed to the new idea, but the report Jones and board officials turned in said that the group wasn't interested in such a plan.
>
> They felt that book-keeping and administrative problems involved in the project were too great, and that they didn't have the time or expertise to oversee it.[137]

The feisty Fiona Nelson would receive the Order of Canada in 2015 for "a life of volunteer work devoted to the well-being of children, notably in the fields of education and health". During this early confrontation, she didn't mince words:

> What she believes happened is that the administrators "called in four principals and made the difficulties involved in such a plan seem so monumental that they decided they didn't want it". An experiment in local financial control is something she sees as "absolutely essential," however, and she says now that trustees will just have to make sure that such an idea gets a fair trial.[138]

The second battle concerned the solicitor's report of March 22, 1972, which, according to the Community Schools reporter, "had been requested at the last minute by the financial committee, and was at the board under questionable circumstances".[139] Because the solicitor's report seriously impacted SEED, it was included verbatim in the Shukyns' book about SEED that was published the following year.

The Board's Finance Committee had requested the solicitor "to report to the Board on what the Board's statutory obligations are as far as the delegation of authority for the running of a school such as the Laneway Community School is concerned."

The solicitor explained:

> The recommendation of the Special Committee re Alternatives in Education is that the Board approve in principle the operation of the Laneway Community School under the aegis of the Board. The dictionary meaning of "aegis" is protection. It would, therefore, be contemplated that the school would not be under the charge or jurisdiction of the Board.[140]

Though Laneway was focused on basic skills, and ALPHA was to be a non-graded *Hall-Dennis* school, this solicitor saw them as "similar in concept." In the view of the report, their similarity lay in their common determination to operate "independently of existing board schools" and to be run by a "staff-community council."

To ensure the survival of learning conditions they felt their students needed, the parents who started these schools wanted control over their locations and staffing. Quoting from the Schools Administration Act, the communication concluded:

> The Board has no power to finance or support the Laneway Community School nor to operate the ALPHA school under the proposed form of organization.[141]

This report, submitted only the day before the March 23 meeting, seems to have been quite a bombshell. According to Ellen Murray:

> What Nelson objected to was the fact that the problems had never been raised before, in spite of the fact that ALPHA had been discussed six months previously and approved, and Laneway had already passed committee. A few words in committee could have prevented any legal problems.[142]

In the face of trustees' objections, the head administrator himself, Ronald Jones, agreed that the "legal points . . . were relatively technical and could be ironed out by co-operation and some changes in wording".

Reporter Ellen Murray concluded: "Although the episode is probably due more to administrative inefficiency than sabotage, it did demonstrate the lack of sympathy between the board and administrators."[143] Despite the elected trustees' challenges to it, the solicitor's report remained on file, to affect what would happen in the future.

The easy road for trustees to take had been to declare alternative schools like ALPHA and SEED to be *experimental*, a term that *Globe and Mail* reporter Loren Lind declared was so popular in those times that "the use of the word itself will make school administrators look bad if they oppose it".[144] But there was a risk to this. The wording of the solicitor's report subtly shifted control of such "experiments" to the administration:

> However, the experimental educational programme contemplated for these schools could, subject to any necessary approval from the Department of Education, be conducted under the jurisdiction of the Board in schools under its charge in accordance with the present legislation.[145]

For example, the Solicitor described SEED as an "experiment" that was "under the direction of the administration", ignoring the partnership of the board members, teachers, students, parents, and volunteers that created and operated it. SEED's coordinator Murray Shukyn warned:

> In his report, the solicitor quoted at great length from the Schools Administration Act and concluded, "A board may not delegate to committees comprising parents, teachers and others, the responsibility for the selection of staff and for the establishment of policy."
>
> It seems that the basic concept of meaningful community involvement in decision-making has been negated by this interpretation of the statutes.[146]

SEED saw the solicitor's opinion as an "interpretation" of the Act, and so did a majority of the elected trustees. Shukyn described how Nelson counselled the SEED Community, pointing out that "both ALPHA and Laneway had in fact made recommendations for staffing that the board accepted. She was of the opinion, having spoken with a lawyer, that the SEED community could form a committee to recommend specific staff appointments, in spite of what the board's solicitor had said".[147]

Thus, public alternative schools that did not yet exist gave SEED some needed backup, in effect creating precedents for their precedent. By pushing for Board funding, independent Laneway opened up the Board to ALPHA's proposal. ALPHA's acceptance made Laneway's inclusion almost inevitable.

But SEED had good reasons to worry. It was a successful Board initiative, addressed a youth problem, and drew a community of students and teachers so excited about education that they had created and supported it during evenings, weekends and summers without accreditation or pay. Even as one arm of the Board of Education supported the creation of more new alternatives, SEED was coping with an administrative attempt to impose four damaging top-down decisions on the system's pioneer:

- SEED was to be moved from its collegial home at the YMHA to some empty classes in a high school
- the community's ability to hire its staff was being contested
- Shukyn, who had been with the school since its beginning and had worked his first year as a volunteer, was to be transferred
- there was to be "closer administrative supervision of all aspects of the program".[148]

Without consideration for what the nature and needs of its educational "experiment" might be, the school was to be moved and the experimental conditions and personnel changed by administrative directive.

The administration's direct interventions in SEED in 1972 seemed to reflect administrative "sabotage" more than "lack of sympathy", particularly in the transfer of Murray Shukyn, whom Globe and Mail reporter Loren Lind described as "the man most responsible for getting it going".[149]

Shukyn was heartbroken, but strategically, he advised the SEED Community to let him go and focus its limited energies on keeping its location and on fixing its Achilles heel, its undefined community decision-making powers:

> The SEED community has historically been involved in decision-making by consent and trust, and no process has been established to ensure a community voice in decisions except as a reaction to those imposed. It seems to me that to guarantee the integrity of this program we must devise a process whereby we are involved and unite to ensure its implementation.[150]

Guided by recommendations of an ad hoc committee and by a report from Fiona Nelson, the SEED community "formulated unanimous recommendations about the hiring of staff, which were quickly accepted by the board and implemented by the administration".[151]

In a speech to SEED's students, parents and teachers, Shukyn explained the often implacable but usually non-malicious process of administrative thought. It seems that the directive to move SEED came from the Director of Education and the Finance Committee:

> School enrollments are dropping, producing vacant classrooms in many of our secondary schools. These rooms are heated, maintained, and available at minimum cost. The problems of housing two distinctive programs with differing philosophies under the same roof, though apparent, were never discussed.[152]

This is a serious, on-going problem in large education systems: major decisions that affect programs are often made for reasons unrelated to programming. This struggle shows that, as community and alternative schools were supported by some administrators and politicians in the public board, others moved quietly to rein them in.

Such moves and counter-moves characterize the ambivalent relationship the public board has with its alternative schools, one in which conflict and crisis recur, in the words of AERO's Jerry Mintz, "like clockwork". Allen Graubard documented this dynamic as it occurred in the USA:

> Many experimental alternative schools within the public system are now beginning, and many of these are free schools. However, they are necessarily enmeshed in the public school bureaucracy and under various constraints and pressures because of this. In the private free schools . . . one finds a situation of real independence. These institutions are built by people who have not asked educational "experts" to design or approve an "experimental program".

In Graubard's view,

> The key to these institutions is that they are almost always the result of voluntary grass-roots efforts to build schools where children and young people are not oppressed by the arbitrary discipline and total power characteristic of most public schools and where the possibilities for experimenting and searching for new and better ways for children to live and learn can be explored.[153]

Initiated by parents, teachers and students, but funded by the public board, Toronto's alternative schools were examples of both kinds that Graubard described. This was the unusual opportunity that Toronto presented at the time. Grassroots governance was gaining a toehold in Toronto-area public schools, through community-controlled initiatives designed to help disadvantaged students to achieve literacy (as with Laneway), and attempts to try different and democratizing pedagogical formats (as with MAGU, SEED and ALPHA). The existence of the *Hall-Dennis Report* and the presence of supportive trustees and administrators fueled hope that economically accessible alternatives would find a permanent place in public schooling.

In a press interview with this author after Murray Shukyn's death in 2016, Toronto administrator Dale Shuttleworth recalled that, after Shukyn was pulled from SEED, he sought Shukyn out to help parents, teachers and students to develop still more schools. While SEED was designed to give students all the freedom they could handle, subsequent high schools were focused on helping struggling students. Shukyn would advise on many initiatives for youth over the years, and was instrumental in the creation of SOLE and SUBWAY, and in the eventual formation of the Alternative Schools Advisory Council (ASAC) in about 1980.

The visionary educators and feisty parents and students who were swimming upstream to start alternative schools found support from a number of liberal-minded people of influence. Professors from OISE supported MAGU and ALPHA. SEED had the backing "of a large group of socially prominent parents", including several university professors, as well as world-famous social thinkers like media guru Marshal McLuhan and urban critic Jane Jacobs, who had inspired the Stop Spadina movement.[154] In the battle against established power for the survival of challenging social initiatives, high-profile allies come in handy.

6:

STARTING ALPHA

> *For release to all media--September 21, 1971:*
>
> People for an Alternative Elementary School is a group of concerned people who have been meeting for the purpose of establishing an alternative educational experience for primary school children in Toronto.
>
> Our goal is to form a public-supported school to become operative in September, 1972. We are now forming policy and program decisions, and hope to petition the Board of Trustees by early winter.
>
> General meetings are taking place every other Tuesday evening for the purpose of developing our educational philosophy and building our school community. We are meeting on September 28 at 8:00 p.m. at the Ontario Institute for Studies in Education, 252 Bloor St. West, Room 201.
>
> (*The ALPHA Community press release, September 21, 1971*)

Signed by OISE professor Roger Simon, a note attached to the press release requested parents to visit MAGU in North York "for the purpose of seeing an alternative school in operation."

A discussion paper attached to this release was also found in the TDSB archives. The paper expressed a "growing dissatisfaction among parents and teachers in Toronto with the existing public school system and the lack of alternative educational opportunities for children of primary age." It also expressed the frustration of teachers who found it difficult to work in schools "where discipline has priority and the individual needs and desires of each child are often ignored altogether."

The paper evoked the language of John Dewey and the *Hall-Dennis Report*, as it issued the following invitation:

> The school we hope to initiate will need children and committed parents and teachers to develop a community for living and learning.

Three out of the fifteen oral history informants I interviewed were involved in those preliminary discussions. Thirty-six years later, the three participants recalled those meetings:

> *I was involved with ALPHA before it started. My wife and I . . . saw an ad in the Globe and Mail I believe . . . I can't remember where the first meeting was, but the second meeting was in our house and more people were in our house than we could comfortably accommodate. I think there were about sixty people that turned up to this meeting, in our house.*
>
> *I remember the discussion year, the year before ALPHA started, my wife and I hearing about it and coming . . . a big room and coffee there, and people sitting around in chairs every week and discussing issues and so on. And I remember taking turns chairing and trying not to have a chair at all.*
>
> *People would come and go. There would be a central core and people would come to find out what was going on. A lot of people wouldn't come back, and others would stay and participate.*
>
> *Even who came to those early meetings, it was quite diverse. There were people who came and had a formal political perspective on things; and there were some of the people in the group whose expectation was that you could hold a meeting and bring your kids, so the whole question of how you could have a meeting and have kids in the room at the same time was trying to be worked through . . . getting hell from the cleaning staff because the people were leaving the place a mess and sanitary napkins and diapers were in the OISE trashcans. It was a pretty messy process.*

Roger Simon would later talk about these discussions with Mark Golden of *Community Schools*:

> "There was a lot of negative discussion at first," he recalls. "People didn't want a school like other schools. And they didn't want to be a second MAGU. Some MAGU people were there but no one wanted to listen to them. Everyone mostly told stories about what the schools had done to them and might do to their kids."[155]

One can sense a kind of group therapy taking place, something that is not just about the children.

An early argument was over the question of whether this would be an independent free school or a public alternative school. Writing for *Community Schools*, Mark Golden later outlined his understanding of how this question was settled:

> ALPHA parents had not wanted a free school. Free schools were basically elitist, available only to a small and relatively privileged part of society. They wanted a publicly-funded school, hoping to use their political influence to set a precedent for other parents.[156]

Unlike Kozol, Graubard and other free school educators from south of the border, most of ALPHA's co-founders felt cautiously optimistic about collaborating with Toronto's government on their visionary initiative:

> *I think people thought it was a moment of possibility, where one could actually work within the system, and have the system be flexible enough to make that possible and then potentially influential. I don't think that was unrealistic, actually. I think that it was a very interesting moment.*

In 1971, the Stop Spadina Movement had saved Chinatown, Kensington Market and the garment district (ALPHA's eventual neighbourhood) from demolition.

> *The success of that, and the sense that citizens could take control of their own lives and initiate policies that*

> *best met their needs was an extremely important political factor in motivating people to think about going to the public system for the creation of alternative forms of education for their kids. . . . Stop Spadina wasn't just about stopping a freeway. It really was about questions of local control.*

"Local control" was vital to the concept of the new alternative elementary school. The press picked up on all-day kindergarten and self-governance: "The main feature of the proposed ALPHA school is that it would be run by the parents and the staff, although coming under Board of Education auspices."[157]

Community control by parents and staff was a step beyond the *Hall-Dennis Report*, which relied on the benign authority of principals to ensure that a school would reflect its community's needs and concerns. Part of the activism of the sixties involved defending and rehabilitating run-down neighbourhoods, and creating intentional communities to develop ecological, equitable and sustainable economies. Simon later told *Community Schools* that ALPHA was proposed as "a real community instead of a geographical community":

> We wanted more than just a school: we wanted a general sharing of resources. In fact school was sort of a bad word; the original idea was a community center, the integration of education and other things. Not field trips into real life but letting kids do real life things within the community."[158]

According to an ALPHA co-founder, the group that gathered to discuss ALPHA's creation also faced the task of presenting

> *a vision of an ALPHA Community . . . so that it could be accepted in the public system as something that was a really solid option—a group of people who knew what they wanted and were making demands on the School Board for it.*

They discovered that building a cohesive community around this proposal was not a quick or logical process.

> *One of the things that certainly happened is that a small group articulated a vision—this is inevitable—a small group articulated a vision of what we wanted—exactly what we did I can't tell you but I know we did it—and as we got more people involved, because obviously we needed more than five or six families involved, opinions got more diverse and so the coherence of the vision got more diverse and the fault lines and contradictions of what people wanted started to appear.*
>
> *The coherence of those demands internally, really within the ALPHA "Community" was a fiction. Documents are very self-consciously written to present a public face for a political process, and I think . . . they should only be read on those terms.*

As this co-founder indicates, this proposal wasn't just a vision or a wish list, even though the community it envisioned didn't yet exist. It was the first step in a complex political, administrative, cultural and historical process.

Working with the successful example of MAGU's proposal, the group had the assistance of Toronto Board of Education administrator Dale Shuttleworth, who had entered the system "to try to serve as a change agent and social entrepreneur".[159] ALPHA's founding community, many of whom, he noted, "were professionals and war resistors", was the first group of parents he worked with.

> This involved numerous town hall meetings where educational theories and ideologies were debated, often with great emotion. I represented the school establishment and, at least initially, was not to be trusted; I became the apologist for everything that was wrong with institutional schooling. I found this to be rather ironic. . . . The final result of all the meetings and debates was the drafting of a proposal to be presented to the Board of Education.[160]

The document that arose out of the deliberations in these coffee and diaper-scented rooms was called *The ALPHA Experience*. It would turn out to be surprisingly durable.

The ALPHA Experience

A certain yellowing paper, printed with purplish ink, laid the groundwork for fifty years of democratic schooling at ALPHA. These original drafts of ALPHA's proposals are crumbling relics that were created using a Ditto machine, a reproduction process that predated photocopiers. One draft provides the source for the name ALPHA, an acronym for *A Lot of People Hoping for an Alternative*. A handwritten scribble attributes the name to Maureen Joy. Hers is the only name on the document. This would be typical of most official ALPHA documents, unsigned group creations with no designated representative or leader.

The ALPHA Experience, submitted to the December 16, 1971 meeting of the Toronto Board of Education, reflected many of the ideas contained in the provincial government's *Hall-Dennis Report*. It echoed the mainstream *zeitgeist*, asserting that technological change was making inevitable a "complex society of the future". With a shorter workweek, citizens of the near future would have more time to participate in cultural and democratic processes and must be educated "for a rich personal life".[161] Such ideas about quality of life and social responsibility contrast with today's mainstream ideologies, in which ever-increasing productivity and worker availability 24/7 spawn an anxious drive for increasingly elusive "success", even for young children.

The word *values* appears ten times in *The ALPHA Experience*. The school isn't proposed just for academic accomplishment, but "in order to reflect and nurture the values" of cooperation, diversity, freedom of expression, autonomy, social responsibility, and affiliation. Its statement that "competition in the program will be de-emphasized" challenged a prevailing cultural dogma that has become even stronger in recent years than it was in 1971. Yet it wasn't out of line with its time, when the values of materialism and competition in a shrinking world were being seriously debated in mainstream forums.

Some of the most striking departures from public school norms reflect *Hall-Dennis* recommendations—for example, that the program be "nongraded," with "no norms of skill acquisition and no formal evaluation of a child's performance". In 1971, the proposal already committed to accommodate, "different learning styles". It noted that pressure on students to constantly perform in front of others "often has detrimental effects".[162]

A key element of *The ALPHA Experience* was governance by a "staff-community council", something that the Community Schools movement in Toronto wanted to see in all schools. *Hall-Dennis* had vaguely recommended such councils. Some of the American parent-created free schools, including Kozol's Black-operated Roxbury School, operated this way. ALPHA co-founders also noted the influence of A. S. Neill's *Summerhill*:

> ***Co-Founder 2****: There was a certain amount of discussion and publicity about Summerhill that influenced some folks, but not everybody, in terms of the people who were interested in ALPHA. . . . I think Hall-Dennis was just as important as Summerhill, in terms of people thinking about what they wanted for their kids.*
>
> ***Co-Founder 1****: Alternative was the word that was used most of the time. Certainly, the initial concept* [for ALPHA] *was along the lines of Summerhill. That was very much talked about in the initial formative stages.*

In his 2002 history, *Free Schools, Free People: Education and Democracy after the 1960s*, Ron Miller describes an *alternative school* as a de-politicized *free school*, "less suggestive of counter-cultural lifestyles or radical politics" and consequently more acceptable in public education.[163] The carefully apolitical language of *The ALPHA Experience* may have eased its passage, but it was also a reflection of a founding community that had not reached specific agreement on its learning structures.

But the press often identified ALPHA as a *free school*. The term was used without explanation, showing the broad public awareness of the concept of free schooling. Writing for the Toronto Citizen about the proposal the Board had approved, Ellen Murray speculated, "The school will run pretty close to the usual free school model with strong elements of a kind of community control built in."[164]

With the backing of reform-minded public school trustees, ALPHA's creators began to lay an administrative groundwork for pedagogy and governance. Writing in the *Globe and Mail* a few months later about the TBE's "experimental" schools, education writer Loren Lind found this groundwork important, especially in view of the aforementioned crisis SEED was experiencing: "ALPHA, unlike SEED, has a charter that spells out how the parents want the school to be run."[165]

Relations with the School Board

During the period of discussion that led to the drafting of *The ALPHA Experience*, the ALPHA Community had already begun a collaborative relationship with politicians and administrators. According to a co-founder:

> *We had done our homework with the trustees, and we worked very very closely with* [Graham] *Scott and* [Gordon] *Cressy, who also then developed support with the other trustees. . . . We worked closely with the board to draft a proposal that the board would see as acceptable. If you have the trustees behind you ahead of time and you have the Board with you ahead of time, you go into the meeting pretty well sure you're going to get passed, which is the only way to go about this kind of thing.*

The final proposal submitted by the ALPHA Community to the December 16, 1971 meeting of the Toronto Board of Education (TBE) included a detailed budget, and had already been thoroughly examined by officials.

A parent whose child entered the school in September, 1972 commented:

> *The people who founded ALPHA were very adept in Board of Education politics, and we worked through the trustees. They understood working with the trustees to get the administrators working better. Which we did. It*

> *doesn't take that much, especially back then when the trustees had a lot more power than they do now, you actually could get things done.*

Press and Board Minutes showed Fiona Nelson to be a firm defender of alternative schools. One co-founder recalled: "Gord Cressy and Graham Scott as trustees were absolutely instrumental in strategizing for this." Another parent from the early years affirmed:

> *I think it was that Board and it was the trustees who were elected, and it didn't take that much to start a school. I think it's much harder now.*

Until the December 16, 1971 meeting of the Toronto Board of Education, ALPHA's creators worked with a Board subcommittee called the *SEED Sub-Committee* that had been formed by the Toronto Board to work with that alternative high school. That evening, the name was changed to the *Sub-Committee on Alternatives in Education,*[166] indicating that the majority of the trustees foresaw that alternative school creation would be an ongoing process.

Mark Golden of *Community Schools* would later write that the ALPHA proposal passed with "very little discussion",[167] but Board minutes show an unsuccessful motion by trustee William Charleton to delay it. According to the *Globe and Mail*'s Loren Lind, it "had a rough passage".

> Trustee William Charlton, who later became board chairman, argued loud and long against approving yet another new school without having established a policy on approving new schools.
>
> His objection won the support of Herbert Barnes, William Lang and Robert Orr, but the vote was 14-4 in favour of ALPHA. The board approved the school "in principle", with the understanding that 4- and 5-year olds would be able to attend all day.[168]

ALPHA's initiators and the trustees who supported them had already sought an opinion on the administrative viability of the all-day kindergarten. The administration reported that it was doable:

> The Chief Accountant reported that it was his opinion that this would present no problems with respect to Metropolitan grants, as they are based on pupil days and the Board now obtains grants on the basis of one pupil for each two pupils who attend on a half-day basis.[169]

Again, the designation of "experimental" proved to be handy, if problematic. Some in the press saw it as inequitable, but it's notable that Ontario's first attempts at all-day kindergarten were carried out in the play-friendly, non-judgmental, multi-age environments of Toronto's early alternative schools.

Anything goes?

At the December 16, 1971 Toronto Board of Education meeting where the ALPHA proposal was passed, the trustees confronted the question of the kinds of diverse initiatives that could take place under a public school umbrella. Does diversity and community control mean that anything goes?

Writing for the community newspaper *The Toronto Citizen*, Ellen Murray reported trustee Charleton's argument for delaying the ALPHA proposal:

> Decisions on funding an alternative type of school, he held, should not consider the philosophy of the petitioning group, but merely its size. If it is (or has the potential to be) large enough to form the basis of a viable school, then it should receive funding. Charleton argues that if the Board funds a group's proposal as an "experiment" and "evaluates its progress", then it is not really supporting either community control or diversity in education.[170]

The same meeting that approved ALPHA referred another proposal to the newly renamed "Sub-Committee on Alternatives in Education".[171] According to Ellen Murray,

> Some [trustees] seemed to feel that the policy he [Charleton] suggested had already been adopted de facto because the Board was giving serious consideration to a proposal for an alternate school from the conservative Parent Action League [PAL] and the Committee against Moral Pollution in Schools [CAMPS]. If the Board is flooded by requests from similar groups, we'll be able to judge whether such a policy does exist or not.[172]

This reporter saw the ALPHA group as "made up, for the most part, of articulate intellectuals". She asked, "Would the Board be willing to finance a group not from the avant-garde middle class?"[173] An ALPHA founder recalled this proposal, presented by a "homophobic right-wing minister" and a teacher who was a "right wing public voice for education for years throughout the seventies":

> *They presented a proposal for a parent-run, extremely right-wing program, under the same logic of course that we were going for, that parents had a right to define the educational possibilities for their children. There was some pause about what we were doing and what that potentially was opening up in terms of possibilities within the city, but the Board voted them down at that time. . . . So we knew the structure of what was being opened up in the city had some points of contradiction in relationship to the larger spirit of what we were trying to do.*

In arguing for their public school, ALPHA's parents used the 1948 *United Nations Universal Declaration of Human Rights*. Article 26 states: "Parents have a prior right to choose the kind of education that shall be given to their children." It could theoretically support initiatives that are narrow, bigoted and pedagogically unsound if used outside its human rights context, and if a Board of Education does not have policies to contravene them.

However, politicians and civil servants who observe Article 26 are obliged to weigh any proposal within the larger human rights context. Article 29 states: “These rights and freedoms may in no case be exercised contrary to the purposes and principles of the United Nations.” The take on “diversity” that Charleton seemed to express, in Ellen Murray’s account, was that a willingness to fund one alternative should mean a willingness to fund any proposal. This was a minority position on the Board, “ignored by most trustees”.[174]

American alternative school proponent Mario Fantini was similarly dismissive of such arguments with respect to public alternative schools.

> Some may ask whether a Nazi school or an antiwhite one for Blacks could exist within the framework of a public system of choice. Obviously, it could not. The concept speaks of openness. It values diversity, is democratic, and is unswerving in its recognition of individual worth.
>
> Within these bounds, however, there is a full spectrum of alternative possibilities with new educational and learning forms. Schools could, for example, emphasize science or languages or the arts; they could be graded or nongraded, open or traditional, technical or nontechnical; they could seek a multicultural approach or work to strengthen particular ethnic and group identities. Each, however, must meet the standard principles which are fundamental to a public school system of choice.
>
> Respecting the rights and responsibilities of others, for example, cannot work if the option being promulgated is based on a system which advocates the imposition of one’s own values on others.[175]

In a similar spirit, the Toronto Board of Education continued to take an interest in the nature of the alternatives that would fall under its umbrella, to exercise its judgment, and to make its decisions proposal by proposal.

Writing in *Canadian Forum* magazine, trustee Fiona Nelson recounted that, as the Board moved toward replacing the "very old" Balmy Beach school, they heard depositions from CAMPS and PAL, who wanted the replacement to be a "traditional school" with "no frills". The "WASP, very 'Orange' predominantly working-class"[176] neighbourhood of Balmy Beach had a history of notoriety in terms of race relations, being a major Toronto locus of anti-Semitic activities, including an active pro-Nazi Swastika Club in the nineteen-thirties. But counter-culture people had also moved into what was then an area of affordable older homes.

CAMPS and PAL had collected a thousand signatures in support of a school to teach Christian virtues, but "another group petitioned the Board saying that the previous petition had been signed by many non-residents". Nelson hinted that, in the face of these competing factions, resolving the issues in Balmy Beach "may take a while".[177]

The various factions who spoke to the Balmy Beach initiative brought the arguments into the open where community and political processes could deal with them. The upshot was that CAMPS and PAL didn't get their school, but during the next few decades over forty pedagogically-based alternative schools would be created in Toronto's public school system.

Parents Hire Teachers

After approval in principle of their proposal on December 16, 1971, ALPHA's founders worked out the details with trustees and administrators. The December 16, 1971 agreement between the ALPHA Community and the Toronto Board of Education recognized that the "ultimate responsibility for our staff rests with the Board".

The teachers would be "supplied from within the system", but were to be hired by a "selection committee of 8-10 people including parents involved in the school planning, a trustee or two", and "sensitive and supportive" administrators.[178]

While the location of the school was still undetermined, the parents set about to hire three teachers to work with the ninety students who would be waiting for their new school on September 1, 1971:

> ***Co-Founder 2****: How people thought about what an appropriate teacher would be for their vision of what the school is—this was really crucial to the early years of the program.*
>
> ***Co-Founder 3****: I guess I was on the committee or just sitting in, because I definitely remember the couple that got the job. . . . They were friends—good friends but not partners. . . . They both had applied from the Toronto Board, but they worked in different places. I remember them coming and saying they were very interested in doing this and had some background in trying to be alternative in the classroom and very specifically saying that they would come if both of them came. . . . The third fella I remember was from . . . down East.*
>
> ***Co-Founder 2****: My memory is that he was hired as . . . the hiring Committee's fantasy of what an alternative school teacher should look like and how he should behave, because he had this kind of loopy communal persona, kind of looked like Santa Claus in a way, except his beard wasn't white—he had a big beard. Very gentle and good with kids, really communicative with the kids. And I think there was a lot of investment in a certain kind of persona, which was a fantasy of what the school might look like.*

The education writer Loren Lind reported that the school communities of both ALPHA and SEED were being permitted to select staff in an "amicable ad hoc agreement that will avoid setting any clearcut guidelines for the future".[179] Through the years, though the Board often filled part-time and temporary positions without consultation, ALPHA's procedure for community-based teacher hirings persisted until the new millennium.

No mention was made of a principal in *The ALPHA Experience*, but in early 1972 Loren Lind reported that ALPHA parents

> were forced to accept at least minimal supervision by a certified principal under a ruling by solicitor Douglas Gilmour. "We would try to make it a general oversight, a tolerant one", education director Ronald Jones promised them last March.[180]

During these days of pioneering alternative school formation, trustees began to spell out what the role of the principal could be with respect to a self-governing site. *Report No. 2 of Special Committee re Alternatives in Education*, signed by trustee Fiona Nelson and passed by the Board on April 13, 1972, is specific about the relationship between principal and school:

> The Solicitor is of the opinion that to fulfill the requirements of the Schools Administration Act, such schools [as Laneway and ALPHA] must have supervising principals to be responsible to the Board for their operation. It is not a requirement that the supervising principal must be in attendance at the school at all times during the school day, but be available for consultation if the need arises.[181]

Location

Like SEED and Laneway, ALPHA's founders wanted a non-traditional location. An ALPHA parent explained to a reporter:

> Alpha was approved as an innovative and experimental school, which necessarily will make the Alpha group of children a minority in a shared facility. This would unquestionably lead to conflict amongst the parents, staff and children of the two groups. The experience of the North York Board of Education with MAGU (a similar project) located in Wilmington Public School, shows that this is a very real problem.
>
> Any experiment in education, by its very nature, generates many difficulties. To add the additional burden of sharing facilities to such an experiment, may very well prove fatal to it.[182]

Assigning an alternative to empty classrooms in existing schools was economical. The on-site principal who went with a shared facility was a comfort to Board supervisors, but not to the alternative. It's easier for an off-site principal to simply "be available for consultation". For an on-site principal, indifference or resentment at being saddled with an extra school could quickly turn to nervousness or hostility when they observe situations that contravene their ideas of how a school should run. Watching MAGU struggle with this situation, ALPHA's founders stood their ground. Ultimately, trustees assented to the rental of space in the Broadview YMCA.

7:

CHAOS

Getting Started

When ALPHA commenced in September, 1972, there were no doors to open. The teachers were hired and 100 students were ready to register, but the renovations that would make the Broadview YMCA suitable for an alternative school weren't complete. One small article in a Toronto daily newspaper reported: "The hundred pupils who registered at the ALPHA school . . . have been going on field trips while waiting for the renovations on their quarters to be completed."[183]

In the generous spirit of the time, the Holy Trinity Church let ALPHA's hundred students use it as a home base, while their parents finished work on the top floor of the YMCA. One of these parents recalled:

> *I'm an architect and I was kind of—volunteered I suppose to rearrange the space in a more suitable way for ALPHA. So that's what we did: change a few walls around, painted the doors bright colours and basically created what was the ALPHA School for many years.*

A later *Toronto Life* article described ALPHA's home at the Broadview Y:

> It's on the third floor of what must be the oldest Y building in Toronto: the floors creak, the washroom partitions are made of good old-fashioned wood and nothing is modern except the educational philosophy.[184]

An original ALPHA student, who started in 1972 at the age of five, and was recently interviewed for this thesis project, said that they had "many pleasant somewhat fragmented memories of those years".

> *I remember early on there was lots of play, lots of fun stuff. I don't think as a child I had really a lot of understanding about different forms of education, beyond a bit of nursery school that I think I'd done. . . . I remember when we moved upstairs to the top of the YMCA. I remember the big room with the big geodesic dome and the big wooden blocks, rooms around the side of that. . . . I had a lot of fun there.*

On December 2, 1972, ALPHA was still getting good press. A newspaper article described Todd Glover, "a super-intelligent youngster . . . a student at ALPHA, a free school under the aegis of the Toronto Board of Education run largely by the parents of the children attending it." He is described as "the only 12-year-old campaign coordinator in the municipal election" and he is responsible for the "deployment of 150 volunteer workers."

> He was given time off school after his resource teacher—a canvasser for the Spencer-Leckie team [probably a parent volunteer]—asked him if he wanted to work on a political campaign.
>
> "Politics sort of intrigues me," he says. "It's the organization . . . and seeing how it works."[185]

The brief reference to ALPHA in this article gives a glimpse of the school's political connections. According to Michael Valpy, writing in the *Globe and Mail*, Bob Spencer and Dan Leckie were "running as school trustees on a campaign stressing community-controlled schools."

Since this was ALPHA's first year, one can hardly credit the school for Glover's precocity. But the article demonstrates how the school was following up on the charter's commitment to encourage initiative, autonomy and social responsibility, and hints at the school's connection to the life of the city as "knowledge of the society of which one is a part".[186]

Disorientation

Even as Valpy's favourable article went to press, there is little doubt that ALPHA parents were feeling the strain of putting their school into effect. The number of parents who actually showed up regularly to help out was disappointing.

Said one informant from the early years:

> *I think there were a lot of parents who could talk about educational ideas, but the idea of getting there and working with a bunch of really wild and not terribly obedient kids was a little more than they could really cope with.*

And, as it turned out, many parents were not happy with the school they encountered, as three teachers and a small coterie of active volunteer parents grappled daily with the problem of programming for ninety students in a big room.

That same year, 1972, Allen Graubard published *Free the Children*, in which he warned,

> People often have differing ideas about the school, even within the generally shared free school framework; and these differences frequently lead to serious conflicts that can result in splits within schools and the spinning off of new schools.[187]

Certainly, this happened during that first year at ALPHA. Dale Shuttleworth even recalled some parents "threatening to establish a BETA alternative school (Better Education Than Alpha)".[188] The reasons given for conflict varied among those who had come together to create a school.

> **Co-Founder 2**: *One of the first splits at ALPHA was between people who had a more communitarian focus in relationship to what they wanted from the ALPHA Community, and those who wanted a particular kind of schooling experience for their child.*
> **Co-Founder 1**: *We ended up really with these two factions fighting and very much the issue really was over the amount of structure. . . . You could call it "how free should a free school be?"*

> ***Parent 1972-76:*** *In terms of the whole free school vs. other models, there was a lot of conflict among the parents over what exactly the direction ought to be, and many people left after the first year because they really couldn't face the reality of what a free school meant. They couldn't stand the fact that kids were just running around. They felt they weren't learning anything. In fact, not only the parents left; the teachers left, too. The survival into the second year was very precarious.*

Under the pressure of meeting the daily needs of children in this "unstructured" environment, the "fault lines" in the parent community cracked open. According to a co-founder, the parents found among themselves a wide "diversity of points of view, commitments, ideological forms, fantasies, visions for what's important for your kids".

> *I had set up communal showings of Frederick Wiseman's High School in my house, for people to come and discuss notions of schooling. I'm sure every ALPHA parent could look at the school that was in that film and say: "That's not what we want". . . . But in relationship to what our visions were of ALPHA and what we really wanted, I think there were a lot of differences.*

ALPHA parents had (and continue to have) two main avenues of constructive influence. First, they could spend time at the school and, through their work and programming, co-create the school with other parents and teachers. Their second opportunity for influence was the parent/teacher meeting, usually held monthly, where problems were discussed, and decisions made. During ALPHA's first year, it would appear that the parents had not worked out this structure any more than they had worked out the in-school structures:

> **Co-Founder 1**: *The meetings were (pause)*
> **Co-Parent 1972-76**: *interminable. (much laughter)*
> **Parent 1972-76**: *They really were. They went on for hours.*
> **Co-Founder 1**: *The structure—boy, I don't know—I think there was a chairperson, and the chair tried to*

accommodate what everybody wanted to say, but everybody wanted to have their say.

Since the arguments documented by early reports and minutes are about adult concerns, it's hard to know what the day-to-day life at the school might have been like. One parent, who left after the first few months of the school's life, conceded, "It certainly wasn't all bad."

Certainly, there was an activity-based program, a reasonable amount of equipment, not great; like a lot of these kinds of programs, not so good for kids who hang back and need support—those kinds of kids would tend to not do so much and kind of get lost, a bit of running around. . . . I have memories of a lot of motion and scrambly kind of things, a few fights with the kids that were in the Y but didn't go to ALPHA. When you walk into activity-based classrooms you have the sense of a noisy productivity thing. I think I had that experience.

There was also some extraordinary programming going on. During the first year, students went "once a week, winter and summer" to Maggie's Farm, a rural site operated by the Ontario College of Art, to work on building structures:

Parent 1972-76: *We built some of these things in a sort of barn . . .*
Researcher: *Well, that's playing with structures, eh. Not just some little things on a table.*
Co-Founder 1: *These were things they could actually live in. They could camp in them. That's a different thing.*

According to the school phone lists, enrollment plunged from 90 students on October 5, 1972, to 40 students in January, 1973. Mark Novak documented a similar phenomenon in the first year of the school he studied, a school that was definitely not ALPHA but an older, suburban school: "Approximately 30 percent of the 'like-minded,' 'homogenous' parent and student body left by Christmas."[189]

He listed some observable problems: "To many concerned parents the school remained stubbornly incomprehensible and apparently chaotic. Lack of adult supervision, callous use of supplies and the absence of any ongoing, regular program unnerved and provoked even the most progressive parents."

Novak described his own sense of disorientation upon experiencing a newly-formed free school:

> I confess that I felt strange throughout the day. The apparent freedom of the children impressed me; for example, they roamed in hordes and in small groups, in and out of rooms with little adult supervision. I feel that my own disorientation resulted from the students' mobility, their sheer numbers, and the apparently casual organization of the room.[190]

In my experience, this kind of disorientation is commonly felt by people who encounter a public free school for the first time. The students' erratic mobility conflicts with our sense of what is "right" in school, based on a dozen years of our own experience (whether or not we enjoyed it or felt it was right). It's a recipe for unease. Such disoriented, concerned parents, who often have not previously worked with children other than their own, are the people ALPHA has relied upon, from its beginning, to solve the very problem that disorients them: how to work with students in a non-coercive public school environment.

Buckling Down

Researcher Mark Novak also pointed out: "any social experiment spins off complications and displays growing pains in one form or another".[191] In ALPHA, the remaining parents buckled down to grapple with them.

Dated January 9, 1973, there is a report entitled the *January Committee Recommendations*. Teachers and parents met together with a facilitator for three days to "consider the communication between the teachers, the parent involvement in ALPHA and possible solutions." They came up with a proposed *Constitution* to recommend to the parent/teacher body.

This Constitution created the role of Chairman and ALPHA's first standing committee, the Policy Committee, which primarily "deliberates and recommends policy", adding the caveat "note this is not a decision-making body". It defined ALPHA's voting membership: primarily contracted teachers and parents. Students seldom took an interest in these political matters, but they could participate if accepted by the Policy Committee. It also provided for a non-voting membership of "all others; with right to speak". The quorum was thirty voting members and Robert's Rules could be used by the chairman as a "last resort".

This committee's description of the teachers' role was:

> 1. To implement policy decided by the community. The fact that all three teachers are also on the Policy Committee insures [*sic*] harmony between policy and implementation
>
> 2. to convene curriculum groups
>
> 3. teachers' contracts will be renewed annually.[192]

An interesting expression of the Parent Community's authority over the running of the school was the role of Coordinator, created "to insure [*sic*] that the teachers' collective responsibilities to the entire school are met". The Coordinator was paid out of the Board budget for secretary/administrator. This could only have been done in an era when administrators worked primarily on school-generated matters, rather than on paperwork generated by the bureaucracies above them. Under the constitution, the Coordinator also operated as a "floating teacher", liaison with the Board, and coordinator of volunteers. This position was chosen "by the contracted teachers and will have two permanent parent [volunteer] helpers".

"Other Recommendations" of the January Committee include, under the rubric of "Curriculum", that consultations with parents would establish children's interests and needs, in addition to parent expectations, and determine the kinds of resources parents can bring to the school. Under "Parent Involvement" it was made clear that parents were expected to give time during the school day or on evenings and weekends (the YMCA site gave seven-day access) or at home. The *January Committee Recommendations* also included "Requests to the Policy Committee", one of which was to make recommendations on "the concept of freedom in the school".

The Teachers: Shock and Aftershock

The January Committee structure was adopted, but the school continued to bleed out. One oral history participant left ALPHA after the first six months,

> *. . . because not only what was happening around the teachers, but the level of conflict within the group, and some despair about people getting it together, and having my kids in the middle of that . . .*

Parents in those early days recalled that the teachers presented problems that couldn't be ignored, or left to the "professionals" to sort out:

> *In the middle of the first year, the teacher that people had fantasized most about in terms of being a stable alternative school teacher, that was going to be the main teacher in the program, had had an affair with one of the mothers in the school and left the province.*

A decade later, a book on Toronto alternative schools dryly noted that, during this first year at ALPHA, "Some parents appeared to be more interested in working with the community of adults than in working with the children in the school."[193] One participant joked: "the early problems were all about the mundane things of life—sex, drugs and rock'n'roll", and mused:

> *In hindsight, there was a lot of acting out of a particular version of a lifestyle that was part of the vision or fantasy in terms of what the school meant. In other words, the school meant more than just a program for one's kids. It also meant something about people's*

> *identities, and who they were and what they were projecting into the kind of school that they wanted for their kids, as is the case in eighty percent of those kinds of choices. . . . You had those kinds of issues going on together with all the problems of a community that really wasn't all that coherent to start with, because of the way in which a whole bunch of diverse people came together and we got put together for political reasons in order to present a unified voice. And so we were in a position of then "Okay, now we have to work out our problems, now that we have a real structure within which to do it." And it wasn't so easy to do.*

Since half the enrollment had been lost, the teacher wasn't replaced. While the parent community held "interminable" meetings and struck committees to deal with the problems, a serious falling out occurred between the two teachers who had declared themselves to be inseparable.

According to one informant:

> *I definitely remember coming into the school maybe in December or January and looking at them and they were in two different rooms and people were saying they don't even talk to each other. They wouldn't even be in the same room together.*

As recalled by a number of early members, this rift occurred when a teacher from the pair who were hired together formed an alliance with a parent: "a very very dynamic guy, very powerful guy within the social context there. A hippie-type guy, middle-aged . . . " An ALPHA co-founder pointed out:

> *In the decision-making in those kinds of settings, one person can become very powerful. And I think it's a concern because, certainly in the three alternative schools I was in, we worked very much in a collective way, but there were unfortunate times, two or three times, when individuals really were able to control the meeting, and that indicated a problem.*

The first teacher's affair and subsequent abandonment of his post had been a shock, but this other alliance may have been as damaging, as one informant stated: "They were pretty much a couple, and they dominated the meeting."

This is a recognized pattern. American psychiatrist Scott Peck's work on building intentional community has been used by the Albany Free School's Chris Mercogliano[194] and by critical pedagogue bell hooks[195]. Peck identified such alliances as a "common pitfall" that was "highly likely to interfere with a group's mature development". Peck didn't suggest that people can't become close to those they meet in a community context. Rather, he explained that they mustn't permit their involvement to cause them to "exclude" the other community members or to "lose sight of the central task of building community". [196] When such an alliance gets out of hand, community members need to do the uncomfortable work of confronting the dynamic and reclaiming democratic control.

The Press: Rushing to Judgment

Ironically, while some administrators supported ALPHA parents in their agonizing struggle, their allies in the radical education press became judgmental. A fault line could be seen between writers who primarily advocated community control for local schools and the parents who were working on alternative educational models.

Months before ALPHA opened, reporter Ellen Murray had pointed out that the "Board's administration, if not the Board itself, have been hostile to the Community Schools Workshop and what it represents: involvement and control by people over their local schools." She suggested that because "ALPHA involves very few people, it doesn't relate to any existing school, and it has an ambiguously experimental status", and therefore Board officials might have considered it "a safe way to deal with the community control issue".[197]

In early 1973, Mark Golden of *Community Schools* agreed with this analysis.

> ALPHA's survival seems guaranteed: the Board is proud of its alternatives (they *are* easier than changing the whole system).

Golden blamed ALPHA's problems on the unwillingness of middle-class participants to make the changes in their jobs, homes and family situations that would enable them to support the school.

> I wonder how much change we can make for our children when we don't make changes for ourselves. And how much energy we can spare for changes so limited.

Golden declared ALPHA to be a "success as a school," but a "failure as a community school."

> ALPHA needs the community to run its educational program. A breakdown in the community concept directly affects the kids in the school, and that concept has broken down. ALPHA has never been able to develop the kind of shared responsibility that was its goal.[198]

Only half a year into the creation of a school that was a new paradigm for all of the families and professionals involved, it would seem a little premature to announce success or failure of any kind. Though Golden was critical of ALPHA, his descriptions of the school in operation in early 1973 showed engaged, friendly children. His article opened with an anecdote about a multi-age group of students playing *Krypto*, a math game that involved using addition, subtraction and logarithmic functions.

> The winner most of the time was Kyla. She is only 4 so she just had to say what number the card turned up was. It was pretty nice.[199]

ALPHA's co-founders deeply identified with the Community Schooling Movement, but the feeling wasn't mutual. The activists of the Community Schools Workshop were committed to specific, racialized neighbourhoods, where the parents' deepest concerns were for strong literacy education. Very much in this camp was Laneway which, Golden noted, benefited from the precedent set by ALPHA.[200]

In an era of fragmenting neighbourhoods, ALPHA's founders chose the common strategy of the 1960s: forming community around common purposes. One thing they agreed upon, (which may not have resonated with most local school families) was that coercion and stratification constrained the intellect and harmed students—as many felt they had been harmed. They also believed that their children were entitled to good lives as children, rather than wanting only to arm them for a hostile future.

Such rifts between caring activists were difficult and divisive, but they expressed a vibrant culture around education. ALPHA's founders didn't see these movements as contradictory, but complementary. Its members would always identify ALPHA as a community school.

Finding a Way Through

Whether they left or stayed, the five study participants who were adults involved with ALPHA during 1972-1973 used the word "chaos" to describe this initial year:

> ***Co-Founder 1****: You see we were trying to be very democratic, so we had these meetings, and everybody had a say, and it was too democratic. It was just so democratic that it didn't work very well, quite frankly. The Board of Education became very concerned. They dropped in a headmaster who was our then Superintendent of Education at the time. But he became the principal of ALPHA because they felt that somebody had to take control of this thing, I think.*

It was fortunate for ALPHA that the principal assigned to it was the Superintendent of Public Schools, Mike Lennox.[201] Since self-governance and self-regulation were its core concepts, this school needed to find its own way. Lennox happened to be a powerful administrator who was interested to see if local control could work.

One of the co-founders recalled that Lennox provided

> *one of my all-time favourite lines from an administrator. He was quoting to me constantly that "anything that was educationally desirable was administratively possible".*

In contrast to the "foot-dragging" and "information withheld" that reporter Ellen Murray described as lack of "sympathy" in the bureaucracy,[202] friendly administrators like Lennox and Shuttleworth defended the independence of the struggling alternative schools and gave them the time to find their way through the chaos.

The Path to Community

American psychiatrist Scott Peck has worked with concepts of intentional community for several decades. In *The Different Drum: Community Making and Peace*, he documented his experiences with community. These included intentional communities like the independent Christian faith known as Quakers, temporary communities formed through workshops, and communities that crystallized out of crisis such as war and disaster.

Peck hypothesized:

> Groups assembled deliberately to form themselves into community routinely go through certain stages in the process. These stages, in order, are:
>
> Pseudocommunity
> Chaos
> Emptiness
> Community.
>
> Not every group that becomes a community follows this paradigm exactly. . . . But in the process of community-making by design, this is the natural, usual order of things.[203]

ALPHA was, by self-definition, an example of "community-making by design". There's a correlation between the process Peck describes and the stages that ALPHA went through in its first years. ALPHA's *pseudocommunity* stage was identified by a founding member as a "fantasy". Yet it had led to a proposal that could be accepted by the Board of Education, and which is still a pillar of the school.

Perhaps *pseudocommunity* could be seen as an aspirational stage. Articulating a group's aims and ideals, it's a first step on a new path, but not yet tried or proven. Characterized by "conflict-avoidance" and "the lack of acknowledgement, or the ignoring of individual differences", *pseudocommunity* is a wavering, temporary stage. When difference can no longer be denied, it quickly falls over the brink into *chaos*.[204]

Those who lived through the first year at ALPHA might be interested to know that Peck sees the *chaos* stage as "an essential part of the process of community development", a time when problems are brought into the open, and the only exit from the bland pretense of *pseudocommunity*. According to Peck, as long as members try to "obliterate" the opposite point of view or to "heal" or "convert" one another, the stage of *chaos* prevails.[205]

Peck observes that a group's first attempt out of chaos is often to "escape into organization".[206] ALPHA's archives from this time show a labour-intensive effort to do just that.

Emptiness

Scott Peck claims there is only one road out of chaos and into community: through what he calls e*mptiness*: the "hard part, the most crucial stage of community development". In Peck's vocabulary, in order to come together in *community*, people in a group need to empty themselves of expectations, preconceptions, prejudice, ideology, and theology: "the need to Heal, to Convert, to Fix. Or Solve."[207]

Reports from the ALPHA archives give some perspectives of the hard-working parents who remained in the school. In the

March 27, 1973 Minutes of General Meeting are listed four pages of parental concerns, but there is no indication that the students themselves were concerned about spending much of their time in rambunctious play.

One parent "felt that the children were happy." Another worried that the "children were drifting and that the environment we had hoped for was missing . . . we should perhaps hire someone for a short time to look for the freedom and creative atmosphere we had all originally anticipated for ALPHA." Another felt "a kind of spiritual leadership was absolutely necessary from someone with a positive and creative attitude, who would disregard the unimportant details and provide the environment which was vital".

The voices of the remaining teachers are included in this document, and they are respected. But their inability to resolve their conflict and work together was a deal-breaker. In March, hiring season at the Board of education, the teachers demanded to know whether they would be rehired, so they could find other jobs if necessary. Regretfully (after first passing a motion that "if either teacher was rejected, they might re-apply at a later date if they so wished") parents designed a ballot to vote on which teacher, if any, should be rehired. They voted to let both teachers go and start afresh the next year.

Even as ALPHA seemed to atomize, new patterns of activity formed among parents gathering to work things out and carry on from day to day. For the families who persisted, the governing principle seems to have been that "anything that could be done to keep the experiment alive should be done".[208]

The conclusions of the *ALPHA School Special Sub-Committee Report, May 23, 1973* listed these major problems:

> 1. Deep conflicts around philosophy and who indeed makes up the real community are still unresolved . . .

2. Many people making up the working committees and the general "community" have little firsthand connection with what is really happening. Decisions therefore tend to be made by people who are not deeply affected by them—perhaps on hearsay from other adults and children. . . . This often makes the working committees and general meetings reprimanding bodies in the eyes of those deeply involved on a day to day basis.
3. There is not on the teaching staff a person sufficiently experienced and competent in the use of processes to create an open community with a cohesive spirit or élan.

With half the families gone and the remaining teachers on their way out, ALPHA's community was indeed experiencing *emptiness*. They had no way of knowing that they were not alone.

Surviving that First Year

ALPHA's problems and solutions were also encountered at other free and alternative schools. In 1975, Mark Novak would publish a book that showed parallel problems in the older Toronto school he called ASPE.

South of the border, 1969 had been a "wild and tumultuous year," as Mary Leue expanded her home schooling practice to create the independent Albany Free School in New York State.

> Parents battled over educational philosophy and practice, kids from opposite ends of the socio-economic spectrum thrashed out their own issues, and several city departments (building, fire, and education) all vied to shut down this funky, radical, and penniless storefront institution.[209]

In his 1975 study, *An Organizational Explanation of the Failure of Alternative Schools*, Terence Deal of Stanford University states: "Eighteen months has been generally accepted as an average life span for the alternative schools of the late 1960's and early 1970's."[210] His study of three new alternatives led him to conclude that the most critical factor in this failure was that "they were not able to cope with the organizational problems produced by new authority patterns and by highly complex educational processes".[211]

Independent of Peck's work on community, Deal observed a parallel process in newly created alternative schools:

> . . . a series of developmental stages which led ultimately to dissolution, to a reversion to more conventional education or, in a few cases, to novel compromises in the educational process or the distribution of authority.[212]

Deal named the stages *euphoria*, *crisis* and *dissatisfaction*. In the schools he studied, Deal saw two factions form:

> one group favoring the original "innovative" charter of the school, the other pressing for a more conventional program and more traditional patterns of organization. [213]

Like Peck, Deal found that a group's response to the third stage (which Peck called *emptiness* and Deal called *dissatisfaction*) was "critical". The final stage, which Deal called *resolution*, could have one of three outcomes:

> They may refuse to alter their course and either fall or split apart or voluntarily disband. They may become highly conventional in their governance and approach to learning. Or they may stumble intuitively into some form of compromise in their authority structure and educational program. [214]

This pattern uncannily resembles the experience of ALPHA's founding community.

ALPHA's Third Way

The diverse complaints of those leaving ALPHA gave rise to contradictory rumors: that the school was hopelessly chaotic, or that it had, in Deal's words, "reverted to conventionality".

But interviewees from this time agreed that two lines of thought persisted. One recalled:

> *There were the ones who were, perhaps, the academics that had been involved with the OISE group, discussing things. . . . There was also, I guess you could maybe characterize them as, the hippie contingent. They tended to be more extreme, left-wing, more tolerant of the chaos which . . . was very high and not everybody could cope with that.*

Committed members of both contingents worked together to find a way out of the chaos. Some participants indicated that the departure of the more colorful and ideological counter-culture characters probably helped the school to find cohesion. (Several recalled a draft-dodger who sometimes referred to the gun he kept in his car!)

Yet Molly Wills of *School Progress* quoted one of ALPHA's first teachers as saying,

> If anything, ALPHA is closer now to the *Hall-Dennis* philosophy than it was before the "unstructured" group left.[215]

Like the intentional communities Scott Peck worked with, and the alternative schools studied by Terence Deal, ALPHA would be created over time by people with different ideas, working together to define a third way that was a group creation. During the latter part of ALPHA's first year, the extended community many had hoped for began to create itself, as parents attacked massive problems together. ALPHA's Community laboured over them even after school had ended in June.

July 30, 1973 is the date of a document titled *alpha 74*. It contains *Operational Guidelines for the ALPHA School Commencing in September, 1973,* as well as a bare-bones two-page *Constitution*. Together, these documents articulated what the founding parents had learned about the needs of the school.

Responding to pressure to move ALPHA into empty rooms in a school, the *Operational Guidelines* defended ALPHA's YMCA location, which had been renovated with much effort only a year before:

> After a first year of growing pains which left much to be desired in many areas of ALPHA's activities, we feel that some stability is finally being established and the consistent location is one of the key factors for both children and community, which strengthen this stability. (*Section 1. c*)

The *Operational Guidelines* aimed for a school enrollment beginning at "65 children with an age range of 5 to 13 years," and staffing at "two Board of Education paid teaching staff and a secretary/coordinator". This size was "more manageable than the original 90 in terms of the organization of volunteers, resource people and children".

A detailed description of the teaching role included a hard-earned lesson:

> Teachers must have the ability to work with each other and with volunteer parents and resource people.

The Principal's role was affirmed as a figurehead rather than an authority, exploring *Hall-Dennis*'s germ of an idea that the Board of Education administration would mentor local governance rather than ruling directly.

The Operational Guidelines laid down the principle:

> Day-to-day functioning of the school will be administered by a group of people who work in the school on a regular basis and are thus in constant touch with the needs, problems, and practical aspects of what goes on. (*Section 4. b*)

Included in the staffing structure were

> 4 unpaid voluntary positions in the school each day, which will carry the same responsibility towards the ALPHA Community as the paid teaching positions. (*Section 4. e*)

The volunteers, together with the two board-paid teaching staff, would represent "the minimum core which ALPHA requires to function." In ALPHA's democracy, "teachers and parents are answerable to the group as a whole".

The Coordinator was responsible for seeing that ALPHA's staffing ratio was maintained, a role that was seen as "supportive rather than an authoritative one". Yet strong measures were proposed to ensure that parents would meet their volunteer commitments of "at least one half-day per week as a condition of their children's enrollment". (*Section 5*)

> "Consistent failure to fulfill commitments must be investigated and action must be taken by the group to correct this situation. This may mean a parent will have to withdraw his child." (*Section 4. d*)

There is no evidence that such a policy was enforced; the school struggled to maintain enrollment. If the policy had been protested before the Board in any era, it would likely have been struck down on the grounds of equity of access. As Mark Golden pointed out:

> You've also got to let people into your school. And if that changes the nature of the school—if some of the new people want to let the staff run the show, if they want a baby-sitting service . . . well, you just have to struggle it through.[216]

There was no golden age when everyone felt that there was enough, but volunteerism and parent involvement would continue to be central to ALPHA. The responsibility taken by ALPHA's parents was as necessary as it was pioneering: when *alpha 74* was released on July 30, 1973, the school had no staff.

Equally extraordinary is that after the spectacular chaos of ALPHA's first year, the Toronto Board of Education let the parents try again to hire a suitable teaching team. Their tentative hiring of Susan Garrard, a teacher with a new baby, who wasn't sure she wanted to work full-time, marked a turning point in the life of the school.

Before the fall term began, the volunteer parents made a strong effort to draw the new teachers into their midst:

> ***Susan Garrard:*** *When I was first hired, we hung out at this farm during the summer and I was just amazed that these parents who had just hired me had read all the same books as I had: Paul Goodman and of course John Holt, George Leonard's Education and Ecstasy. . . . There were all those sixties writers, and then there were others that were a little more specific about schools in New York City. They were all coming out at the same time.*

In August 28, 1973 a small news item announced:

> A summer-long search has led to the hiring of two teachers for ALPHA school—Toronto's first unstructured elementary school. . . .
>
> Earlier this summer, Toronto Board of Education had expressed fear that ALPHA, located in the Broadview Ave. YMCA building, might not open this fall because of a lack of teachers.
>
> The school will open with about 55 students Sept. 4.[217]

A parent who was part of this arduous year said:

> *I think the survival of the first year was rather precarious. We lost a lot of kids and parents. . . . But it did survive. One of the remarkable things about it is that it found a way through that precarious path on the route to get to something.*

8:

NO CAPTIVE AUDIENCE

Founding Teacher Susan Garrard

In April, 1973, a group of ALPHA mothers who volunteered for a day or more per week had listed the "somewhat special personal qualities that will be required of its staff":

> someone who is a really together person, with sufficient self-esteem to give of his/her talents positively and to see others' accomplishments or excellence as signs of hope and strength . . . who feels good teaching but also, perhaps more so, feels good that a child doesn't need him/her; someone with a high degree of interactive skills, because, in the long run, only willing cooperation is going to work.[218]

Soft-spoken Susan Garrard would provide the "positive and creative" mentorship that the parents were seeking. She was not only an experienced teacher, eager to educate differently, she had not only read all the education books—she was already a survivor of chaos.

Garrard had lived in Rochdale College, Toronto's live-in "free university". Rochdale was a locus of the counterculture in Toronto, and incubated a number of pioneering cultural organizations that are now long-standing institutions with national and international profiles. While the "free university" itself crashed and burned, Coach House Press, Theatre Passe Muraille (founded by Garrard's husband, Jim), and the visual arts organization Art Metropole rose from its ashes.

But ALPHA had been let down by a teacher who appeared to be a counter-cultural icon. The group that hired for that second year chose Susan Garrard not for her Rochdale experience, but for her solid ten-year record as an elementary-school teacher, and her references. A member of that hiring committee recalled:

> *One of the memories I have is of interviewing Susan and calling up my uncle who was on her resumé as a reference and asking him what he thought of her. . . .*
>
> *He said you should hire her—a very positive reference. Not her husband* [laughter: playwright Jim Garrard had been known, briefly, as the king of Rochdale!] *but her, yes.*

For all her experience, Garrard found ALPHA a challenge. She described her first week on the job, in September, 1973:

> *I came in there and I thought I was going to have this interested group of children who really wanted to learn, and they were going to have the freedom to learn, and I was going to have so many lovely things for them to learn. I remember setting up an interest center. I think it was creatures of the sea—books and seashells. They actually came and swept it onto the floor. We had this huge space and I set my little work area up in one room with all this stuff that I needed. My kids, who were supposed to be the little kids, went the furthest corner away that they could.*
>
> *I thought that's probably natural; it's hard to get used to a new teacher. But what really worried me was that they played "doggie" all day long. That's all they did. There was nothing educational that I could see. They just kept putting the leash on each other and taking each other for walks.*

Sweeping Garrard's shells onto the floor was an ugly and, as it turned out, atypical act for these children. It may have been an angry, territorial kind of gesture by students who were upset by the disappearance of the teachers they knew. In a school where there was no enforced fear of adults, Garrard wasn't someone they needed to please; she was an outsider.

It's even possible that the children found the tedious "doggy" game so absorbing because of the effect it had on the interloping adults. The new teachers needed to have a success, and children are good at sensing this kind of tension in adults.

> ***Susan Garrard****: I thought: "How long can this go on?" But it kept going on and on. I kept trying to make friends, but nothing worked. So I finally went to their corner and went down on my hands and knees and barked. I literally did, and that's how I made friends, and then they came to my corner. They put the leash around me and took me for a little walk. That taught me a lot because it never occurred t' me in all of our discussions that I wasn't going to have a captive audience.*

Getting on one's hands and knees really doesn't sound like a good idea, in any school. Puzzling about why Garrard's intuition worked, one might think about what adults do when we move into a new neighbourhood. Most of us don't bring gifts to the neighbours, or throw a party right away, or boss them around. Instead, we behave in a non-threatening manner, and watch to see where we can fit in.

When Garrard went to the children's corner and barked, it wasn't a show of submission, but a respectful route into the children's world. The fact that, when Garrard took the leash, she did not lose the respect of the students—that, when she accepted the students on their terms, they began to accept her as their teacher—shows that in this case, it was the right thing to do. Garrard proved to be very capable of making such judgment calls, both with respect to students and adults. Founding parents agreed: "One of the big factors in making that school gel in fact was Susan. . . . They did a lot more than play doggie."

With the help of volunteer parents and teachers, it appears that early ALPHA students undertook a variety of skill-building activities. In a founder's archive is a September-October, 1973 edition of the school newspaper *Alpha Centauri*, "a genuine 'alpha kid' approved publication", which contained a three-page story about a mongoose, comics, an illustration of all the gear a diver needs, jokes, and an interview in which ALPHA students were asked what they thought of the school.

One student compared ALPHA to a regular public school: "In the other school we have to write and do art and all that junk—here you can do woodwork, read in the library, you don't have to do work all the time." Asked if he "just plays around all the time," the student replied: "Here I'm always bothering myself to do something."

Another offered that her favourite activity was "doing puppets" but complained that "they still don't have the cards in the library fixed. . . . I looked for trains and there were no cards in the T to R."

A third child compared ALPHA to her two years at Sunflower, a short-lived private free school:

> Sunflower was just fine, it was more free, like at ALPHA, you can't really go out so much, at Sunflower it was so hot nobody was hardly ever inside, and there was always a lot of fights, somebody's always swearing. . . .
>
> I like ALPHA, but I liked Sunflower better. We were going to dissect a baby snake and I missed that. I was learning more there, but I've only been here two weeks so I can't tell yet.[219]

These interviews show students having different points of view than adults might have—for example, what constitutes "work." The former Sunflower student felt she was "learning more" in her previous independent school where she spent most of her time outside and there was plenty of conflict. It's interesting that the student valued freedom over protection from fights and swearing, showing that a child's idea of what is needed for security and safety may differ from adult perspectives.

As the child frustrated by the incomplete library organization noted, students need their tools available to them in a reasonably ordered environment—a condition that, A. S. Neill regretfully noted, the adults, not the children, must largely maintain.

Freedom, not License

George Dennison pointed out, "When adults give up authority, the freedom of children is not necessarily increased. Freedom is not motion in a vacuum, but motion in a continuum."[220] The task during ALPHA's formative years was to build such a culture, such a continuum.

Sylvia Ashton-Warner described landing in a new school of privileged American children, heady with the "intoxication" of life without limits:

> I like children's voices, high, wild or low, solo or in unison, but the beat and boom of stereo and the hitting of the suffering piano in the foyer . . . what is this thing, freedom, supplied to the children in over-spilling glassfuls, in tankards, in brimming kegs? Must glorious freedom mean all this? Is this, indeed, freedom? If it is, what good is it?[221]

Such chaos wasn't uncommon in the American free schools, one possible reason why ALPHA's original parents tried to distance themselves from the term. So did Summerhill's A. S. Neill. But Neill respected New Yorker George Dennison, who wrote of his First Street School:

> Let me replace the word "freedom" with more specific terms: 1) we trusted that some true organic bond existed between the wishes of the children and their actual needs, and 2) we acceded to their wishes (though certainly not all of them), and thus encouraged their childish desiring to take on the qualities of decision-making.[222]

Rejecting the chaos of many of the free school experiments, ALPHA also needed to pursue its own solution to the problem that Neill posed as the distinction between *freedom* and *license*. Susan Garrard recalled that ALPHA's students would frequently approach adults with their conflicts. Adults found it "exhausting" to respond to all the students' needs in this area. Also, "We didn't feel it was our place to do this."

This isn't just a matter of ideology; it can be difficult for an adult to make a just decision in children's conflicts, which are vital to them but often incomprehensible to us. Neill asked, "Are we free enough to keep from butting in on the life of another, however young that other may be? Are we free enough to be objective?"[223]

In free schools, it was felt that the best role for adults was to help students develop skills to resolve differences so that their relationships could carry on in healthy ways. But, as in the larger society, before a conflict resolution system could be created, more basic issues of governance within the school needed to be clarified.

Two institutions grew out of ALPHA's early search for social organization, *Meeting* and *Committee*, both referred to, quirkily, without an article in front of the name.

Does Anybody have Anything to Say?

After his visit to ALPHA early in 1973, Mark Golden reported that regular student meetings at ALPHA were happening during the first year, and that the children were proud of them.

> Hey, I said to someone, this is pretty nice.
>
> Oh, well, they said, this is nothing. The real thing is the meetings.[224]

An ALPHA newsletter from October 2, 1973 noted the following:

> We have decided to have a kid's meeting every Monday morning at 9:30, for two reasons:
>
>> to let them talk about what they want to do and what they like and don't like;
>>
>> to let them know what's been planned for the week.[225]

Susan Garrard described the development of these general meetings of the students and the adults present at the school.

> *It was sort of based on Summerhill's weekly meetings . . . but the children were too small to handle*

all those issues and they'd squirm and wiggle and not pay attention. So we instituted daily meetings: tried to have short, sweet daily meetings where it's much more—immediate. . . . Being kids, they all had to have their turn. So we always kept a list of who had had a turn as chairperson, and they would choose the next chairperson. Later on, it got to be that, if you were a little kid you'd have to choose a big kid, or if you were a girl you'd have to choose a boy.

Then that evolved as well, because the child was finding it hard to be the chairperson. Some of them were five and the kids would be fooling around. So the kids at the meetings talked about this problem of nobody listening during the meeting, so they decided to have a shutter-upper. So the chairperson got to choose a shutter-upper. And again, if you were a boy it had to be a girl; if you were a little kid it had to be a big kid. That always was changing too, but I think mostly if you were a little kid chair, it had to be a big kid shutter-upper; if you were a big kid it had to be a little kid shutter-upper.

That went on for a long time, but the shutter-upper just made more noise, yelling "Shut-up!", so we discussed that whole problem and came up with a Separator. That still works today. That's what happens. They choose somebody to be the Separator and they separate people who are fooling around.

At the kids' meeting, it's "Does anybody have anything to say?" and that's what every chairperson throughout history has said. . . . And that's the way it starts.

And it's pretty much the same with the parent meetings. There's no agenda. Sometimes there's a chart paper up or something. When parents come in, they can put something up. Or a teacher can put something up that they want to discuss that evening.

The structure Garrard described about chairing student meetings has carried through to the present: a rotating chair and separator with the gender and age balance maintained. When a small child is chair, the older separator will guide them by whispering in their ear to keep their attention on their job.

The quotation above shows an aspect of ALPHA (and free school) culture that not all parents are comfortable with: the language used is blunt, like "shutter-upper." As in Summerhill, swearing would often be tolerated, though not without frequent objections and discussions.

In ALPHA's archives is an undergraduate research paper containing a 1989 interview with a twelve-year-old recent graduate.

> For about two weeks we spent the meetings discussing swearing because one little kid didn't want people to swear. We decided you could swear if you really had to.[226]

The recurring controversies about swearing show how a school can work out a community standard for a controversial behavior that its families disagree on. Few adults like to hear kids swear, but adult behavior often contradicts standards they expect of children. At ALPHA, family cultures range from no one swearing to all ages cussing freely. In the wider culture, the common home pattern is one where the most powerful adults swear, but children are forbidden. Free schools reject such double standards.

Speaking practically, to forbid and penalize swearing sets up a challenge that can actually increase its incidence on a playground outside of teacher earshot. Like all unnecessary rules, a swearing prohibition targets children with emotional problems rather than helping them. But figuring out together what they can live with, is a profound lesson in democracy that students can buy into.

The swearing rule has evolved. What students settled on at meetings over the years is that no one is allowed to swear *at people*. It's a sturdy rule, harmonizing with prohibitions against name-calling or abuse in any form.

Helping children to understand why it's okay to swear into the air when you stub your toe, but not to direct that vitriol at a human being of any age or status, is an excellent curriculum for fostering emotional self-control.

Like other free schools, ALPHA's justice system and governance structure puts adults on a par with students. Adults model respectful meeting decorum, and children gain experience in working out the community origins of law—what Neill calls "practical civics".[227] Except for safety rules and unavoidable Board of Education regulations, the rules of ALPHA are set by the General Meeting, including those that govern the meeting itself. As at Summerhill, each adult or child has one vote.

> ***Garrard:*** *We discussed endlessly about the rules of the Monday morning meeting. "You must sit on your bum," or "Can you sit on another person's lap during the meeting?" We'd probably change the rule again the next Monday, but we were discussing these kinds of things endlessly.*

Since students generally attended all meetings but volunteers couldn't, children were more aware of the rules than adults.

> ***Garrard:*** *The kids had a million rules, but we would never write them down. Parents would come in and say, "But this is too confusing for us. How do we know what the rules are if they're not written down?" But well, we'd say, "Cause we might change them tomorrow. This rule is only good until we change it to something else." The kids all knew the rules and the parents didn't need to. They were always asking for that: "I mean, it's a school, after all."*

Fluctuating rules frustrate people who are getting used to ALPHA. But the rules themselves matter less than the act of making them. It's an aspect of non-authoritarian creation and enforcement—students often remind one another (and adults also) of rules without threats or punishments being involved.

Through Meeting, differences in political influence between Board, teacher and student are discussed, and community reaction to non-negotiables such as safety issues and Board regulations can be heard. Even in matters where the school and the children have little power, discussing where the power does lie can help students understand their society and engage in critical thinking.

Conflict and Behavior Problems

When children are allowed to move as their energy rises, and slip into fantasy according to their nature and stage of life, the need for control and discipline is greatly reduced. In a free school, or what the educators of Reggio Emelia call "an amiable school, where children, teachers and families feel at home",[228] child-friendly expectations mean fewer behaviour problems.

This isn't a "lowering" of standards; there are simply fewer confrontations in a school designed around children's needs. Where children can wear hats, drink water, or go to the bathroom when they need to—where they can move around, curl up and read, or play—the relationship between students and adults is quite collegial. This exchange between two former ALPHA students captures some of the ambiance:

> ***Student 1972-1976:*** *I also really enjoyed the slightly more level playing field in terms of the power dynamics. Just the healthy sane relationships with adults and all that, I think stuck with me.*
> ***Student 1974-1982:*** *It's kind of like you had to go into another mood with adults when you were outside of school.*
> ***Student 1972-1976:*** *Yeah.*
> ***Student 1974-1982:*** *Because when you're not at ALPHA, adults expected a certain deference. That just didn't go at ALPHA, wasn't part of what we did.*
> ***Student 1972-1976:*** *It wasn't a lack of respect or anything; I think it was more kind of egalitarian.*
> ***Student 1974-1982:*** *Yeah, like: "Hey, how's it goin', forty-year-old guy?" Not: "Oh, hello sir."*

American researcher Anne Swidler noted that, with fewer rules to enforce and a minimum of arbitrary conditions set, free school teachers are not as "subject to escalating challenges that go with successful defiance"[229] that happen in classrooms.

A school that most students see as a good place may not be comfortable for most adults, and may offend our culturally conditioned sense of order. Based on their individual situations, each free school works out ways to keep the place habitable, to encourage independence and responsibility, and to avoid creating a sense of a servant class that picks up after the students. But they are not quiet or tidy places.

Meeting is a good place to work out whether the school or the individual needs to make the adjustment—or whether something can be worked out. Neill notes that, with their single vote, Summerhill's adults speak up for themselves:

> Our Saturday night General Meetings, alas, show the conflict between children and adults. That is natural, for to have a community of mixed ages and for everyone to sacrifice all to the young children would be to completely spoil these children.[230]

In the fall of 1973, ALPHA's students and the people who took care of them still had to figure out what to do when the agreements made at Meeting were broken. They needed ways to deal with disruptive behavior and interpersonal conflict. ALPHA needed a justice system.

Committee

During ALPHA's early years, a long-standing non-authoritarian method of conflict resolution and community-based discipline was worked out by students, teachers and parents.

Susan Garrard describes how it came about:

> *Summerhill would also deal with discipline problems at Meeting time, but we found that was totally unworkable—it was really unwieldy. In the meantime, kids were always coming to us: so-and-so did this and so-and-so did that . . .*
>
> [A staff-member hired on a LIP Grant] *had heard about groups that had a "committee" system. So we tried it and called it "The Committee" and that was a very very important part, for the kids took over that . . .*
>
> *I remember we started out with four kids, and we had to make it five because of the deadlocks. . . . I would make up the list, who would serve on it, and of course in the*

> *Monday morning meeting we discussed endlessly about how this would work--how many people would be on it, how long they would serve . . .*
>
> *Anyway, it ended up that I would make up the list and knowing the kids I'd try to mix it up between boys and girls and vocal and not-so-vocal. And just post the list: "This is the Committee for this week. If you have a problem, call Committee on the person."*

The 1986 *ALPHA Parent Handbook* included an explanation of how Committee works:

> *It is ALPHA's internal disciplinary and dispute resolving body. A staff person or parent "takes" committee and invites each person involved to tell his/her side of the story. The children—3 from the older group and 2 younger—listen, question, and decide on a punishment or a warning. Punishments usually have to do with extra cleanup duties or being prohibited from using certain equipment for a period of time.*[231]

As with Meeting, some of the practical arrangements around Committee would change as conditions at the school changed, but it remains an important part of the structure of ALPHA today. To students, it carries the weight, but none of the outlaw glamour, of the classic visit to the principal's office.

> ***Student 1974-82:*** *I think Committee was a very powerful tool because the community as I remember it was so tight-knit. To have the ostracism of your friends was a major threat. So often if you threatened to call Committee, then the other kid would back down.*

Thus, students would learn experientially the foundations of democratic law—not in the will of authority, but rather in the protection of individuals and community.

The following exchange gives several perspectives on how Committee was perceived and used, as students, teacher and parents from the founding community searched their memories:

> ***Student 1975-78:*** *I think it happened quite a bit. It was a big threat, I think. "I'm going to call Committee on you" was like—*

> ***Garrard****: A lot of times Committee was never held, but it was like saying "I'll tell my mom on you."*
> ***Student 1975-78****: It was a threat. To get them to stop doing what they were doing.*
> ***Garrard****: I would do it too. I'd say, "If you don't stop that, I'll call Committee on you." So that usually that was enough.*
> ***Student 1975-78****: Obviously from a kid's perspective, I don't remember it being that chaotic and us being that bad (laughter).*
> ***Student 1972-76****: I also remember there were adults around and at the end of the day, they had some authority.*
> ***Student 1974-82****: Yeah, there was always one teacher who sat in on Committee.*
> ***Student 1972-76****: Yeah. I only have really vague memories of the Committee concept, but it seems to me I always kind of had a sense that the adults were more or less in charge—that this was perhaps a formality. (Several groans.)*
> ***Parent 1974-1990****: I never felt that way. I don't know.*
> ***Student 1972-76****: Well, this is a little kid's perspective, so I'm not sure.*
> ***Garrard****: Sure, sure. But that's always been the hardest part: that the teacher is there, but they have to give it over to the kids, no matter how agonizing the process is, they have to take it over, and you are just there to facilitate.*

This exchange reveals that adult authority isn't absent from the school. George Dennison describes the attributes of *natural authority*: "adults are larger, are experienced, possess more words and have entered into prior agreements" from which "children intuit a seriousness and a web of relations in the life that surrounds them". He writes that "the natural authority of adults and the needs of children are the great reservoir of organic restructuring that comes into being when arbitrary rules of order are dispensed with".[232]

As Garrard noted earlier, students spontaneously took their problems to adults. In long-standing free schools, adults fulfill their responsibilities as mentors, models and caregivers, while the students learn to take charge. In ALPHA's Committee, the students trust in the memory of the adult who chairs Committee, to ensure that the steps are properly followed, and each student is able to give an opinion.

ALPHA's egalitarian ways invited all participants into problem-solving. A carpenter hired through a LIP Grant also worked with students and contributed to the development of ALPHA's conflict resolution process.

> ***Garrard**: He had just heard about a Committee system. Because we were talking about the disciplinary system of Summerhill, of the whole school talking about somebody and giving them a fine, usually, because they boarded there. So a fine wouldn't work for us, and also it takes so much time to talk about all of these conflicts, you know. These are little kids. So, no, we just thought of a smaller group dealing with it—that was his idea—and it just developed from there. We just worked it out.*

The adult role in this case was to respond to student requests for conflict resolution, and to research restorative alternatives to the authoritarian structures that no one wanted. A system that had worked well at Summerhill needed to be adjusted for ALPHA's younger children. The students discussed and voted on every step of working it out. Their willingness and skill with the system during any particular era, and the time adults have to support them, gives Committee its credibility.

> ***Parent 1974-1990**: I remember endless meetings about rules—why you could call Committee. They would change, and that was fine too. But to look at a little kid who was chosen to be on the Committee that week and see the smile—the power that child felt, and the importance of being part of that method of governance—I thought that was always very important.*

Not every problem goes to Committee. With caregivers and experienced children, pupils daily practice strategies for getting along. If an adult or another child sees a conflict getting out of hand, they can intercede with ALPHA's non-judgmental question "What's happening?", at which point each child in turn articulates their feelings to the other. Thus, daily, students witness or experience negotiation and mediation. The *STOP rule* is used world-wide, in all kinds of schools. While common cries like "no!" can be part of a drama or fantasy, a signal like "stop" immediately freezes an unwanted action. At ALPHA, Committee is seen as a serious step, almost a "last resort" because everyone really would rather be playing or making or learning.

Though the discussions that created Meeting and Committee seemed "endless" at the time, the system they worked out remained in place, with problems and adjustments, for decades. This is the strength of community building and of governance through consensus. With many inputs and continuous feedback through working-out periods, the structures can be quite sturdy. Consistently, democracies need a governing body, a justice system, and rules to enforce respectful participation, and there must be latitude for them to be worked out in ways that fit the community of the day. During the year 1973-74, ALPHA set itself on that road.

Compassion and Critical Thinking

Chris Mercogliano wrote that, like Summerhill, the Albany Free School uses the general meeting for both conflict resolution and for governance. In contrast to Summerhill's weekly meetings, a general meeting at Albany can be called at any time.

> In order to empower the kids to hold up the end of the bargain of "freedom not license", Neill's famous phrase from Summerhill, and also to give them a nonviolent way to work out their differences, (which were many in that initial period), Mary and the others instituted a "council meeting" system. Accordingly, anyone who wanted to resolve a conflict

> or to change school policy could call a general meeting at any time. This enabled student and teacher alike to make new rules or change old ones, provided they could garner sufficient support for their position.[233]

The tools of governance at a free school can take up a lot of teacher and student time, but they are a vital part of the school program. Neill explained the educational value of self-governance:

> The educational benefit of practical civics cannot be over-emphasized. At Summerhill, the pupils would fight to the death for their right to govern themselves. In my opinion, one weekly General School Meeting is of more value than a week's curriculum of school subjects. It is an excellent theatre for practicing public speaking, and most of the children speak well and without self-consciousness. I have often heard sensible speeches from children who could neither read nor write.[234]

Such opportunities to make judgments sometimes about others but most often about oneself, comprise a vital curriculum. They nurture the *critical thinking* that is so important, in theory, to educators—and which adults also need to practice.

What's important isn't just that children often "win", but that their opinions are aired, acted out and challenged in authentic real-world terms, rather than being humoured or obliterated by higher powers. Jerry Mintz argues that "no matter how large or how small the sphere of power, it is critical that it is never thwarted, co-opted or counteracted."

> Democracy can't be faked. Children absolutely know when they're being given real power and when they aren't.[235]

Though Meeting makes decisions by majority vote, the school ethic is to work toward consensus, between two or among eighty. Winning and losing are part of the picture, but they are less central and far more complex than our competitive culture makes them out to be. Confrontations that occur in children's meetings and committees seldom cause shame or embarrassment because children tend to place the incidents on a direct and personal, rather than a moralistic, plane. Adults are expected to do the same.

In his account of life at Lewis-Wadhams school, Herb Snitzer described the free school approach to ethics that works with the child's sense of justice, egoism and need for community:

> No one around here identifies as a virtue patience, forbearance or tolerance. No one defines virtue at all, which is not to say it does not exist. There is a lot of talk about and thought given to being oneself, fulfilling one's own wishes, finding one's own ways of ego and body satisfaction, and not interfering with others. This leads to much noisy argument, meetings about who did what and to whom, and had he a right to. On the other hand, it also seems to lead in the end to a live-and-let-live attitude . . . an ambience of extraordinary patience toward all but the most outrageously wounding behavior or the most relentless invasions of privacy. I don't know what name to give this ambiance. Call it compassion, perhaps.[236]

Compassion among children doesn't take the form of a permanent atmosphere of love and peace, and it certainly does not involve sublimating desire. It takes the form of both self-respect—the ability to stand up for oneself—and forgiveness for transgression.

In this way, real democracy and real community are very different from the comforting civility, the serene "tolerance" of *pseudocommunity*. One of the factors that may drive people away from practicing direct democracy or engaging in community processes is the difficulty, in a repressed culture, of learning to express oneself honestly, to listen openly, and to confront. There is no destination, where every community member will be in sync; it is always in process. Free schools are places where learning rights and responsibilities as an individual in a social group is always on the curriculum, for adults and children.

9:

LIVING AND LEARNING

This is all well and good, a parent may say, when their kid has spent three years building spaceships, marrying all the toys to each other, being called Committee on for pouring soap and sand into the water table, and chairing the odd meeting.

> *But what about literacy? What about teaching? What about school?*

Jerry Mintz sums up the observations of humane educators from Tolstoy to Neill to Mercogliano to Garrard:

> People are natural learners. Children are natural learners. They don't need to be "motivated" to learn. We have no way of predicting what kinds of things each one of us is going to want to learn or do, and in fact, the words "learn" and "do" pretty much blur together—learning isn't in some separate compartment.[237]

Many of ALPHA's early parents and teachers agreed that a child's learning doesn't necessarily correlate with teaching:

> ***Co-Founder 1****: My wife had been very involved with formal education and felt that children learn, rather than are taught. Given the opportunities, they will learn anyway. So that was the whole philosophy that I personally was interested in, about ALPHA.*
>
> ***Susan Garrard****: My own two children, who went there for ten years, received almost no instruction, really, if you think about it. But I don't think it makes any difference in the long run.*

Peter Gray observes that many children at Sudbury Valley learn to read and write "with no formal instruction at all, primarily through age-mixed play with older children".[238] Urban activist and educator Matt Hern notes:

> We are happy to trust a one-year-old to learn to speak an intricately complex language like English without being taught, yet somehow we believe that four years later she cannot learn reading, writing, geography or anything else without being taught.[239]

Hern argues: "The kids that I know (and I dare say all kids) do not want to grow up stupid, ignorant, lazy or illiterate. No one does. Everyone wants to be knowledgeable, competent, confident, articulate and literate".[240]

But that doesn't doom teachers to unemployment, or make their workday a long nap. To the contrary, schools have deep, often-neglected responsibilities that curriculum checklists don't address. John Dewey and Ontario's *Hall-Dennis Report* placed their discussions of education within a broad context of *living and learning*.

George Dennison wrote: "The proper business of a school is not, or should not be, mere instruction, but the life of the child."[241] He argued that a narrow focus on learning is inappropriate in schools, which are charged with the care of the young.

> The proper concern of a primary school is not education in a narrow sense, and still less preparation for later life, but the present lives of children—a point made repeatedly by John Dewey, and very poorly understood by many of his followers.[242]

This holistic sensibility, this respect for life and its needs, underlies all humane approaches to education—from Tolstoy to Montessori to Neill to Dewey to ALPHA.

The "Normal Way"

Susan Garrard had arrived at ALPHA knowing that she could no longer teach in the "normal way":

> I hated what had happened to me in school and I thought: "I was such a good student, what must it have been for the other kids?" I went into teaching to change the system from the inside.

The "normal way" was described by John Dewey as "teaching by pouring in, learning by passive absorption".[243] Friedrich Froebel, who founded the kindergarten system, "warned against using the child as you would a piece of wax, to be molded into a shape that others desired".[244] Critical pedagogue Paulo Freire called it the *banking* concept.

> In the banking concept of education, knowledge is a gift bestowed by those who consider themselves knowledgeable upon those whom they consider to know nothing. Projecting an absolute ignorance onto others, a characteristic of the ideology of oppression, negates education and knowledge as processes of inquiry.[245]

This is the brutal, but common, metaphor of the child as a passive receptor, a *tabula rasa* (blank slate), a *sponge*, an *empty vessel* to be filled. It hasn't been proven that children benefit from this treatment. Jerry Mintz argues that the proof goes in the other direction.

> The prevalence of this notion exists in spite of modern research that continues to prove that the brain is aggressive and ready to learn, that children are natural scientists, observing and cataloguing and quickly understanding the world around them. So, as study after study refutes the idea that children are lazy, what if we all stopped to look at school from another angle? Maybe the problem doesn't lie within the hundreds of thousands of discontented children; maybe the problem is inherent to the one, overarching system meant, somehow, to serve them all.[246]

A Child's Work

There is one item that children insist must be on their curriculum day after day, though most adults trivialize it, discourage it, worry about children "wasting" their time. Neill noted, "Every child under freedom plays most of the time for years."[247] So in striving to "foster *initiative, inner-directedness, freedom of expression, and autonomy*"[248] for their students, as stated in their charter, ALPHA families had to accept that their children would spend much time in play.

Susan Garrard respected play, which a number of educators call "a child's work". In an interview for Recess Magazine in 1986, Garrard would describe play as "a pooling of the children's resources":

> She says: "The kids basically play. Many people have a problem with the amount of time that they spend playing but whenever I get discouraged about it, I just go and listen in on their conversations as they play and I find that their dialogue is amazingly rich. In fact, it is far richer than any lesson I could prepare for them. What they are doing is sharing all of their knowledge, their experiences, their imagination and their ideas. Children are very resourceful."[249]

Vivian Gussin Paley noted such a lesson in her observations of kindergarten students who had assigned themselves the difficult work of processing the events in New York City on Sept 11, 2001.[250] The emotions and ideas children need to work through come from their lives and from the often-problematic greater culture, and are not always easy to hear. Paley observes that the kind of community-building children undertake during play, and the expansion of the fantasy world to include their various interests and issues, often accommodate children who have very deep emotional or "special" needs.

Garrard's respect for play would define ALPHA as a *free school* despite numerous challenges posed by locale, resources, the constraints of working in a public school, and parental worries. While concerns about how their children spent their time were often expressed, the pro-play aspect of ALPHA received the unqualified support of some parents:

> ***Parent 1992-2002:*** *You don't need to keep them busy. You don't need to make them do anything. They exchanged and interplayed and spoke and made things up and got along and fought and figured it out all by themselves. So you really don't need to be controlling and manipulating people at all. And they learn by playing. They're awfully little; let them play.*

Neill didn't understand why it is that children play, but the fact that they are driven to spend much of their days in fantasy engendered his respect. He found a "vague moral idea behind the disapproval of play", and "fear of the child's future."

> Fear is at the root of adult antagonism to children's play. Hundreds of times I have heard the anxious query, "But if my boy plays all day, how will he ever learn anything; how will he ever pass exams?" Very few will accept my answer, "If your child plays all he wants to play, he will be able to pass college entrance exams after two years' extensive study, instead of the usual five, six, or seven years of learning in a school that discounts play as a factor in life."[251]

Much later, psychologist Peter Gray would gather reams of interdisciplinary research to analyze how play supports children's intellect, mental health and democratic skills. Relevant to both Summerhill's and ALPHA's social goals is his argument:

> Children cannot acquire democratic values through activities run autocratically by adults. They can and do, however, experience and acquire such values in free play with other children. That is a setting where they are treated as equals, where they must have a say in what goes on, and where they must respect the rights of others if they wish to be included.[252]

Peter Gray also observes:

> Everywhere, to live in human society, people must behave in accordance with conscious, shared mental conceptions of what is appropriate; and that is what children practice constantly in their play. In play, from their own desires, children practice the art of being human.[253]

It's hard to imagine a more urgent, relevant curriculum.

A Community for Living and Learning

All that said, teachers teach all day at ALPHA. It's their job. Students need adult support, in a rich environment. But it's hard to put aside cultural habits and figure out non-coercive ways to work with students, especially when the school is overwhelmed by needy children and anxious parents.

John Holt mused, "If (the teacher) gives up being a boss, he must to some degree find himself an entertainer . . ." He compared the role to restaurant staff trying to please a customer who would not be pleased, or to a mother trying to feed a fussy baby:

> It does indeed wear us out, for the same reason that being a cop in the classroom (except for people who like being cops) wears teachers out. We have no more business being entertainers than being cops. Both positions are ignoble. In both we lose our rightful adult authority.[254]

In a consumer culture, it can be a struggle to free ourselves of service paradigms where parent and student sometimes act as fretful consumers. The traditionally under-resourced education system ensures there will be plenty of dissatisfied clients, in any public school.

In its second year of operation, grounded by Susan Garrard's calm, ALPHA's methods would coalesce. Garrard described her personal technique, a strategy special to a site where students are largely self-occupied, or working and playing with peers, volunteers, or other teaching team members:

> *I usually just went around and fished. If you weren't building something magnificent, if you were kind of at loose ends, then I'd say, "How about some reading now?" I had my own little list of whom I'd worked with. . . . And also, I would roam around and say, "Come on, let's do some math!"*
>
> *I remember* [a volunteer parent] *told me my first week there, I think: "Don't ask them!" Because, she said, it's just as easy to say no as yes. So say "Come and do some math!" so it's harder for them to say no. That was a good trick.*

Thus, Garrard worked with students one-on-one or in small groups, while the other teacher and the volunteers offered programming, and supervised children doing creative work and playing. When the teacher who had been hired with Garrard in the summer of 1973 "couldn't cope with the set-up", a parent, also a teacher by profession, took over as the second teacher. This parent/teacher's approach was different from Garrard's:

> *I'm not good at floating in an amorphous situation. I think that's one of the reasons as a teacher there that I instituted such a thing as "math time." If you want to do math, come to me in the little room at 11 o'clock, and we'll do math together. . . . And kids turned up, you know?*

This parent's memories of teaching at ALPHA are a snapshot of a point in time, the spring of 1974:

> *I remember having a very hard time as a teacher in the six months or so that I was there, trying to get a grip on it, because I'd actually been trained as a secondary school teacher, in a completely different mode. . . . And I was also feeling that we needed to have a male and a female teacher. . . .*
>
> *Susan and I were teaching and there was no model for the boys. So I resigned at the beginning of May, when we had to. After that, things just really gelled, and it was*

> *really wonderful, and I was so sorry that I'd put my resignation in at that point because somehow we'd gotten into a rhythm and the whole thing was really working. I remember thinking about how to structure learning in the school, because there was a considerable push from some of the parents to offer lessons to the kids. So what I finally decided to do was offer math-time or science-time, and whoever wanted to could come to whatever we were going to be doing, and it actually began to work quite well.*
>
> *The kids were interested. We did plants under lights, and on one occasion we did a volcano. I guess I mostly remember them coming to math time, because they really seemed to like math. About five of them would come, and we'd sit around and talk about math problems together and it was a wonderful way to learn. I learned stuff from them, too.*

In early 1974, a year after it had lost its staff and half of its enrollment, ALPHA started to hum. Literally hum; it was, and is not, a quiet place. Here is a description by *Toronto Life* reporters who visited in 1975:

> The kids spend much of their time working together in a single large room: painting, working on puzzles or projects, chatting or reading. If afternoon field trips are planned, every child from four to 12 has a vote on whether or not to go. Mornings are spent on the three Rs. Teacher Susan Garrard works with each of the younger children individually. Older kids often work in small, seminar-like groups, or on their own projects.[255]

bel hooks observes: “Conversation is the central location of pedagogy for the democratic educator. Talking to share information, to exchange ideas is the practice both inside and outside academic settings that affirms to listeners that learning can take place in varied time frames (we can share and learn a lot in five minutes) and that knowledge can be shared in diverse modes of speech.”[256]

Conversation opens up the process of learning and teaching. It enables cooperation, the real glue that holds human societies together, and the way that most of the work of the world is done. ALPHA's motto became *sharing education*. Not only did parents become educators, but the students, in a class where they shared knowledge rather than competing for marks, became educators too.

The Basics

Most educators agree that the one tool that they must somehow share with students is literacy. A classic free school trope, even more than the geodesic dome of the seventies, is kids just hanging around reading. A kid who can't yet sprawl over a couch and read a book is likely to be among the ones sitting in a small group with a teacher, working on that very skill.

Math comes in at a close second. In ALPHA, with science and social studies often organically following and branching out from kids' interests, the day-to-day persistent programming is often focused on these basics.

One quote of Neill's always startled me: "We have no new methods of teaching, because . . . the child who *wants* to learn long division will learn it no matter how it is taught."[257] Who on earth wants to learn long division?

Then, working with ALPHA's kids, I'd see them do math every day: counting toys, haggling over trades, dividing treats, playing card and computer games. Some kids love numbers and see them as an interesting puzzle to solve. Even some kids who struggle with math at first are relieved and intrigued when they discover its consistency. Unlike English spelling or watercolor paint, number facts are something you can count on.

Susan Garrard described how an intern introduced math books into ALPHA, noting that in mainstream education circles of the time, math books "were really frowned upon."

> **Garrard**: *I would never have had the nerve to introduce them on my own because it was seen as the lazy teacher's way.* [The intern] *was working with a mathematics professor at Waterloo who was a big fan of math workbooks. So she convinced us to buy them.*

> **Parent 1974-1990**: *I remember working a lot with the kids with math-books. . . . It was good because somebody would be ahead of someone else and they would work back and forth with each other, because it was the same book.*

This old-fashioned pedagogy turned out to be easy for students to use cooperatively with teachers, fellow students and volunteers, or on their own.

> **Garrard**: *Actually, it worked really well, because it was one thing they had. It was their one structure: they had a math book, and they could actually work their way through. It wasn't me at the front of a class of thirty-two saying, "Okay, we're going to do page 56 today." They all just took out their math book at any time and they could do it on their own or anybody could help them. Anytime could be math time. And they could see that they were actually doing something and making some progress.*

Workbooks aren't a panacea, and are certainly not the only approach to math at ALPHA. Manipulatives build understanding of the realities underlying numbers. The ancient abacus is a marvelous tool. It makes little sense to force page math on a kid who still struggles with writing. But when a kid feels the ambition to take on a worksheet, they'll work to get their printing under control.

Teachers who detach themselves from the rigid judgments in canned curricula find that children who learn the basics later are not, in fact, "left behind". Award winning teacher John Taylor Gatto says, "reading, writing and arithmetic only take about one hundred hours to transmit as long as the audience is eager and willing to learn. The trick is to wait until someone asks and then move fast while the mood is on."[258]

Daniel Greenberg describes teaching a dozen Sudbury Valley students all the skills of reckoning—addition, subtraction, multiplication, division, fractions, decimals, percentages and square roots—in twenty hours of lessons.[259] Jonathan Kozol encapsulated the issue:

> Twelve years of lockstep labor in the field of math or language arts are manifestly wasteful of a child's learning energies and learning hours. Freire teaches basic literacy in forty days. No child who is not brain-injured or otherwise impeded in his powers of comprehension needs six years to learn to write ten sentences with reasonable cogency and power. The three-year French or Spanish language-block required by most high schools and by certain of the college-entrance stipulations can usually be transcended in three months by methods such as those used by both Illich and by the U.S. State Department.[260]

Ivan Illich maintained, "Most learning happens casually, and even most intentional learning is not the result of programmed instruction." He found free time essential to consolidate basic skills, observing, "Fluency in reading is also more often than not a result of such extracurricular activities."[261] If Illich is right about this, the many hours of homework children now endure may be doing academic harm, as well as draining joy from after-school hours.

In Sudbury Valley and Summerhill, rough-edged but bucolic schools with large properties where students spend their days in discovery and play, a child's free choice lasts through their childhood. The same conditions existed at the Stelton Modern School, where Jimmy Dick didn't learn how to read until he was ten. In an interview on AERO's website he recalled:

> I was more interested in making crystal set radios and working in the shop. . . . I remember very well wanting to read a book called *Smokey*, which was about a horse and a cowboy. It's a very touching story with beautiful pictures. . . . Some famous cowboy wrote it. . . .

> When I visited [one of the Stelton teachers] later on and said "Gee, you were the one to teach me how to read", she told me, "You came to me with this book and I said, 'Oh, do you want me to teach you how to read?' and [you] said 'No, I want you to teach me how to read *this book*.' Nothing else."
>
> When I read that book, I read everything from then on. My only regret was that I'd missed reading all the kids' stories. I had to do that when I was much older because I went right onto reading serious books.

Jimmy, finally drawn into reading by an interest in cowboys, became a pediatric doctor. Unlike speech and social skills, in which infant neglect will have a permanent impact, literacy can be acquired at any age, once a person is developmentally ready. All over the planet, adults become literate when they have the opportunity.

But as early as 1972, Kozol pointed out some sociological consequences of an approach to literacy that was too casual, for families who know that their child carries extra risks of growing into a life of hard labour, unemployment or exploitation. He challenged "the haphazard, libertarian approach of many of the counterculture schools".

> I was convinced that they would shortchange children and drive away poor people. I also feared that they would inevitably drive away large numbers of black parents who were otherwise devoted to the moral and aesthetic aspects of the Free School.[262]

Kozol found that "as many as ten or fifteen children out of twenty-five or thirty" pick up reading in the course of living, and rigid instruction programs "devitalize" their relationship with literacy. But he emphasized,

> For as many as one quarter or one-half of the children in a Free School situation, it is both possible and necessary to go about the teaching of reading in a conscious, purposeful and sequential manner.[263]

Kozol wasn't calling for a return to the rigid methods from which his students at the New School for Children in Roxbury had fled. With typical passion, he wrote:

> There has got to be a way to be "free" without being maniacally and insipidly euphoric, and to be consistent, strong, effective, but not tight-assed, business-like and bureaucratic. Either discretion represents a falling-off from our original and authentic vision.[264]

In early decades, when there was plenty of literacy on offer but little pressure to take part, some ALPHA students put off reading for as long as Jimmy. But over the years, beginning in the early 2000s, ALPHA responded to concerns related to class and diversity, and to the worries of parents and students.

Literacy teaching still supports individual development and learning styles. ALPHA doesn't risk creating a learning block by forcing literacy on young children who are not ready. But, drawing from Kozol, and respecting members of its teaching team who have long worked proactively and progressively, literacy teaching at ALPHA is more strategic and more visible.

ALPHA still relies on its community members to support and tutor kids, to help them feel safe, to bring in enriching projects and to support the teachers so that they can concentrate on the students who most need them.

The Role of Parent/Educators

An ALPHA co-founder explained the contributions of volunteer parent/educators:

> *You would have more resources, more bodies per student and consequently the pupils would get more exposure to the learning process.*

A former student commented:

> *It's an interesting contrast with A. S. Neill, because he wanted to get the kids away from the parents.*

Neill saw his puritanical, patriarchal, class-ridden European culture as so toxic that adults, including himself, had to step back so that children, whom he saw as "innately wise and realistic", could recreate natural human community without being twisted by adult neuroses.

However, the American urban free schoolers Jonathan Kozol, Mary Leue, and George Dennison saw that to "free the children" in American inner cities involved working closely with their parents. Parents often were involved in the creation of the schools. One aspect of ALPHA that its original argumentative parents seemed to agree on was that they wanted to be part of the school, at least in principle.

> ***Co-Parent 1972-1976:*** *I think we felt that school was an artificial construct—that it separated the children from their parents in an unnatural way, and that we felt that we wanted to be a part of their lives, of their educational lives as well, and that it was a much more holistic and a much more natural way of educating our kids, for us to be involved with them.*
> ***Co-Founder 1:*** *But the other reason was that it was also felt that there were tremendous resources available, amongst the parents—amazing possibilities there.*
> ***Parent 1974-1990:*** [Our child] *went to a cooperative nursery school and those were probably happening in a lot of places. It just became a natural thing to do.*

Community and alternative schooling were fed, in part, by cultural movements to de-institutionalize relationships in society. ALPHA's founding parent community embraced parent involvement as a matter of conviction.

ALPHA's early parents carried the school through two years of unstable staffing, negotiated with the Board of Education and the YMCA, and continued to take considerable responsibility in the classroom. The *Operational Guidelines* of 1973 declared: "In the sense that the community exercises control over the school, ALPHA is a real community school."

The alumni students who were interviewed found this aspect of ALPHA's identity overwhelmingly positive.

> ***Student 1975-78****: I just remember having a lot of comfort knowing that everybody, even Susan, wasn't just a teacher—'cause she was somebody's mom. Everybody was somebody's mom or dad even if they weren't your mom or dad. They weren't as scary as other teachers and stuff because they were all moms and dads of someone. They treated you more like a kid and a parent than like some scary teacher.*

Parents made substantial contributions to pedagogy, supporting various activities that made the school feel like a home-like place:

> ***Student 1975-1978****: The parents were I think a bigger part than they are at the public schools. . . . Somebody's dad used to come in and do Scary Story Time every week.*
>
> ***Student 1972-1976****: As a child, I think I enjoyed a variety of adults coming into the situation and doing fun things. I remember just enjoying all the activities and the field trips and the craft stuff that we used to do. It was pretty varied.*
>
> ***Parent 1974-1990****: One of my favourites was I had kids painting on both sides of plastic. It was messy, but it was good. I did a lot of food organization, a lot of camping trips, potlucks.*
>
> ***Co-Founder 1****: One of my roles was to take a bunch of children up to a place called Maggie's Farm . . . run by the Ontario College of Art. . . . Once a week I would take a bunch of kids up to Maggie's Farm and they would build themselves shelters.*

A note from 1973 asked for programming initiatives and listed several that were under way: reading and language arts, evening ceramics workshops, a play to be produced, a botanical garden, shelter-building, a vivarium, computer programming, and use of YMCA facilities for Phys Ed. In a chronically understaffed public school, reliable volunteers make a difference not only to the children drawn to their activities, but to the school as a whole. When such a parent was on scene, said Garrard, "finally I could focus."

When volunteerism wasn't sufficient, the parent community began to raise funds and ask for contributions from parents to help pay for support personnel. ALPHA held its first annual rummage sale and took full advantage of the extraordinary employment programs that were available at the time.

During ALPHA's early years, the Toronto Board of Education didn't interfere with its staffing practices, or any of the DIY (Do-It-Yourself) initiatives to supplement its very challenging staff levels. (Garrard recalls it as two teachers to sixty-four students in the 1970s.) In 1986, a provincial review would take a positive view of such practices:

> The reviewers were generally impressed with the quality of human resources available to pupils in alternative schools and programs. These ranged from parent volunteers who performed many tasks in the alternatives to extra staff paid for by the parents themselves.[265]

Toronto's policies were in line with what Fantini in the US articulated: that alternative schools could not "carry a price tag that makes it more expensive than what already exists".[266] By mustering the resources it needed, the school was allowed to figure out and demonstrate the conditions needed to carry out its pedagogy, without making demands on the mother system that would be unfair in terms of equitable resource allocation.

This placed extra responsibilities on the shoulders of ALPHA parents, which got complicated. On one hand, our society values a DIY ethic where people take responsibility for their choices. But looking through an equity lens, some families drawn to or in need of ALPHA are financially constrained, or caught in life situations that make it very difficult for them to support the school.

In practice over the years, I would describe the community ethic at ALPHA in French socialist Louis Blanc's 1839 phrase: *from each according to his abilities, to each according to his needs.* Some who contribute a great deal don't find this equitable, but to honour every gift, however small, has been the best way to keep both morale and participation high.

Teaching as a Team

In a cooperative spirit, ALPHA's personnel could self-define their roles, contribute ideas, instigate projects, and function as part of the team. A carpenter, initially hired on a grant to build that classic dome, worked with students, and made key suggestions leading to the formation of Committee. A university student, whose academic project was to work at the "experimental" school, remained on ALPHA's staff list for three years, and contributed to the school's pedagogy.

Open, welcoming, and possessing an eternal faith that adults and children could figure out their roles, Garrard proved to be the answer that the team of mothers in April, 1973, had been seeking: a teacher with "sufficient self-esteem to give of his/her talents positively and to see others' accomplishments or excellence as signs of hope and strength".[267] She did her work as her own babies crawled about people's feet, soon growing up to be students themselves.

Teamwork allows people to bring their full talents to help with the considerable work involved in a school, as well as providing role models to transmit the school's values. In Deborah Meier's words, children need to keep "company with adults who exercise these qualities in the presence of adults-to-be". Team-teaching has been essential to Meier's work in creating learning communities in public schools in New York City and in Boston:

> Within these communities, teachers are encouraged to talk to each other, debate things of importance, and use their judgment on a daily basis. Parents

> meet with teachers frequently and press for their own viewpoint. Sometimes they make trouble. Kids learn the art of democratic conversation—and the art of passing judgment—by watching and talking to teachers whom the larger community shows respect for and who in turn show respect for their communities. Principals are partners with their facilities and have the respect of their communities. Everywhere you look, in such schools, people are keeping company across lines of age and expertise.[268]

In ALPHA, where students can wander and choose to work with an assortment of staff and volunteers, team teaching is a natural and necessary approach. During the seventies, a staff team formed around Susan Garrard, including board-funded teachers and teaching assistants, teaching aides paid through fund-raising efforts, and interns, all of whom were often listed simply as "staff" in the school phone lists. Parents continued to be a powerful presence, if not always reliable.

The Tail that Wags the Dog

The question of assessment in education looms large in the eye of the public. It could be seen as the tail that wags the dog.

"But are they learning anything?" parents anxiously ask, even if their child is only seven (school-starting age in high-ranking Finland). The absence of quantified *outcomes* in free, experiential, holistic, conversational, and organic learning worries adults acculturated to public schooling. It places non-mainstream schools at a disadvantage in political arguments about education, despite the fact that the results of standardized tests in mass, curriculum-driven systems are often less than reassuring.

George Dennison described how his First Street School was extremely *accountable* to its families:

> We did not give report cards. We knew each child, knew his capacities and his problems, and the vagaries of his growth. This knowledge could not be recorded on little cards. The parents found—again—that they approved of this. When they wanted to

> know how the children were doing, they simply asked the teachers.[269]

Recommendation 74 of the *Hall-Dennis Report* was: "Abandon the use of class standing, percentage marks, and letter grades in favor of parent and pupil counseling." AERO's Jerry Mintz finds this "more effective than measurement-based testing".

> The Deweyan concept of reflection, of having to evaluate or review what experiences you have had, has been shown to be one of the ways you are able to reinforce what you learn. According to brain research, having regular sessions in which a person reflects on and evaluates their time spent . . . puts the learning they've done from short-term into long-term memory.[270]

The family/teacher conference, often child-led, has been the method of assessment at ALPHA for fifty years.

Special Needs at ALPHA

ALPHA's non-judgmental, non-standardized school community has included students with various disabling congenital conditions, with terminal illness, and many on the autism spectrum. Many children living with such challenging conditions can benefit from a small, social school. Often, the child and their caregiver (if there is one) become beloved contributors to the school, their very presence guiding students toward greater empathy and inclusion.

To successfully accommodate a child with such needs, parents and schools must weigh whether ALPHA's fluid, social, active atmosphere is helping or hurting, whether there is enough support, and whether better options are available. However, there is rarely enough support for children with special needs. A school system can only address this injustice by hiring enough humane people-oriented helpers to support children with high needs properly.

The most common "special need" that alternative schools are expected to meet is the school system's need to accommodate children with disruptive behaviours. A 1982 policy would state:

> Alternative schools are under increasing pressures from social service agencies to take students who have difficulty or who have dropped out of regular school . . .
>
> Because the schools tend to be small and less impersonal than regular schools, many students adapt well. On the other hand, because of their size, alternative schools face the danger of having to absorb too many "difficult" students too quickly.[271]

It's interesting that "impersonal" is seen by officials to be "regular." Children who adjust smoothly to depersonalization are seen as normal. Perhaps some *special needs* are created by the school system itself. For instance, active boys were seen as healthy—until they were compelled to sit in schools, for long hours and years, from a very young age.

George Dennison argued that "*every* child is plagued by apparently special problems and unmet needs".[272] His insight, if applied in public schools, could make a difference to all children.

Many of Summerhill's early students were "problem children sent in despair by parents and schools". Neill stopped offering psychotherapy, observing that "freedom . . . was the active agent" in Summerhill's success at "curing" most of them.[273]

Observing progressive classrooms in the United States and Britain, John Holt noted that freedom often works because, given such leeway, children can heal themselves, and their community facilitates the healing:

> If, that is, we give them time and space to do it. If we don't pile new problems on the old. If we don't make the fact that they have a problem into a bigger problem. . . . As is shown in rather different ways by the work of A. S. Neill and Ronald Laing, people, and above all children, may not only have much greater learning powers than we suspect but also greater self-curing powers.[274]

But it doesn't always work out. Since healing and growth happen through working and playing in the children's community, a disproportionate number of children with serious emotional problems can undermine the school culture that is the main agent for socialization. Their adjustment period could entail months or years of acting-out behaviors that, without proper support, are hard on other students and the school.

Susan Garrard recalled that at ALPHA,

> *from the first day I went there, we had so many, way out of proportion* [to our numbers] *and with not just some special needs, huge special needs.*

A parent recalled one student who

> *would just fly off the handle and hit somebody over the head with a two by four or something like that. It was quite difficult to manage.*

Another recalled:

> *The first day there, with my precious child, some kid dumped a can of paint on another child's head—it was chaos.*

These families kept coming, but some parents withdrew their children from alternatives after such incidents, and reported to friends and family that such schools did not work.

In their history of Wandering Spirit Survival School, Sharon Berg and Pauline Shirt report even greater challenges:

> The TBE had continually asked WSSS to enroll a high percentage of students with special needs, many of them non-Native. It needs to be pointed out that Vern Harper, Pauline Shirt and Bill Lewis each independently claimed that as many as one third of the students at WSSS were officially identified, or gave strong indicators for designation, as Behavioural or Learning Disabled. At the same time, there were no additional Board personnel offered to support these students.[275]

Knowing that their students' families needed support to cope with the inter-generational trauma of colonization, the founding Parent Group of WSSS "extended their mandate to serve not only students but the parents and community at large".[276] They received no financial support from the Federal Government or the Board for this vital decolonization work.

Based on Neill's work and, through him, on Homer Lane's work with profoundly troubled adolescents, the free school model includes a commitment to children with "special needs". Sometimes, however, a child is never able to meet the challenges of agency, flexibility and responsibility that students carry at ALPHA. To recognize that a child needs greater supervision and treatment is not to give up on the child as a person. It is simply to need a different kind of school.

Many children manifest the natural and necessary neurodiversity of humanity, or experience anxiety and trauma in their lives. With good care, many grow into adults who no longer show signs of "special needs". But some will need tolerance and support all their lives. All schools need to be places where people can learn to give that support and tolerance, and to work out the boundaries that make it possible. The schools need support and funding from their governments and societies to do this vital work, for in every neighborhood and every social class there are young people facing traumatizing lives and deep challenges.

10:

LOCATION, LOCATION, LOCATION

The ALPHA Community loved its home in the old Broadview YMCA. It allowed access to the swimming pool, gym facilities and a playing field that hosted the "ALPHA Olympics".

More than most schools, the Y was what Albany's Chris Mercogliano would call a "permeable vessel, meaning that there are frequent exchanges between it and the outside world".[277] Trips to the beach at Lake Ontario and to the demonstration farm at nearby Riverdale Park were easy to organize, and the Broadview area offered many opportunities for the out-of-school programming vital to the concept.

> ***Student 1972-76****: There were trips every week. We used to go on so many field trips. I loved it. It was great.*
> ***Parent 1974-1990****: It was important just to find out about your neighbourhood.*
> ***Student 1972-76****: All kinds of interesting places: lots of workplaces we would go and see, where they make shoes . . . factories and stuff.*

Several community members moved to the affordable area to be near to the school, and local kids began to attend. One informant was a neighbourhood kid whose parent found the school at a time of desperation:

> ***Student 1975-78:*** *I had started kindergarten at the public school near my house, and I wasn't there for very long and I hated it—with a passion. I hated the teacher, I hated them making us sit there and we couldn't move and we had to hold our hands in our laps-- and I came home and told my mother that I quit and I was never going back again. So I guess she in a panic had gone*

> *looking for an alternative school and found ALPHA. . . . I asked my mom how she found it, and she couldn't quite remember, but she said she thought she either just flipped open the phone book or just word of mouth through parents that she knew and kids and that anybody could go there. There wasn't any kind of process or application. It was just word of mouth, and she looked it up and found it and that was it, probably.*

Other informants managed to commute to the school, even as small children.

> **Student 1972-76**: *I remember for my first couple of years at ALPHA, my sister and I used to travel by ourselves on the subway and streetcar from basically the Annex, Bathurst and Bloor area, all by ourselves, little tiny kids in ways that I can't imagine anybody would allow six and five year-olds to do today. But it was always okay.*
> **Co-Parent 1972-76**: *I think you were a little older; you were six and seven.*
> **Garrard**: *Seven seemed to be the age when they could handle the streetcar by themselves.*

Except for some reverberations in the press, there was no sign of discontent with the site at the Broadview Y. Those who felt the working class neighborhood was a problem had left, talking to reporters on their way out. Not only were students comfortable with the building itself, they also formed relationships with local stores and restaurants. Many kids in this era had the run of their neighbourhoods, and ALPHA's older kids could go abroad at lunchtime, and take responsibility for a younger child.

> **Student 1974-1982**: *At the Broadview Y, we had a rule that if you wanted . . . to go down to the corner of Broadview and Dundas to buy your lunch, you had to have a big kid go with you. So that was a really important thing to do. You felt pretty fancy if you had a big kid going with you to buy lunch.*
> **Student 1975-1978**: *I hung out with so many kids from ALPHA when I was there that all the adults in my life*

> *were familiar with ALPHA. Even the kids that I hung out with in my neighbourhood seemed to be—there was enough on the street and around in the Bain Co-op and stuff that went to ALPHA and their parents were involved, that I remember going to Susan's house sometimes.*

ALPHA was not only home, it was starting to look like a real neighbourhood community school. But with continual pressure from the Board to move into an existing school space, it had to constantly defend even this most basic, substantive aspect of its existence. Without open hostility, this is how administrative pressure wears down all kinds of community-based initiatives—forcing them to revisit old struggles even as new challenges constantly arise.

Yet ALPHA's original community acknowledged the Board's financial dilemma, with respect to accommodation:

> ***Parent 1972-76****: We wanted to be outside school premises. The School Board was, unfortunately, under a lot of pressure, with schools getting emptier, not to pay any rent on any outside facilities at all.*

The Search

After five years at the beloved Broadview YMCA, ALPHA finally had to move. The building was to be demolished.

With a thoroughness typical of this early school community, ALPHA's parents assembled a brief that was ten pages long, including results of visits paid by the New Space Committee to six private properties and the two school sites that were offered by the Board of Education.

The schools offered up by the administrators weren't happy with the idea of sharing with ALPHA. One principal was "sympathetic," but the spaces were "inadequate," the host school was "growing and our accommodation would have to be considered temporary".

In the other school, "the principal stated to us initially that he did not feel the schools could be compatible". The classrooms on offer were in use and "scattered about the school".[278] This principal wrote a letter to Trustee F.P. Nagle stating the dilemma from the viewpoint of the "host school" and the principal, who would be delegated the extra responsibility for the alternative:

> With the introduction of ALPHA to such a visible position, this community will experience three formal programme schools and one alternate school existing in very close proximity. There must be no lessening of the community's expectations of educational achievement for their children. Can the community rationalize the two systems without weakening its support and faith in the existing educational programme? The children of three formal school programs will see an alternative educational system. How will they view a programme which uses in many instances opposing methods to achieve its goals?[279]

This letter also "question[ed] the safety of young students in the ALPHA Programme" in a schoolyard that was shared with three other schools. Referring to the experiences of Contact and SEED in shared school spaces, this principal suggested "a more freely structured educational system does not achieve optimum development in a structured environment".

Meanwhile, ALPHA's New Space Committee found a house at 633 Broadview Ave. that could meet "all its criteria and would also conform to Board specifications". Rooted in the Broadview neighbourhood, they were eager to succeed. Appendixes to the committee's brief included detailed floor plans, budgets and copies of relevant legislation. But this time, the Board of Education couldn't be convinced:

> ***Garrard****: Then the Board officials said "Are you nuts? There's no way we are paying rent." But we kept looking all year for a space. They would say, "Oh, we've got this great open space and you get half of it. And the other school gets the other half of this open space"—with not even a wall! That kind of nonsense.*

> *Or "There's a classroom vacant here on the second floor of this school. And then there's another one. . . ." It was just silly. That was very very stressful.*

The Board of Education's initial offers seemed to show little regard for the needs of either the alternative school, or the host school. ALPHA parents had talked to teachers at MAGU, where the children's interactions with the host school and principal were problematic. They talked to staff at SEED, who were "quite bitter about the move into Board space and [felt] that such a move led to the deterioration of the school". At Contact, the teachers related how staff at the existing Board space "cheered the day we moved out".[280]

Brant Street

In the end, however, the persistence of ALPHA's community, and the goodwill of administrators, resulted in a permanent location for the school. An article in the Toronto Star indicated that the decision to move the school from its neighbourhood in the east to the west side of downtown was seen by many ALPHA parents as a defeat. Trustee Judith Major told the parents:

> I'm uncomfortable in being put in the position of an enemy of alternative schools. But I must warn you that the halcyon days are over.[281]

Made only a few years after the alternative schools' hard-won beginnings, this is a chilling statement, and a sign of struggle to come.

But at ALPHA, the community's persistence had resulted in the Board finally offering a space that respected the school's autonomy and identity.

> ***Garrard:*** *I remember after we had looked and looked for the whole year at all these spaces, there was nothing. So we ended up back at the Board with the superintendents and things.*
> *They said, "Well, what'll we do now?"*

> *Then someone said, "What's happening with that old Brant Street building?"*
> *They had other clients there, but they were easy to move. As soon as we went in there, we said: "We're home." It just felt like that.*
> ***Parent 1974-1990**: It smelled like a school, though.*
> ***Garrard:** It did—it was hard. After what we'd looked at, boy, it was pretty good. But we had said we wouldn't go beyond Parliament Street and here we were, west-enders.*
> ***Parent 1974-1990**: I did some research with the kids one time. We went to the Board archives and found photographs of Brant Street. It was never built as a real school. It was meant to be a book depository but there were some immigrant students. Because there were photographs of students sitting at desks in that building. But it was never built with the permanence of a regular school building.*
> ***Garrard:** I believe too that the reason it has those big windows is so it could be turned into a factory, if it didn't work out. Because it was in that district. But the big windows are wonderful.*

Though, on the whole, the new location worked out well, the students noticed that the change affected the way that the school operated.

> ***Student 1972-1976**: I remember in the early days, I guess because I was younger, it seemed a lot freer. I think I was sensing that the whole thing was becoming more structured with time. At least I remember perceiving that.*
> ***Student 1974-1982**: I remember that happening when we moved to Brant Street. It was really exciting that we had this new building, and then there was also a feeling of some major changes that were starting to take place.*
> ***Garrard:** The space made a huge difference. We set it up then that the Big Room was the littlekids room and the Quiet Room was the bigkids room. They didn't have to stay there, but the littlekids' stuff—the toys and stuff—were in that one room.*

> And later, when we were really cramped and everybody was complaining . . . we put in to have the third floor and we got it. We moved the bigkids to the third floor. So we had the littlekids on the first floor, Downtown Alternative School on the second floor and the bigkids on the third floor. That was a huge, huge thing.
>
> It really put a lot of structure into ALPHA that was just necessary because of the physical thing. And you couldn't just swing back and forth between bigkids and littlekids then, because it was up this big staircase. Just communicating, running up those stairs just to say something to anybody there was amazing.

ALPHA's move in 1977 to the Board-owned site at Brant Street removed what had been an ongoing irritant to the Board of Education, and an annual tussle for the school community. Relations seemed to settle for a while into arms-length congeniality.

Most Rewarding Year

In May, 1979, the Toronto Board of Education published a collection of *1978 Annual Reports* from nine public alternative schools. ALPHA's submission to this document opened with a joke:

> Despite the fact that we are the second oldest alternative school with the Toronto Board, this is the first year we have presented a written annual report. If this is the beginning of a trend, we may end up issuing report cards to our students![282]

Dated October, 1978, the tone of the report was open, relaxed and assertive. It indicated that the move from Broadview Y during the summer of 1977 had not damaged the school in terms of enrollment. Both locations were solidly working class, so in those days families could find places to live and work near the school.

From 33 students in 1976-77 at the Broadview Y, enrollment increased to 45 in 1977-78, the first year at Brant, to 48 in October, 1978.

"Most of the children who lived near the Y were able to travel to the new location on the King streetcar. . . . ALPHA continues to draw families from across the city." The upbeat report stated, "we feel that we have just completed our most rewarding year." It showed pride in a "strong senior program".

It is interesting to quote this document at length, because of its description of the operations of the school:

> Initially, ALPHA attempted to make all levels of the school work at once as it had a mandate for JK to 6. It was not truly appreciated that children function best at ALPHA by growing into it. The strength of the senior program stems from the fact that children are staying at ALPHA past 2 level and from the fact that the present staff has special skills in this area.
>
> The staff, Susan Garrard, responsible for the junior program, Mike McCarthy, responsible for the senior program and Irene Thomas, hired by the parents and responsible for six to eight year-olds who are in transition, have formed a strong, supportive team.
>
> Families continue to work in the school one half day each week. Their role is to assist the children in the activities the children wish to undertake. They supplement the teaching staff and, in some areas, act as teaching assistants. The families are also responsible for the ongoing operation of the school.
>
> An administrative committee, known as the Sieve, is elected annually, and is composed of five parents and three staff members. The Sieve meets monthly to set the agenda for monthly general meetings. The Sieve is responsible for the parental involvement in the school, the variety of programs offered, the hiring of staff and fundraising.[283]

The school was open about the responsibilities its parents and teachers had taken on. A parent/teacher team unequivocally hired the staff. They hired and paid additional personnel. Volunteers worked directly with the students and volunteerism was considered to be high at this point with "at least three family representatives there each day."

> Parent participation enables the children to arrange visits to the neighbouring factories, to swim on a regular basis, to sew, to cook, to attend the theatre, to produce their own plays and to write their own newspaper. The children have also been able to take part in other religious and cultural events than their own.[284]

The school was happy with the building on Brant Street, which it shared with Hawthorne, the French Immersion school. ALPHA looked forward to "building a new playground jointly with Hawthorne through Ryerson Polytechnical Institute." They "wince when the Board considers ALPHA and Hawthorne to be one school for that purpose" of allocating equipment, but they otherwise seemed to be on good terms.

> We have had excellent support from the Board. Dale Shuttleworth has been especially helpful. Les Birmingham has been a good principal. We have found most Board departments easier to deal with than they have been in the past.[285]

This report reflected that most parents were content with how the students were doing:

> Regarding the children, we can say with confidence that they are developing a sense of responsibility onto themselves. Visitors continue to be amazed that the children move from activity to activity freely, respectful of their peers. There is no harassment, little bickering, and no physical abuse. There is peace, a sense of purpose and calmness about the school which reflects the happiness and self-confidence of the children. The daily meetings, held at 2:45, permit all the children to meet and discuss the events of the day and to plan and prepare for the next. Discipline at the school remains child-centered with a committee formed of a staff member and children on a rotating basis, acting as arbitrator.

The optimistic report noted a single dark cloud on the horizon—the prospect of staff cuts at the TBE. ALPHA's staff "has little seniority" and "losing 50 per cent of our staff would be catastrophic". This problem would soon impact the ability of schools and teachers to choose one another, a major problem for alternatives.

As 1980 approached, daily life at ALPHA had settled into a rhythm. A brochure published by the Board in 1979 declared unequivocally "Parents run ALPHA".[286] ALPHA's "most rewarding year" was also the year when the Toronto Board of Education adopted a policy encapsulating what it had learned since MAGU and SEED had started kicking its doors in 1969. While a few trustees and administrators had held them open, over twenty alternatives had poured into Toronto's school system—and more were on their way.

11:

STRUCTURING FREEDOM

The community-based creation of publicly funded schools was truly unique, something that would be christened *The Toronto Experience*. The high water mark for Toronto's alternative schools may have been a document that was issued in 1978, entitled *General Policy for Alternative School Programs*. It outlined a policy foundation for collegial, arms-length relationships between local schools and the public administration.

Co-authored by Dale Shuttleworth, and then adopted by the Toronto Board of Education on February 9, 1978, the *General Policy* emphasized that Toronto's alternative schools were the self-generated products of local democracy:

> Alternative school programs in the City of Toronto may be unique in North America, because in almost every instance they were initiated by groups of parents, teachers, students and other interested persons who approached the Board of Education for support of experimental programs within the system. By comparison many other school boards have designed their own alternative schools, administratively, with a minimum of community involvement.

The *General Policy* pointed out that autonomy and shared control over decisions affecting the schools were essential elements in the Toronto approach. The document further identified grassroots creation and operation as the essential elements in *The Toronto Experience* that made it unique in the world.

> The most common characteristic among the secondary and elementary schools in Toronto has been shared responsibility for major decisions affecting the operation of the school. (This usually would include parents and teachers at the elementary level and teachers and students in the secondary school.) In this regard, such vital functions as budget and staffing have been shared with Board administrators. Otherwise, each alternative school has its own separate identity and approach to curriculum and program within Ministry guidelines.[287]

The *General Policy* positioned Toronto's alternatives within an international movement. It quoted Mario Fantini's description, in *Public Schools of Choice,* of the public school as "a place that has to deal both with diversity and the needs of universal education". It declared a commitment to meeting the needs of what Fantini described as the "critical mass of dissatisfied customers who are converging on the schools and saying it is not working for them".[288]

The nine-page typewritten *General Policy* was conversational, clearly written, and intended to be "of assistance to parents, teachers, students and the community at large". It included clear regulations to ensure that alternative schools would remain fully public and fair. They were to receive no more funding per pupil than "any other school at the same level in the system" and could not "restrict enrollment beyond the regular considerations which apply to any other school".[289]

The *General Policy* quoted the Canadian educator John Fritz, in his publication *My Encounters with Alternatives*, who listed the purposes of alternative schools as follows:

> 1. They provide continuing educational opportunities for students who drop out of or prove disruptive in the regular school.
>
> 2. They serve students who for a variety of reasons find the regular high school inadequate to their needs and who are interested in exploring opportunities in alternative schools.

3. They explore possibilities in developing new school procedures or plans for subsequent wider applications in the system.
4. They develop alternative programs in keeping with the diverse needs of student clients and parental conceptions of the type of schooling preferred for their children.[290]

Fritz's ordering reflects the education system's priorities, but early elementary school creators would likely have listed them in exactly the reverse sequence. In its initial approach in 1971 to the Toronto Board of Education, the ALPHA Community had offered itself as "an educational experiment for Toronto schools":

> It is our belief that in order to obtain any educational or other form of social progress, new programs should be created on an experimental basis within the system. It cannot be done all over the system at one time. To this end we will be an educational experiment for Toronto schools. . . . In addition to serving as an experimental program, we see such an opportunity as fulfilling a function as a potential resource for expanding the context of teacher training and curriculum development.[291]

This was not experimentation in the sense of imposing a risk on a vulnerable population, something that happened too many times during the twentieth century. This "experiment" involved a group of parents, teachers and students working together to develop a best practice, while keeping a watchful eye on the children they cared about.

A Bright Flame of Innovation

An ALPHA co-founder recalled his early hope that the creation of alternatives within the public system "would have an impact on the very structure of what was happening in the school board".

> *I think that was what was meant by radical reform; it was a change within the system, not overturning the system, but people aspired to those changes having an*

> *impact, in ways that would alter the entire system. It's what Michael Apple came to call a number of years later "non-reformist reforms". Nobody's fooling themselves: this is reform, it's not revolution. But there's a hope for it being more than just simply a minor reform that doesn't change anything.*

ALPHA's supporters within the public school administration shared such hopes. In 1981, Dale Shuttleworth delivered the keynote address to the London Educational Alternative Program Conference in England, entitled *How Can Alternative Education Affect the Mainstream?—The Toronto Experience.* Shuttleworth listed three distinct alternative school types which had organically developed to meet the needs of diverse constituencies:

- *Learning-Style Alternatives* that included ALPHA and SEED, interested in trying different "approaches to learning",
- *Socio-Economic Alternatives* like Laneway that grew out of needs identified in inner-city neighbourhoods and were characterized by a "smaller teacher/student ratio", and
- *Cultural-Linguistic Alternatives* which at the time had only two schools: Wandering Spirit Survival School and the French/English Hawthorne II Bilingual School.

Shuttleworth called public alternative schools "a bright flame of innovation sweeping across . . . the western world", and expressed hope that the grassroots control they pioneered would continue to "play a leading role in the identification of, and response to, human need, particularly with reference to minority interests".[292]

As the eighties dawned, Jonathan Kozol in the US would also feel that those who created pioneering schools in the 1970s were changing the monolithic institutional culture of public education. In 1982, an unusually exuberant Kozol issued a revised edition of his book *Free Schools*, which he retitled *Alternative Schools*. He wrote that the free school "remains a vigorous and still expanding institution".

Speaking of the United States and of Boston especially, Kozol wrote, "More important, however, is the transformation that the Free Schools themselves have been able to provoke within the public schools."[293] He listed activists who had moved from the free schools into places of prominence in American public systems, and saw this as a sign of reform to come.

The ALPHA Constitution

By the late seventies, daily life at ALPHA had formed a rhythm, and working partnerships were being sustained. The school managed to maintain its arms-length relationship with the Toronto Board of Education. In 1979, a Board-published brochure declared unequivocally that "parents run ALPHA".[294] But much remained to be resolved about how the parents would run the school.

At the turn of the eighties, decision-making hit a snag that would result in ALPHA forging a unique democratic path. In 1978, as it had in 1973, ALPHA's Constitution declared that "the ultimate decision-making body is a meeting of the community as a whole". It continued to define itself as "horizontally" structured, without hierarchy. However, the governance strategies during ALPHA's founding decade of the 1970s showed a conventional approach to democratic organization.

> ***Parent 1972-76****: Early on, I think we were much more Robert's Rules of Order at our meetings—parliamentary procedure. I was the chair, so somehow I must have been elected to that. I don't think there was a huge executive, but certainly the meetings were probably more structured. It's interesting that the long-term trend was to less and less structure at meetings.*

ALPHA's bare-bones constitution had been amended several times during the 1970s, as ALPHA worked on its processes. The 1978 constitution shows that there was still some investment in an executive committee. To clarify that it was not the decision-making but a house-keeping body to work with the staff on small day-to-day issues, it was called *the Sieve.*

As of June 1, 1978, ALPHA's constitution defined the ALPHA Community as "a group of parents who believe in sharing the responsibility for the education of their children". It declared that the parents would have an "obligation to participate in the governance, administration and philosophy of the education of the children in ALPHA School". Its page-long list of "Objectives" remained consistent with the original proposal to the Toronto Board of Education, defining a "desirable educational environment" as one that would support:

> 1. Children and adults in their efforts to define, pursue and achieve their own educational goals. . . .
> 2. Constant encouragement so that each child can grow in his/her own direction and at his/her own speed. We particularly support multi-age grouping. . . .
> 3. The continuity between school and home, so that living and learning are not arbitrarily separated. . . .
> 4. The child's total experience of himself/herself and his/her world, so that he/she will be respected as real and viable and valuable. . . .
> 5. A view of the child as unique and non-comparable, non-measurable worth; such an environment requires the elimination of arbitrary standards and goals.[295]

Under this constitution, the voting membership included all parents, all staff, and children and volunteers "who apply to and are recommended by the Sieve committee".

The Sieve was a standing committee elected by written ballot, composed of chairperson, current and previous coordinator, treasurer, all staff, and two parent members. There were some periods in these early years when the investment of a limited authority in structures like the Policy Committee and the Sieve seemed to work, but at other times they became dysfunctional.

The Sieve

The Policy Committee, founded in early 1973 as the school flailed in confusion, had often brought detailed proposals to the ALPHA General Meeting for ratification. According to the hand-written *ALPHA General Meeting Minutes* from Sept 10, 1975, it appears that the Policy Committee had taken on an executive function:

> The status of the committee was discussed and there was no objection to giving it the power it seemed to have assumed. That is to deal with sensitive issues and make important decisions that cannot wait until general meetings.

After the early years of intense policy work had passed, the parents created the *Sieve* to figuratively blow off the administrative chaff, so the parent meeting could chew on the grain.

> **Susan Garrard:** *We had monthly parent meetings and we instituted an executive meeting in between because we were finding we were getting bogged down. We all wanted to talk about real issues at the parent meeting, but there were so many business issues—Board of Education issues and things that we had to deal with, so we instituted what we called the Sieve, which was really an executive committee, but we didn't want to call it that. It was to sift through the business so that we wouldn't burden the General Meeting with that. We would just report to the General Meeting so in the middle of the monthly parent meeting, we would have a Sieve meeting, and we would report.*

But the parent community was unwilling to delegate even a small amount of decision-making power.

> **Susan Garrard:** *I was frankly tired of going to twice as many meetings for no reason. Because you'd bring anything back and someone would say "Just a minute! We want to decide that again." Or "Let's discuss that again."*

Eventually though, the problem of having an unacknowledged quasi-executive came to a head. The Parent Meeting of June 18, 1981 confronted problems presented by the Sieve, in the context of a serious conflict that involved parents and a staff-member. The minutes recorded a "lengthy discussion" in which, among 39 recorded points, it was noted:

> – structure we're working in does not coincide with the philosophy of ALPHA . . .
> – problems never came to the community as a whole, negative comments on both sides continued back and forth between a small number of parents and staff, the problem is the structure of the Sieve . . .
> – problem with decision-making process—group makes arbitrary decisions that create problems . . .
> – minority speaking for majority and manipulating community
> – concern of parent body not to allow people to take control
> – people who have power are trying to give power up
> – palace revolt, parents taking more power, teachers' role has been redefined . . .
> – teachers must function within trust-accountability . . .[296].

On June 23, 1981, an amendment to ALPHA's constitution dissolved the Sieve.

Community Governance

The dissolution of the Sieve seems to have set ALPHA on the road to a workable whole-community governance model.

> **Garrard**: *We abolished the Sieve, and we went back to a much more primitive system where it was "Okay, there's no executive. We will have monthly meetings and they'll be on the first such and such of whatever month, and as long as they are duly posted, and everyone comes, and we'll choose a chairperson at that time. We really opened*

> *up, and that was very important. That still goes today, and it's worked very very well.*

Part of ALPHA's maturing governance structure may have been the acceptance that, since most of the parents had full-time commitments elsewhere, they couldn't involve themselves enough in their community school to become the full education partners that the founders had envisioned. ALPHA's unsuccessful experience with the Sieve, however, showed that the parental role could not be delegated to a few highly involved parents.

ALPHA's founding ethic was based on direct democracy, communitarian and participatory. Though the school was guided overall by decisions made in the monthly General Meeting, it was becoming clear that those actually present in the school had to be trusted to carry on their day-to-day collaborative work. A letter written by an ALPHA teacher during this time of conflict explained:

> For the children and the staff, this is a full-time occupation, and we work out ways of living and learning together. The parents are the governing body, and they are asked to act as supplementary staff in the school, to attend meetings, and to serve on committees. This is not their full-time occupation. They must fit these responsibilities into their busy schedules. So it is that many parents fall short of meeting these obligations. . . . Nevertheless, ALPHA has managed to thrive with this system, due mainly, I believe, to the feeling of goodwill and support which we share. Few schools could boast of a more thoughtful and interested membership.[297]

The Albany Free School had also realized that direct democracy required real autonomy and partnership on the part of the workers and students. At the independent Albany,

> only those actually present in the building could determine the school's day-to-day operating policy. Others were welcome to attend meetings, and advise and make suggestions, but that would be the extent of their power.[298]

With the final abandonment of any form of executive, ALPHA laid aside structures that sometimes facilitated troubling practices of parental *oversight* as opposed to *participation*.

In a democratic school, many small decisions are made on a day-to-day basis. Community-minded individuals do this work autonomously, in harmony with agreed-upon values, prioritizing the needs of students and staff. But to deal with matters of import that must be brought to the group as a whole requires much more than a lack of concentrated power in a designated executive. It needs a solid group decision-making process.

It's a delicate balance. Years later, Susan Garrard would say:

> *"Every time you introduce a bit of structure, by whatever means, you lose something, so I was always trying to figure out a balance."*

Drawing on his varied experience, Scott Peck made similar observations: "Committees and chairpeople do not a community make." While some formal organization is necessary, Peck doesn't see it either as a solution to chaos or a doorway into community.

> An organization is able to nurture a measure of community within itself only to the extent that it is willing to risk or tolerate a certain lack of structure.[299]

Some folks think of non-hierarchical communities as leaderless groups. However, Peck saw a community as a "group of all leaders".[300]

Creating a Community of All Leaders

As ALPHA dispensed with its last vestige of an executive, it benefited from the experience of a gentle, rebel Christian group that has for centuries practiced governance by a "community of all leaders."

Susan Garrard credited ALPHA's consensus governance to a community member who, when interviewed, seemed unaware of having made such a vital contribution.

> ***Parent 1980-1991:*** *Everything I know starts with the Quakers, and it's all about leveling power and speaking truth to power and creating safe places where anyone can speak and be listened to well, with no mediator between you and whomever. There's no creed, but you're coming together because you share a powerful common belief in your place in the world and where you're going. So the Quakers have lots of really good group process, amazing group process, amazing structural process. They would form a committee because there was a felt need, work on it, and when the felt need stopped, they'd lay the committee down. They don't keep things for the sake of structure. It's all just calm and careful but not powerful—not about power. It's very consensual, and there's a lot about just taking the time to let the group form.*
>
> *People were developing those kinds of processes and structures a lot* [in movements for peace and equity], *in those days. That whole sense of belief in the group's power and ability and capacity to think well and deliberate together, that you don't need a couple of people to go away and make an important decision. You actually can reach consensus and it's not unwieldy. I think maybe that's another piece of it: that you not only form the group by going around and letting people know who you are, but then you demonstrate that you can discuss big items together and come to a conclusion that's worthwhile.*

This is the format that persisted in the monthly parent/teacher meeting. For many, the ALPHA meeting has been their first experience of participatory or consensus democracy.

> ***Parent 1980-1991****: I remember kind of, in the first go, saying, "Believe me: this will work. It will be okay. We won't be here until eleven o'clock listening to one person talk. It will be all right. And it worked. People quite loved it, and then they asked me to do it again. And again and again. So it became a thing.*

To be very different in background and opinion, yet all be *friends*, to listen far more than one speaks, to seek resolution, to debate seeking neither victory, loss, nor compromise—this is what is to be a part of a consensus-based community.

ALPHA's Quaker-influenced meeting model has governed by custom since this time, as the embodiment of the ALPHA "staff-community council" called for in *The ALPHA Experience*, the founding charter that laid down the original agreement in 1971 between the school and the public Board of Education. The vagueness of the original proposal gave ALPHA the space it needed for the decade-long job of figuring out what would work for this community school.

Consensus governance isn't well-known, but it's a venerable and deeply democratic model, and useful even in diverse settings. Quaker chronicler Neale Brayshaw described the careful process of working together for consensus:

> This willingness to *wait* or *persuade* until a large measure of spiritual unity is reached is one of the most cherished possessions of Friends, saving them as it does from smart scoring of debating points or impatience in pressing for a decision. It has to be admitted that often, in deference to timid individuals, a desirable forward step is overlong delayed, but once taken, it meets with general acquiescence free from the bitterness which might at an earlier stage have arisen had one side carried its point by force of majority. Not infrequently it happens that those who have been against the proposed step will help to carry it out.[301]

Brayshaw described consensus as an expression of the holy spirit, which arrives as a Quaker meeting "waits upon the Lord".[302] Several community members from ALPHA's post-1980 period expressed the arrival at consensus as "magic".

Again, Anishinaabe ways need to be acknowledged here, whether or not these educators in the 1980s were aware of them.

A decade before, Wilfred Pelletier had described consensus democracy in Anishinaabe governance:

> I can remember as a boy, when we sat in council, we came to unanimous decisions. Everyone agreed. And if one person objected, we didn't suppress that person. What we did was ask ourselves a question: "Is it possible that we don't see this thing the same way as the other person? Let's explore ourselves.[303]

Devoted to the concept of a sacred light within each human being, the Quaker faith also rejected hierarchies and developed ways to coax out this light in the expressions and decisions of its people. When Indigenous liberty set a match to European discontent and sparked revolutions, perhaps it influenced the formation of this sect that arose in the seventeenth century.

However it was that these new/old ways made their way to these Great Lake shores, during ALPHA's early decades the talking circle format became familiar to activists, especially those working on peace activism and in support work on Indigenous issues. Some of them ended up bringing their children to a little democratic school called ALPHA.

In Quaker and Anishinaabe processes, strong personalities receive less positive reinforcement, and the shy people don't need to struggle as much to be heard. Quiet people can see themselves as contributors to democratic process and builders of consensus.

> ***Parent 1982-1996****: I'm very aware of a role to play here when other people are speaking who are more overt. That there's a significant role to play in being present and listening and enjoying the exchange. . . . This is it, too. . . . And I did really discover it at ALPHA.*

Other families had a different lesson to learn from the process, as another parent/informant expressed:

> *One of the things that are important I think that ALPHA taught me and taught my children is to step back and listen a bit rather than dominate.*

Those with little experience of working in community credit ALPHA with transmitting a vital life skill:

> ***Parent 1982-1996****: I think my first experience of it was there, at ALPHA. . . . I think I had a sense of something that I wanted that had to do with community and . . . I feel like I learned something about community at ALPHA that has grown and informed and I've taken with and brought into play, and a really major major current in my life. And my kids, too. We live with people, you know?*

To keep consensus-based meetings and relationships working well requires self-awareness, for they contradict the norms of this brash, aggressive European-based culture. Pelletier noted:

> *I see white people attempting to use the same method, but they cannot make it work. For what they do, if one person disagrees, they begin jumping on that person trying to change that person's mind and suppress him.*

Pelletier makes an important point. It hasn't always been easy at ALPHA for highly individualistic people to learn to be good listeners as well as good talkers. Each generation at the school has had to engage in self-examination and struggle, to meet the challenges of its time.

12:

A BLESSED TIME

In spite of a trustee's 1977 warning that "the halcyon days are over",[304] ALPHA would be in good shape during the 1980s. Oral history participants recall this period as a "pretty blessed time". Community governance was working well, and ALPHA appeared to have a comfortable arm's-length relationship with the Board.

> ***Parent 1980-1991****: They gave us autonomies, space—physically and metaphorically. Susan had a good relationship with whoever was our principal; once a year we'd take a little parent delegation up and talk to them or something, and do an accountability piece—check in. But we were really left on our own. So for a free school that's a blessing. . . . I think we did have less ability to pull down resources and get special things, but I think we kind of wanted to be under the radar. . . . So there's a bit of a give and take that you do there with the principal. He doesn't ask you for everything and you don't tell him everything and it's all for the greater good.*
> ***Parent 1982-1996****: I do remember the climate was we were left alone. There were certain minimal things we had to do, and they just left us alone to be and do what we were doing.*

Not all alternatives were doing this well, especially some that shared space and principals with mainstream schools. During the school year of 1980-81, representatives from Toronto's twenty-odd alternatives formed the Alternative Schools Advisory Council (ASAC). They would share ideas and support, carry out public relations with the community at large, and work out strategies for dealing with challenges presented by the Boards and the Ministry of Education.

ALPHA was active with ASAC, as it continued to thrive. It had an easy relationship with its principal, who was shared with (and very busy at) nearby Ogden School. In 1981-82, ALPHA expanded to include grades 7 and 8. The 1982-83 Annual Report announced:

> We are about to graduate our first students who have spent their entire elementary school career at ALPHA.[305]

Regular community potlucks, an annual fund-raising bazaar and community camping trips, monthly parent/teacher meetings and day-to-day involvements wove the school relationships into a web of support and friendship, for those who chose to involve themselves.

> ***Parent 1974-1990:*** *It was a very important part of our lives.*
> ***Student 1974-1982****: As my mom said, it was a really important part of our lives and gave me a very strong sense of community.*

When my own family first entered ALPHA in 1985, it had a strong culture in place, a culture that did not explain itself, but expected new participants to watch and explore. There was still a strong counter-cultural sense to the school, and the meetings were informal and peppered with laughter. Participants who were in ALPHA from 1980 and beyond expressed a strong sense of collaboration with the teachers.

> ***Parent 1980-1991****: We were all focused on helping the kids learn, and we all had a different role to play. . . . I wanted the teachers to be central. I didn't have a philosophical need or a personal need to be there by my kid's side all the time. I really trusted them. I trusted that they had skills. Yes, it was "let the kids play", but there was stimulation; there was some thinking behind what was going on there, and guiding, in the best possible way. And they knew how to do it.*
> ***Parent 1992-2002****: They were informed, and they're professionals.*

> ***Parent 1980-1991**: Yeah. And I wanted them to do that . . . and we needed to be there. We needed to do our shifts. I thought that was really an essential piece of that structure. Not just from a staffing point of view. You needed to have more bodies around to be with these kids in the non-structured organizational mode that we had, but I just think it was an excellent philosophy, that you got to see all these other kids—you got to see them in action. I learned a ton, as a parent.*
>
> ***Parent 1982-1996**: I did too.*
>
> ***Parent 1980-1991**: And as a human being, being in that setting. It was like going to school as well. It was a real gift. But we weren't watching over the teachers; we were participants in the school, and it was a truly cooperative piece in that way.*

Parents in this period also recall collaborating with students. The monthly Parent Meeting dealt with business like fund-raising, logistics and relationships with the Board of Education—house-keeping issues. But issues that mattered most to kids and adults were brought to the daily student-chaired Meeting, which was often referred to as the All-School Meeting. In those years students, teachers and parents, who had come to pick up their children, all gathered for Meeting at the end of every day.

Parents from this period felt that Meeting was "key to how that place worked".

> ***Parent 1980-1991**: All the dynamics got played out there, and approaches to problems got played out there, and it was fundamentally important. So how that got shaped was really everything. Although it didn't mean the kids were in control, either.*
>
> *It was like closure on the day. You'd come to pick the kids up if you weren't there, and you'd get to sit on the floor; you'd get to reconnect, you'd get to have a sense of what had gone on that day, who your kids were playing with or not, what was going on, how the teachers were feeling.*
>
> *I don't remember feeling like it was my place to bring up stuff. . . . It was their meeting and they chaired it, and made it work. I think anything they wanted to bring up got brought up: "I don't think it was fair that this*

> *happened" or I don't know, "I really liked it when we did that" or— I can't honestly remember, except that my daughter Rebecca said this morning: "I remember my first meeting." She said, "I put my hand up three times and I spoke, and you said to me "I think maybe you've had enough to say today."*
>
> **Parent 1992-2004**: *Sometimes the meeting would go ten minutes, and nobody would have anything to say, and other times you'd think, "Is this ever going to stop?" Because there'd be some kid, usually mine, who'd say "And another thing. . . ." But I remember that being more fundamental to what held the school together than I would say the parent meetings were, by the time we were there.*

This daily child-chaired meeting was generally a time of announcements and information-sharing, but there were many lively debates. It ruled by majority vote more than consensus. There was seldom a grudge over a lost vote. People who felt strongly about an issue could bring it up again after two weeks.

Parents and teachers couldn't make decisions that mattered to students without going through the school Meeting. Adults who were dismayed at what our "free" children were up to, made our arguments there. A frequent argument was about toy guns and military games:

> **1980-1991**: *An aspect of it was probably about guns and peace and militarism and hurting people and all that stuff. But another aspect of it was just purely chaos. And that was a big deal and I think that took a few meetings to resolve and I think we put in place some sort of measure and we agreed to evaluate it with the kids, right? Let's try it this way, and of course you try it one way and you can't bring any guns to school, but then they were using everything they could* [to make them]— *and all the sounds and stuff. So we kept having to deal with the manifestations that came forward. Anyway. And it just died out.*
>
> **Parent 1992-2004**: *(laughs) But then it came back.*

The alliances in such issues were not strictly adult versus child, for the chaos caused by this kind of play affected children not involved with the games. Whether or not "solutions" were reached, the arguments over substantial ethical and cultural issues, the political shenanigans, and the group problem-solving were stressful, fun and educative.

When I was an ALPHA parent in the 1980s, adults were appalled as kids spent day after day trading and marketing their toys, cheating each other, and arguing. But we were amused to note that this burst of child-generated capitalism contradicted a label that had once been given by a hostile reporter, who had referred to ALPHA as a communist "little red schoolhouse".

Not all children enjoyed this trade in toys. Some opposed its disruptions outright. Some were highly stressed, and—like gamblers—were obsessed with recovering what they'd lost. Staff time was wasted in constant mediation. Anxiety levels were high.

When parents loaded an All-School Meeting to vote the toys out of school, the students involved in the toy trade protested angrily. They vowed to reverse the decision at the earliest opportunity, knowing that rules made at Meeting could be revisited after a two-week trial period. This is a great practice that can result in consensus after a contentious vote has had a positive result.

We parents made no plans to reload the meeting, but counted on the value of our initiative to improve the kids' school lives and win their support over the two weeks it was in force. In the absence of the toys, the school quickly settled back into collegiality, so students did not reverse the vote.

This is the kind of democratic resolution which is often seen as "magic" to ALPHA's alumni parents and students.

The ALPHA Parent Handbook

In 1988, governance processes and the cultural and community traditions that developed over the years were consolidated into the *ALPHA Parent Handbook*.

Written by a committee of parents and teachers, and possibly cribbed from various uncredited works on education and childhood, the 30-page *ALPHA Parent Handbook*, as well as providing a description of school culture and processes for new and prospective parents, marked a technological milestone. It was the first ALPHA publication laid out using the brand new desktop publishing programs.

The *Handbook* began with a philosophical section that was called "A Young Child Learns":

> Eric Erikson calls the stage from about 5-12 the age of industry. Children learn best when they are active, moving and communicating, sharing, tinkering, putting things together, taking things apart, manipulating concrete materials; in short, using all their senses in activities that are real to them.[306]

In this section, the child was described as an "active learner . . . innately curious" and "unique in the way he/she learns". It set basic goals: "important skills and principles, such as the three R's . . . the basic tools of the culture. Most children come to school to learn these."

But ALPHA's handbook also made it clear on the first page that these would be learned "over a period of time". The role of the teacher was to design a "rich learning environment . . . with much to explore, to wonder about and get active with" and "to assess and guide the learning toward long range objectives".

Assessments were made on the basis of the child's individual learning: "Mistakes are not failures. Evaluations must not be changed into judgments." Meanwhile, holism and self-direction were emphasized: "Play is a child's work" and "aesthetics are the heart of the child's world".

Most important, this section concludes: "Childhood is a stage of life in itself to be enjoyed and savoured: it is not simply something to be passed through on the way to adulthood."[307] Families were welcomed "wholeheartedly", and gently but clearly warned of the responsibility they were taking on:

> Adjusting to our unique and wonderful alternative school is not always the easiest thing to do. There is a lot going on, things are very different from the regular school environment, and a fair amount is expected from you . . . [308]

The handbook, and a "buddy system" that paired new with experienced parents, were instituted to relieve the teaching team of some of the additional layer of adult education that goes with offering an alternative. Because ALPHA is so different from the schools that most parents grew up in, and because their participation is so necessary, families join their children on their learning curve. One former parent recalled:

> *I remember Susan Garrard, the first day when we were there, said the most curious thing to me, I thought. There I was at the locker with the little kids, and she said, "Welcome to ALPHA." And she ended up saying: "and we'll see what <u>you</u> learn." (laughter) And then I thought, "What are you saying to me!"*

Garrard set the example of encouraging parents to learn as their children do—through experience, watching, listening and doing. This is challenging, and parental anxiety increased over the decades. Parent handbooks and eventually a Code of Conduct became necessary resources to communicate the deep history and thought behind the school, as well as laying out practical information and procedures.

The ALPHA School Day, 1980s

Still at this time, in 1986, the *ALPHA Parent Handbook* made it clear that the "staff work as a team", that "staff and parents work as a team to administer the school".[309] The Principal's role is to be "the main liaison between the Board and ALPHA".[310]

Most important:

> All rules for daily living in the school are made by the children in their daily meeting . . .[311]

The structure of Meeting and the disciplinary organ known as Committee seemed to have remained essentially as they were set up in the second and third year. In the section of the handbook titled "History and Structure", Committee was described:

> [It] consists of 5 students and adults on a rotating basis. It is ALPHA's internal disciplinary and dispute resolving body. A staff person or parent "takes" committee and invites each person to tell his/her side of the story. The children—3 from the older group and 2 younger—listen, question, and decide on a punishment or warning. Punishments usually have to do with extra cleanup duties or being prohibited from using equipment for a period of time.[312]

As in ALPHA's original proposal, the "program is individualized by means of child-parent-staff conferences". An interesting milestone occurs as the students begin to mature and gain skills:

> On reaching the age of eight the children have the opportunity to choose the floor on which they will do their academic work, which is the main focus of morning activities. The younger children remain on the main floor and the older children work on the third floor. In the afternoon there is free flow of all students between the floors, and an enormous variety of activities is offered.[313]

In the Daily Schedule, "mornings are considered quiet times and a time when some 'work' must be accomplished." The afternoons are "free time" during which clubs, music, field trips, crafts, gym and swimming are offered.[314] The monthly parent meeting is considered the time "where school policy is decided, information is shared, problems are discussed, and plans are made."[315]

Seven detailed pages in the Parent Handbook list ways in which parents could become involved. Under "Shifts", parents could contribute to the everyday running of the school, academic program, sharing skills, and field trips. "If you can't do a shift" there was committee work, cleanup, having lunch with the kids, fundraising, and community events.

The message the Handbook gave was: "TUNE IN: it's still your school, even if you are not lucky enough to be able to attend yourself."[316]

ALPHA's Alumni Give Feedback

ALPHA's alumni are periodically asked to return to the school to give feedback on how their transition to subsequent schooling went, and how well they felt ALPHA prepared them. Responses from early alumni, many still in their teens, were published in the 1988 *ALPHA Parent Handbook*:

> *I learned a natural respect for other people.*
> *I learned patience because I had freedom.*
> *I learned to chair meetings.*
> *I learned social skills—I was the first to ask teachers for extra help.*
> *Because ALPHA is a smaller school, I learned to get closer to people.*
> *I gained more than I knew at the time. Most kids have a narrow band of knowledge. I can look at issues from different angles.*
> *I learned to motivate myself when I really want to.*
> *I learned to focus in the midst of chaos.*
> *I learned how to relax in school. I do not form mental tension.*
> *Other schools judge you by marks but ALPHA judges you by who you are.*
> *At other schools if you get good marks the teachers like you, but the students do not.*

> *I learned to use my common sense.*
> *I learned to work at my own pace.*
> *I developed social skills here that enabled me to approach high school teachers and say, "I'm scared, I can't cope."*[317]

During ALPHA's fortieth anniversary year, alumni Michael Barker and Ariel Fielding carried out a community-based qualitative study, based on a school photo taken in 1978. Nine alumni from that photo accepted the opportunity to have their pictures taken and their thoughts on ALPHA recorded at length. It can be accessed on the Web under the title *ALPHA Alternative School 1972/2012*: https://michaelbarker.ca/alpha-alternative-school/

13:

WE WON'T LEARN FROM YOU

> *They sentenced me to twenty years of boredom*
> *For trying to change the system from within.*
>
> Leonard Cohen

During the 1980s, the Toronto School Board and the Ontario Ministry of Education issued documents giving the alternatives a positive review, even "acclaim". But a careful reading of these documents reveals an underlying determination not to be influenced by different visions or to permit local control in education.

1982: Alternative Schools, A General Policy

In November, 1982, the Toronto Board of Education issued a shiny new document titled *Alternative Schools, A General Policy* (replacing the 1978 document, *General Policy for Alternative School Programs)*. It proclaimed the Toronto public board as a North American "leader in both the number of [alternative] schools and the variety of programs." It began by quoting one of the most trustworthy thinkers in the free school movement:

> Allen Graubard, in an article "The Free School Movement" in the Harvard Education Review, distinguishes among four types of alternative schools.
>
> 1. The classical free school based on the Summerhill model.
> 2. The parent-teacher co-operative elementary school populated largely by young, white, liberal middle-class families and characterized by a significant amount of parental input into the decision-making process.

> 3. The free high school—actually, a broad category including white, working class high schools for "drop outs" and "push outs", street academies for poor minority youth, and small high schools for relatively radical white students of average or above means.
> 4. Community elementary schools controlled by dissatisfied, usually minority parent groups, and characterized by a somewhat conservative curriculum.[318]
>
> It is significant that Toronto has or has had alternative schools which fit into all four categories of Graubard's typology. As a result, alternatives have been able to meet the needs of a wide variety of students.
>
> Parents and students can choose the type of program they believe is best for them. The Toronto Board appears to be unique in having a policy which permits parents, students and teachers to approach the Board for support in establishing new alternatives and in participating in all decisions regarding the operation of the schools, including such vital areas as budget and staffing.[319]

Even more than the Toronto-based analysis in its 1978 policy, this introductory passage quoting from the American free school activist Graubard recognized the different class interests served by diverse alternative schools. It also demonstrated the remarkable consistency in the range of solutions arising when people are empowered to solve their own problems. Its inclusion in this policy statement gave the impression that alternative schools, and the localized processes that created and sustained them, were in the public board to stay.

Created only four years after the initial 1978 policy and very quickly after Dale Shuttleworth had optimistically moved on to promote change in the neighbouring school board of York, this is an odd document. Students were rarely mentioned. But Section IX, "Administration of Alternative Schools", expended ten pages (a third of the report proper) on "issues and questions" relating to administration: specifically, principalship in those schools that displayed a "predilection for managing on their own with little reference to Board administrators."[320]

By the document's end, it becomes apparent that one strong constituency in the Board wasn't comfortable with the alternative schools. It noted that alternatives had accepted principals at the insistence of the administration, for official purposes only: "The Board's alternative schools have preferred an arm's-length relationship with the system establishment", resulting in "the coining of a new administrative title, principal-of-record." Contradicting the alternative schools' documented preference, the *Policy* concluded: "An 'at arm's length' principal is unlikely to be very useful to students, teachers or the Board."[321].

No hint was given that alternative schools were a burden to the administration. The problem seemed to be the reverse: the administrators' unease grew from their own confusion, and possibly the sense that they were not needed. The policy niggled about issues that apply to any school, like providing "adequate supervision" on field trips, and administrative detail—maintaining records, preparing reports and annual budgets, and evaluating and promoting staff.

The policy's thirty-seven pages frequently quote provincial regulations. Though they look intimidating, those regulations are flexible. A principal's responsibilities in regard to organization, timetabling and "ensuring that courses of study are followed" is to be undertaken "in consultation with staff". The requirement to "maintain proper order and discipline in the school" allows room for local interpretation and discretion.

The 1982 *Alternative Schools, A General Policy* recognized that "it is critical to the successful operation of such programs that staff are chosen wisely and that they are committed to the goals of individual alternative schools".[322] But it didn't support the community processes the schools found necessary for choosing appropriate staff. It quoted the 1972 solicitor's letter that had been called a "hatchet job" by trustee Fiona Nelson, and rejected by the elected Board of the day (see Chapter 5).

That solicitor's opinion had been: "A board may not delegate to committees comprising parents, teachers and others the responsibility for the selection of staff and for the establishment of policy."[323] The trustees of the day had not asked for the opinion, had disagreed with the lawyer's interpretation of the legislation, and had allowed schools to continue their processes. It would be interesting to know how this 1972 letter had been resurrected to direct alternative school policy in 1982.

The *Policy* noted that the Board's original four alternatives (SEED, ALPHA, Laneway and Contact) had worked out "patterns of internal decision-making and administrative authority which contrasted sharply with the administrative structure operating in regular schools". The community processes of these alternatives were "supportive of a basic Ministry and Board policy thrust during the 1970's—increasing parent and community involvement in public education".[324] Yet the document subtly reined them in, as seen in this item under "Conclusions":

> Contemporary alternatives believe that parents, students and teachers should be directly involved in the school's governance, usually through what is referred to as a "community meeting". Such meetings provide the opportunity to air grievances, socialize, express opinions and suggest improvements.[325]

Perhaps it would take a wary person to note that the terms *air*, *socialize*, *express*, *suggest*, are not terms of governance. In contrast, the 1988 *ALPHA Parent Handbook* would describe the monthly parent meeting as the forum "where school *policy is decided*, information is shared, problems are discussed, and *plans are made*." (Italics mine.)

The 1982 *Policy* sees the "school principal as the fulcrum used by both the Ministry of Education and Boards of Education to ensure compliance with their respective policies and to facilitate accountability to parents and students".[326] This is a pretty brutal metaphor that more or less wipes out the power of the kids, parents, and teachers on the opposite end of the teeter-totter from the Ministry of Education.

It's also a frightening position for that single on-the-ground person, the principal, who stands alone bearing the weight of both. However, the *Policy* also signals to the administrator which end to favour. Item 6 specifies that the principal's "duties and responsibilities are those outlined in The Education Act, 1974, the Regulations and in the policies of The Toronto Board of Education". Item 7 obliges the principal to negotiate with the school community only "concerning the most appropriate way to carry out these responsibilities".[327]

Sounding the Alarm

OISE professor Malcolm Levin sounded the alarm. In 1984, he wrote, "Toronto's alternative public schools have demonstrated that participatory democracy and community control can work and flourish, even in a modern progressive bureaucratic urban school system." He warned, however, that schools were still "owned" not by their communities but "by distant politicians and professional administrators who occasionally consult with the teachers, parents and students who constitute the 'citizens' of these schools." He maintained also that local control had been "resisted all the way by those who have a vested interest in centralized bureaucratic structures and control", and predicted that "supporters of democracy in education will have to work even harder just to hold the line".[328]

As a co-founder of MAGU, Levin knew intimately the kinds of resistance that alternative schools had met during their first decade. Now he saw approaching what Michael Apple would later refer to as the "conservative restoration" in education.[329]

Levin warned that "Ontario's government reneged on its commitment to the more progressive principles outlined in the *Hall-Dennis* report and embraced the burgeoning Back to Basics movement".[330] The 1982 *General Policy* was a hint of the way things were going to go. Soon the province would make a stronger declaration of its intentions to recover the power that threatened to devolve to local school communities.

1986: Provincial Review Report

The 1986 *Provincial Review Report of Alternative Schools and Programs in the Public System* would repeat the pattern set by the 1982 *General Policy*, showing that alternative schools seemed to work for families and staff, but not for administrators. The reviewers visited and observed all the alternative schools and programs, and interviewed teachers, principals, trustees, board supervisors, parents, and students.[331]

Their findings seemed to be positive. They noted that the small size of alternatives "permitted a level of flexibility and personalized instruction that is almost unattainable in many large schools" and that "a sense of community could be detected among parents, teachers and pupils who appeared to have more opportunities to share meaningfully in the total schooling process". They "were generally impressed with the level of commitment and the quality of curriculum delivery in the majority of alternative schools and programs".

The 1986 *Provincial Review Report* noted "equality in the decision-making process among parents, administrators and teachers . . . personalized instruction . . . free-flow curriculum based on pupils' interests" and "independent study". Despite "tremendous diversity" in the alternatives, the reviewers perceived the "key difference between alternative schools . . . and conventional schools" to be the "open-door" policies for parent inclusion, the "community as an extension of the classroom", as well as "a governance structure that permitted cooperative decision-making"—all foundational principles for community schooling.

The *Provincial Review* observed: "This alteration of the learning environment required substantial parental involvement at school in the overall decision-making process, especially in the planning of the curriculum and the operation of the school" and pointed out that "with principals who carried out their duties by telephone and/or on-site visits on one day or less per week, the alternative school appeared to reviewers to function primarily as a result of the team efforts of teachers, pupils and parents".

Those without much stamina for government documents might put the *Review* down after fifteen pages, comfortable that the alternatives were receiving a positive report: they made diverse offerings, required little administrative support, were democratic, and performed useful functions within the system.

The first note of trouble was principals' concerns about "their duties as defined by legislation and policy" in alternative schools. Like the 1982 *General Policy*, the 1986 *Provincial Review* found principals to be worried, especially "in situations where the majority of parents and staff decide to proceed in directions that are basically incompatible with the principal's beliefs and orientations".

As the 26-page document moved toward its conclusions, it proceeded to issues of "non-compliance". These ranged from philosophically and pedagogically significant ("a de-emphasis on competition, testing, and the recording of pupil progress") to trivial (the "absence of formal opening and closing exercises, as stipulated in Regulation 262", and the "issuance of students achievement forms that were not signed or co-signed by the principal").

While it affirmed that alternatives were satisfying their client families and creating "meaningful" learning experiences, the 1986 *Provincial Review Report* recommended that the structures that fostered these "trusting learning environments" be replaced by "greater congruence of practice with existing legislation and policies".

The report carefully separated alternative school successes from their different structures and practices. Qualities praised by families, such as "emotional support, sense of community, equal voice in decision making, personal attention, respect, and acceptance" were laid out as discrete facts unrelated to the schools' non-conforming practices, which were named as "definite areas that needed to be addressed". This document saw compliance in detail with regulation as a virtue that needed no justification, and to which these schools needed to address their efforts.

Like the 1982 *General Policy*, the 1986 *Provincial Review* took care to praise an education strategy that gave Ontario a reputation for being forward-thinking. Neither report indicated that alternative schools were causing serious problems, nor that their families or the Board found them less than satisfactory.

Yet they mark a watershed, showing that powerful factions of the provincial and city administrations would not allow successful strategies of progressive, radical and community schooling, which had grown under the umbrella of alternative schools, to inform the system as a whole.

The reviewers perceived "the establishment of alternative schools and programs in the public system . . . to be a strategy of change in response to these two common beliefs":

- People learn in different ways and need various kinds of organizational structures and instructional techniques.
- No one type of school or program is best for all.

Their work would go a long way toward heading off such a "strategy for change" in Ontario's public school systems.

Return to "Normal"

Having watched democratic-spirited and equity-driven movements rise and fall for decades, one sees how relentlessly and automatically things tend to return to "normal", after years of (often volunteer, life-consuming) work to create change—even though based on research, need, argument, compassion, principle, rationality, and democratic right. In 2003, Matt Hern summed up the situation in education:

> Contemporary pedagogy has emerged in response to institutional imperatives: that is to say that how kids are taught and dealt with primarily emerges not from larger ideals about citizenry, but from very immediate and everyday management needs.[332]

This prioritization of management over students can certainly be seen in the 1982 Toronto *Alternative Schools, A General Policy* and the 1986 Ontario *Provincial Review*. After a decade on the defensive, these administrative interests reasserted themselves. They would attempt to regain full control in the 1987 Toronto *Issues Paper on Alternative Schools*. These documents show an administrative culture with no interest in adjusting to the presence of alternative or community schools—even when their own research documented student and family satisfaction.

Despite the successes of small, participatory schools, the management trend was in the opposite direction: toward larger institutions, more top-down management, and more massive, detailed regulation. Staffing practice was an area in which the management culture of the Board powerfully impacted the alternative schools.

Staffing

By the early 1980s, experts at all administrative levels were well aware of the importance of staffing at alternative schools:

> Both in research and in the general literature on alternative schools, one finds agreement that it is critical to the successful operation of such programs that staff are chosen wisely and that they are committed to the goals of individual alternative schools.[333]

The 1986 *Provincial Review Report* recognized that principal and staff needed

> i) a clear understanding of its purposes and organization and how he/she is to function in that learning environment
>
> ii) a desire to be a part of that alternative school because he/she believes in the concept.[334]

There would be no integration of this awareness into the Board's policies and human resource processes. Individual administrators at times did their best to work supportively with alternative schools, but the process was stressful, hit-and-miss, and needed lobbying and negotiation for each hiring.

ALPHA co-founders talked about the impact on alternative schools in the late seventies, when the Board of Education stopped hiring more teachers:

> *A key moment was when the teacher layoffs came and everybody got a number about where their time was to be laid off, in the era of restraint and cutbacks. What that meant is that you could be given a teacher to be put into your program who needed to be moved. If your teacher had a higher number than somebody else, your teacher could be bumped off and laid off, and somebody put into that teacher's place. And so in that moment, the school boards just took that control. That was the beginning of the re-appropriation of the freedom that we had.*

The 1982 *Alternative Schools, A General Policy*, shows that the Administration was well aware of this problem:

> When a teacher who would otherwise not choose this environment is placed in an alternative, it often causes distress, not only to the teacher, but also to the other staff, parents, students and administration.[335]

In 1982, OISE researchers Malcolm Levin and Frances Gladstone documented the results:

> In schools where there has been a constant turnover of teachers who have left either through job dissatisfaction or because they have been "bumped" out, there is a difficulty stabilizing relationships. Thus, the central problem for alternative schools is attracting and keeping teachers who can work effectively with both children and parents in an open environment. This is no simple matter, for just as alternative schools are not suitable for all children, they do not suit all teachers.[336]

The 1982 *Alternative Schools, A General Policy* blamed unions for alternative school staffing problems, writing: "Given the complexity of collective agreements, there appear to be no easy solutions."[337] This seems disingenuous, for hiring strategies were agreed upon for a number of educational specialties and arguably could have been created for alternative schools.

An oral history participant recalled that union support fluctuated: the teachers' union supported SEED, then obstructed the creation of a later school. But when it became apparent that the alternatives kept many potential dropouts in the system, union support returned, "because the alternative school movement was flourishing, and there would be more students in the schools and more jobs for teachers".

ALPHA suffered periodic instability from staffing policies, but in the long run the school got lucky. If the administration had transferred Susan Garrard as it had transferred Murray Shukyn from SEED, this book might never have been written.

Garrard remained ALPHA's rock until 1996, when she retired. Twice during the eighties, the school's teacher choices were hired permanently, so that the first long-standing successful team of Garrard, Sue Hess and Karen Light anchored the school well into the new millennium.

Alumni parents recalled that, as families flowed through the school, the institutional memory that teachers carried was vital:

> ***Parent 1992-2004***: *By the time we were there, there was really a sense of counting on the teachers, particularly Susan Garrard, just for information as the historian, the living archivist/storyteller . . .*
>
> *I can remember a lot of meetings where people said "Susan, how did that go? How is that supposed to go?" And she would never answer "how is that supposed to . . . " but she would tell you a story of it . . . and let you decide.*

Stable teaching teams in alternatives mentor both newer staff and the ever-changing community of parents. They also anchor programming that will attract and meet the needs of families, such as the arts and music anchored by Sue Hess, Karen Light and then Steve Cooper, and the anti-oppression work introduced in the new millennium by Emily Chan.

It's interesting to note that the 1986 *Provincial Review* found it "appropriate" that some "well-established alternatives" had "altered radically the paths that were originally plotted for them," because "the pioneer clients who initiated the alternatives were no longer affiliated with them".[338]

This hints at a strategy to keep up the pressure, and wait out the canny, activist communities whose children would grow up and move on.

Issues Paper on Alternative Schools, 1987

The 1986 *Provincial Review Report* claimed to be "exploratory in nature", but its agenda to bring alternatives into compliance with the mainstream was stated early:

> Subsection 149(10) of the Education Act requires that a school board "ensure that every school under its charge is conducted in accordance with this Act and the regulations". Thus, technically, alternative schools and programs, and conventional schools must be similar.[339]

Based on what this 1986 Provincial Review had designated as "areas which need to be addressed", a draft *Issues Paper on Alternative Schools* was submitted to the April 7, 1987 meeting of the Alternative and Community Programs Committee.[340]

Unlike the carefully positive tone of the *Provincial Review*, the *Issues Paper* threw down the gauntlet. It framed the issue as ideological, stating that the "variety of formal and informal working relationships between the alternative schools and the Board" resulted in "the establishment of two camps: those championing local school freedom and those favouring accountability through a central Board administrator."

The *Issues Paper* stated:

> While the autonomy of alternative schools needs to be respected in the setting of goals, school philosophy, and day to day operations, the teachers, principals, school superintendents, and the Board for each publicly funded school must ensure that the Ministry's policy and regulations are fulfilled in the following matters:
>
> - each school will have clearly stated academic and program goals based on Ministry documents
> - the school program will be developmental and sequential
> - detailed courses of study based on Ministry guidelines will be available in schools
> - formal testing and other methods for student assessment will occur
> - each school will establish and maintain an Ontario Student Record for each student
> - teachers will maintain mark records and daybooks
> - annual reports will be submitted to the Board and to the Ministry
> - there will be an official opening/closing of the school day.[341]

The list was extensive and detailed, making clear that whatever the goals or philosophy, the school day in an alternative was to be minutely subject to Ministry control. "Autonomy" under such conditions could only be token. The agenda expressed in this "draft for discussion" would be resisted by alternative school communities who, as Malcolm Levin had predicted, had to "work even harder just to hold the line".[342]

Justifying your Existence

As the 1990s settled in, ALPHA Community members discovered that administrators and politicians found it surprising and strange to have alternative schools in the system.

> ***Parent 1992-2002:*** *You just have to keep re-justifying your existence. . . . Ten or fifteen years later, lives have changed, people have left, society has changed, new people come in too . . . people discover this thing. Trustees on the Board say, "What do you mean we have alternative schools under the umbrella? How did that happen?"*

The tide of paper that beats at the schools, day after day, is driven by officials and workers in a public system that claims to help students "to acquire the knowledge, skills and values they need to become responsible members of a democratic society".[343] In 1971, critic Everett Reimer observed that a bureaucracy's operations are largely unconscious and habitual, creating a situation in which "the world can be worse than the people who live in it".[344] Toronto sociologist Dorothy Smith saw bureaucracies as governed by *relations of ruling*—powerful, though often invisible, controls in the form of media, law, policy and directives: "the organizers and regulators of our contemporary world".[345]

There are also powerful personal and economic interests at work in bureaucracies, from the tops of the hierarchies to the administrators at their desks. Management cultures then and now are ensconced in ideologies of hierarchy and standardization that richly reward the top echelons. At the workers' levels, any change threatens some jobs, even as it opens opportunities for others.

Against the oceanic pressure of these interests and institutional habits, administrative waters quickly close up behind the odd visionary bureaucrat who makes a ripple during their active period. Some may even get pushed out of the boat.

Administrator Dale Shuttleworth was a vital support to alternative schools, but his role as a "change agent" had been far broader. His projects included multicultural initiatives, after-four programs, and daycare in the schools. (Daycare of any kind was new and controversial in those days.) He fostered the use of empty school facilities as multi-service centers and spaces for community services. The surplus facilities became revenue generators, and helped prevent the closing of local schools.

Satisfied that innovation was well under way, Shuttleworth left the Toronto Board in 1980 to carry on similar work in the adjacent Borough of York.[346] He recalled that by 1994, "I was experiencing increasing opposition from some administrative colleagues and trustees. . . . I felt that my days as superintendent of community services were numbered. Consequently, I announced my early retirement."[347]

Founders of alternative schools had hoped that mainstream schools would benefit from their discoveries, but as systemic opposition to student-centered and community-based education gained strength, the alternatives would be termed *elitist* because the benefits within them were not found in the system as a whole.

Rather than being able to reflect on what they were learning, consolidate their programming, and share their experiences with the system at large, alternative schools found themselves in a permanent struggle for mere existence.

14:

DEFENDING ALPHA

Susan Garrard recalled that, as the 1990s settled in at ALPHA, missives from the Board of Education (which had previously stayed largely in the background) were arriving with greater frequency:

> ***Susan Garrard**: Just over the years . . . everything became more restrictive. I think that's been huge. As the Board of Education had more rules, the curriculum was tighter, everybody was more worried about safety issues—everybody was.*

Under such restrictions, ALPHA's parents were no longer permitted to take students independently on field trips, or to supervise small groups for a period of time. So the casual "free flow of all students between the floors" the "enormous" variety of activities described in the ALPHA Handbook, and the close relationship with the neighbourhood were curtailed.

As Garrard said, everybody was more worried about safety. It was not only the administration, but also the supportive parent community that was becoming more nervous and restrictive. These changes in attitude reflected a changing culture, and an economy that was settling into permanent crisis mode.

Herb Snitzer of the free school Lewis-Wadhams once suggested that "some of the pressures parents bring to bear on children reflect the growing constriction of their own lives, reflect their own anxiousness, their sense of something missing that has to be made up for—somehow . . . I am always pleading for time, and for trust".[348] In those days, Susan Garrard also often noted the loss of trust.

In ALPHA's relationship to the Toronto Board of Education, some issues wore away at the school's identity in small ways. Others hit with considerable impact: an administrative attempt to change ALPHA's location, and the loss of its all-day kindergarten program.

A Done Deal

With all the dramas that sixty families can come up with, life never seems quiet at ALPHA. But when ordinary stress switches into overdrive, it usually originates with the Board of Education.

> ***Susan Garrard:*** *There was a time when, way out of the blue, the superintendent thought he was doing us a great favour by finding us a new home. . . . He just made this great announcement: "You can move to Market Square down by the St. Lawrence Market. You and Downtown Alternative will share a building down there."*
>
> *We said, "We like our old building!" He said, "How could you possibly like it? Those awful leaking windows and over-heating boilers?"*
>
> *We said, "We like it! It doesn't feel like school."*

The two elementary alternative schools, ALPHA and Downtown Alternative School (DAS), had shared the Brant Street building for years. Both were shocked at the announcement. With no consultation, it was presented as a "done deal".

Responding in the "strongest possible terms", the chair of the Alternative Schools Advisory Council (ASAC) wrote: "I want the Board to know that we find the issuing of such a decision with no consultation with the communities affected to be absolutely unacceptable."

> The DAS and ALPHA communities are now in the process of considering the proposed move to Market Lane, and the potential workability of such a move. While the communities are taking time to consider their position on the proposed move, they are unanimous in their opposition to the unilateral decision-making position taken to this point.[349]

The proposed school site was an interesting experiment in urban design. It occupied a single story in a building in the St. Laurence Market area, with retail on the first floor and apartments above. It was a splendid fit for a community school, or for Paul Goodman's idea for mini-schools—or for one alternative school.

But no subsequent neighbourhood housing projects were built with this kind of intriguing multiple use in mind, so the district suddenly needed school space for hundreds of children. After a big new replacement school was built, the original site was empty, leaving the Board of Education with a problem to solve. ASAC's letter tried to explain the problem the Board's unilateral solution presented for the alternative schools:

> Parents and staff of alternative schools spend enormous amounts of time building and developing their own program, and should not have this time and concern ignored when a space challenge presents itself. Alternative school community members want, and need, to be part of the process of decisions which affect them directly.

The schools weren't asking for anything new—this kind of protocol had been in place for two decades, and a consultation process was part of written Board policy.[350] Some families responded quickly and negatively both to the arbitrary decision and the idea of moving from Brant Street. But at their respective meetings, both ALPHA and DAS decided to investigate the Board's offer, before making a plan of action.

> ***Parent 1992-2004****: I can remember, within the parent community, that for a short time people like us who saw it not just as the alternative school, but as our neighbourhood school, were in fact in conflict with people who were already trucking sometimes from outside Metro to come all the way to the school.*

The funky Brant Street location, near Kensington Market and Chinatown, was part of ALPHA's identity, and had drawn many locals to it. As with the old Broadview location, some families had moved to the affordable area to be near the school.

Parents didn't disagree for long. The site visit, a raucous occasion attended by nearly every family of both schools, showed that the Market Lane School, though bright and beautiful, was far too small to share, with no way to physically separate the two very different schools. The Downtown Alternative School and ALPHA communities agreed strongly that being together on a single floor would effectively destroy the ambiance and special pedagogy of both.

ALPHA and DAS had sometimes been in conflict over space at Brant Street,[351] but they quickly found a way to support one another in this situation. DAS voted to solve its space problems by moving alone to the proposed location, and ALPHA parents soon reached consensus to fight to remain at Brant Street.

The Board had insisted the move was a "done deal", but the passion of the parents of both schools prevailed. Their decisions turned out well. DAS expanded, as it had long wanted to do, and was freed of its raucous neighbor ALPHA. ALPHA moved its students to adjacent floors. Space and cultural issues that were ever present in sharing with another alternative elementary school evaporated when the top floor became home base for Oasis, an alternative high school.

A simple consultation with DAS, ALPHA, and then Oasis would have quickly reached this resolution, with excitement rather than stress. It's hard not to note that the Board's "done deal", if it had not been successfully fought, would have upset the students' schooling for years, and could only have resulted in either ALPHA or DAS being absorbed by the other—reducing the number of alternative schools by at least one.

At best, the Board's arbitrary first decision suggested that the community-supported identities and individual pedagogies of the schools were meaningless to administrators. These kinds of stressors wear down alternative schools.

To defend ALPHA and DAS (and help the Board solve its problem) required emergency all-school meetings for each school, the striking of several committees, and an intensive program to educate the resistant administration about the alternative schools. In ALPHA's case, this crisis occurred at a time when both the beloved Susan Garrard and a student were seriously ill. The intelligent and passionate confrontation built relationships between the schools and administrators, but this was done on the backs of the schools.

Contraction

Sharing with Oasis brought a different set of concerns—what to do about teens who smoked, and how both schools could protect a girl who was being stalked. But there were opportunities for synergy, too. ALPHA's kids annually marched their Halloween parade through Oasis. During some years, a volunteer program brought interns from Oasis into ALPHA. The older students benefitted from the affection of the small children as they supported them in their studies.

Meanwhile, at ALPHA, the "experiment" of including four- and five-year-olds full-time within the school day had turned out to be an unqualified success. Toddler siblings accompanied their volunteer parents to school and were a part of ALPHA from birth. Most four- and five-year-olds enjoyed the play and sociability, and participated in meetings. One of the beautiful aspects of multi-age groupings, is that often older students helped to care for the younger ones.

> ***Parent 1974-1990:*** [Students] *adopting the littler kids was a really important part of ALPHA, from my perspective, because I had three children who went to school. I understood the idea of mentoring from an educational point of view, but from a social perspective it was much more fascinating and important, I thought. My* [younger] *kids were there when they were babies, and they grew up and had special attention from different members of the school at different times in*

> *their lives and then went on to pass that attention on to younger kids. It was something I hadn't anticipated in that school setting. But it was vital.*
> ***Student 1974-1982****: Also, to have a little kid who was attached to you and sort of following you around sort of gave you a sense of responsibility. And it was kind of an ego-boost, as well. If you had this little kid following you around everywhere with moony eyes, you couldn't help but think you were somehow important.*

In multi-age school groupings with holistic pedagogies and plenty of time for play, kindergarten kids thrived. However, in schooling, success is no guarantee of implementation. Nor are government promises.

In his history of Ontario education *From Hope to Harris*, R. D. Gidney records that, by 1989, all-day junior and senior kindergarten had support from all political parties.

> The April 1989 Throne Speech looked forward, as a "long-term vision", to the day when the government could make "full-day senior and junior kindergarten" available to all four and five-year-olds. But as a "first step" it announced that it would require all school boards to expand their existing senior and junior kindergarten programs. Attendance would remain voluntary, but the government would ensure that boards "offer half-day junior kindergarten for four-year-olds as well as half day senior kindergarten for five-year-olds." Both initiatives were to be implemented over the following five years. As well, the province would "provide funding for school boards to offer full day senior kindergarten programs, where classroom space permits".[352]

This should have been good for the alternatives—and eventually everyone else—but the opposite happened. Kindergarten expansion, promised in 1989, didn't begin until 2010. Instead of existing programs being expanded, an agenda of equalization across the province was enforced during the early 1990s. Existing full-day kindergartens were cut to half-day.

All-day kindergartens at the alternative schools had always been seen as an equity issue, and had been consented to as an experiment. Alternatives tried to keep their all-day kindergartens, but it was difficult to argue that they should retain them when the rest of the system couldn't. Unlike the move that could have destroyed DAS and ALPHA, this wasn't a "hill to die on". But this issue demonstrates that it is not success, usefulness or need that decides whether or not a program survives in public education. It also shows the culture of standardization that was gaining ground at the Board of Education.

The consequences were surprisingly serious. ALPHA's youngest people, previously fully integrated and able to function and socialize based on maturity and ability, suddenly were a special problem to deal with. The after-school Brant Street Day Care expanded and tried to carry out a "seamless day." But the duplication of resources to meet daycare regulations increased crowding. Yet another set of rules—day care regulations—was inserted into the school.

In the Board of Education's quaint parlance, "half" an education assistant was lost. Parents of kindergarten children lost the support they needed to carry on their working lives, and a class divide was created between families who could afford afternoon daycare and those who couldn't. The seamless flow of siblings into the school—from babes to toddlers to full citizens—was awkwardly stemmed.

Loss of the kindergarten had an unforeseen effect on the school's democracy. ALPHA's end-of-day meetings had been a forum where the community of students, teachers, and parents could discuss vital issues together. A large cohort of parents, picking up young kids, were scattered among the kids and calmed the meeting. Tiny people sat on bigger people's laps. Older students and parents affectionately tolerated digressions from the topic at hand.

> ***Parent 1992-2004****: I can remember stuff like how . . . some issue would be being batted around that somebody had raised of really earthshaking importance in the*

overall scheme, and then somebody would pipe up, "And another thing, when you're on the tire swing you shouldn't actually—" (laughter) It was just thrown in the mix and it was never "that's not on the topic" or "that's irrelevant" or "stick to the subject" or whatever. It was just part of the magic.

Including the smallest children in Meeting was so valued that when kindergarten people were no longer at school at the end of the day, its timing was switched around to try to meet their schedule. A viable solution wasn't found. Meetings, for twenty years a warm, laughter-filled cap on the day, are now a job. One parent informant recalled:

> ***Parent 1992-2004****: I have a vague recollection at some point of a decision to divide the meetings and that something disappeared from the way it really worked before then.*

A few years later, in 1995, ALPHA's program contracted at the upper end, when it graduated its final grade 7/8 class. This contraction had been under consideration since 1988, when the Principal was "concerned about the program delivery for grades 7 and 8 in ALPHA" because "the Ministry is tightening up the curriculum for these grades." At the same time, resources were dwindling in public schools. This loss left a hole at the junior high level, as there was no free school or student-centered model at that level. In 2007, some alumni families would try to fill this gap by starting Alpha II, a grade 7-12 school.

Now ALPHA's upper end is anchored by students of about 10-12 years, the age Neill saw as the most problematic in terms of schooling and social living. He called it the *gangster age* because of the kinds of games his students liked to play, but sometimes the moniker fits in other ways! During decades of experience at Summerhill, Neill observed that this age group rarely attends class and spends time largely in intense play, socialization and sports with their peers.

Interestingly, Neill thought that school democracy needed a good proportion of teenagers: “Good government in a school is possible only when there is a sprinkling of older pupils who like a quiet life and fight the indifference and opposition of the gangster age.”[353] Teenagers, a problematic demographic in public schools, are usually settled old folks in Summerhill, often preparing for school-leaving exams.

When ALPHA had pupils up to the age of grade 8, some of the older students became true elders and mentors in the way that Neill described. Fewer students are in a mellow mood in grade 6, though ALPHA has had some precocious cohorts of that age—including some rock bands, even a cohort of activists.

But Meeting isn’t fun like it used to be, and that does matter. Democracy is hard work. When it’s able to operate without systemic oppression, it can also be spontaneous, delicious, creative, warm, funny, and often magical. It can feel like home.

During hard times and good, ALPHA still offers authentic choices, prioritizes children’s well-known developmental needs, and as much as it can in the public system, respects their needs for sociability and play. So I would say that, despite some compromises, ALPHA continues to meet Allen Graubard’s generous definition of a free school, as a place where “serious effort is made to involve even the young children in decision-making”.[354]

15:

THE CONSERVATIVE RESTORATION

Historian Howard Zinn, in *A People's History of the United States*, describes the resistance movements of the sixties and seventies in these terms:

> There was a general revolt against oppressive, artificial, previously unquestioned ways of living. It touched every aspect of personal life: childbirth, childhood, love, sex, marriage, dress, music, art, sports, language, food, housing, religion, literature, death, schools.

Zinn then notes:

> Never in American history had more movements for change been concentrated in so short a span of years. But the system in the course of two centuries had learned a good deal about the control of people. In the mid-seventies, it went to work.[355]

This response from "the system" was powerful, strategic and global. First, corporations imitated the counterculture that had enticed many apolitical youth to grow their hair and get in on the fun aspects of challenging puritanism and conformity, like sexual liberation, marijuana and rock and roll. To reclaim their grip on popular culture, corporations also had to reassure a concerned public that they were onside with the agenda for ecology and human rights. Coca-Cola would "teach the world to sing in perfect harmony". A few months after the first Earth Day in April, 1970, a 1971 Chevrolet car advertisement proclaimed: "You've changed. We've changed."[356]

Over the decades, though, ecology and human rights were dropped from the agenda. As capital mined the world for cheap labour and resources, work was lost instead of shared; the promise of leisure and economic security was quietly withdrawn. Instead, youth now scramble for a place in the economy, made desperate by permanently high unemployment and high rents. The trappings of life have changed, but, like their grandparents and great-grandparents, the deeply-indebted employed now work long weeks and consider themselves lucky simply to have a job.

As corporations shifted their factories to countries where labor was cheap, they blamed the ensuing struggles of workers on the school system. Diane Ravitch, a former US Assistant Secretary of Education, recalls the influence of a 1983 report entitled *A Nation at Risk*:

> The Commission warned that the nation was endangered by “a rising tide of mediocrity” in the schools; it pointed to the poor standing of American students on international tests, a recurring phenomenon since the first international test was offered in the mid-1960s.[357]

A member of the federal bureaucracy from the time of the first Bush administration (1989-1993), Ravitch promoted strategies to solve this problem with *accountability* through standards and tests, a role she would later deeply regret.

As Malcolm Levin had warned, by the late 1980s this international agenda had penetrated Ontario’s education bureaucracies. In his history of Ontario education after 1950 titled *From Hope to Harris*, R. D. Gidney cited “three major [post-1980] reports which exercised great influence among the province's political and policy-making elites, and which received a good deal of attention from the press as well”.[358] These were *Ontario Study of the Service Sector* (1986), *Ontario Study of the Relevance of Education* (1988), both by George Radwanski, and The Premier’s Council’s *Competing in the New Global Economy* (1988).

Echoing the alarms in *A Nation at Risk*, these reports hammered at a central point: "the urgent necessity to come to terms with the economic and social consequences of globalization and the new technologies".

The mantra that would be broadcast for decades was Radwanski's warning in the *Ontario Study of the Service Sector* (1986):

> To compete effectively in a new knowledge-intensive global economy that relies primarily on human capital, excellence in educating our workforce is our single most important strategic weapon. [359]

Gone were the messages of leisure and equity to be brought by new technologies—a "new grace to life". Now that societies were committed to high technology and there was no way out, the human was "capital", the worker a "strategic weapon" in global economic warfare.

In 1991, an enraged Jonathan Kozol noted that the American education picture he had found so hopeful a decade before had "been turned back a hundred years".[360] Canada's Maude Barlow and Heather-Jane Robertson mourned:

> What has changed is that the school's role is no longer to prepare children to create the future, but to prepare students for an inevitable future over which they will have no control, in which at best they can aspire to adapt to the ruthlessness of the inescapable.[361]

The rising critique—which Barlow and Robertson argued was actually a collection of myths—was that public schools were not serving the industrial system well enough.[362] In 1993, critical theorist Michael Apple referred to this movement as the "conservative restoration",[363] comparing it to the period after the English Revolution when, according to historian Christopher Hill, monarchy and hereditary privilege were reinstated and "educational reforms of the revolutionary decades, at all levels, were reversed".[364]

When the New Democratic Party achieved power in 1990, their goals for education seemed progressive: de-streaming and de-labelling of students, employment equity and anti-racism initiatives, cooperative pedagogy and "changes in governance that would short-circuit local bureaucracies and give greater voice to parents and other lay members of school communities".[365]

However, alongside the equity-driven agenda of dismantling streaming, a new monolith was introduced. This was *The Common Curriculum*, "an integrated curriculum that was outcomes based".[366] As Carol Anne Wien and Curt Dudley-Marling noted,

> Arguably, the broad intention of *The Common Curriculum* as a policy framework was holistic, favouring the integration of curriculum, but leaving the means of teaching the "ten essential outcomes" up to individual boards and schools. . . . Additionally, the stance of *The Common Curriculum* emphasized student ownership of learning and a "shift in curriculum emphasis to more integrated programming and active, inquiry-oriented learning."

But the two researchers unearthed "a second stance" in *The Common Curriculum* that fatally undermined its progressive intent. Wien and Dudley-Marling found this agenda "signaled by the recurrence of a single phrase throughout the second half of *The Common Curriculum* document: 'students will'."

> Not students should, might, could, can, or may, or even "it is expected that students will," and not some or most or many, but "students will." Arguably, what such language did was set up an authoritarian series of commands for teachers and school boards in particular. What happens if students cannot or do not reach these arbitrary markers of learning?[367]

With their emphasis on measurable outcomes, Gidney points out, such strategies were tied to testing, a "minefield" the NDP entered in 1993 by carrying out what would be "something of a minor revolution in Ontario education: the first province-wide, universal assessment of achievement in decades".[368]

The Conservative (Tory) Party, governing Ontario from 1943 to 1985, had instituted the Hall-Dennis Report. Gidney argues that what would be seen as the Harris program in Education was ready to roll before his Conservatives regained power in 1995.

> While there were some important differences of emphasis, all three parties endorsed most of the royal commission report and the general thrust of *New Foundations*. . . .
>
> All in all, then, educational issues played almost no role in the election campaign that began on 19 April and ended, on 8 June, with a smashing victory for Mike Harris and the Progressive Conservatives.[369]

Enthusiastic enforcers of a global education agenda whose foundations were laid by Liberal and NDP governments, the Tories would happily take most of the credit for the transformation of the culture of education in Ontario.

Retreating into Authoritarianism

In the USA this education agenda was similarly a multi-party phenomenon, solidified under President George W. Bush's 2001 *No Child Left Behind* and Barack Obama's 2009 *Race to the Top* legislation. According to Diane Ravitch, the standardized curriculum and annual tests did the most damage to schools that served the communities with the highest needs:

> Eventually, if the school kept failing, it was at risk of having its staff fired or having the school closed, handed over to state control or private management, or turned into a charter school. . . . Many schools 'failed' year after year and as 2014 approached, the majority of public schools in the nation had been declared failures, including some excellent, highly regarded schools (typically, the group that was not making sufficient progress toward 100 per cent proficiency was students with disabilities, and the schools that were likeliest to be labeled as failing, enrolled high proportions of poorer and minority students).[370]

Ravitch explained how this ideology diverts huge amounts of education funding to the private sector: in the form of the curriculum and tests themselves, consultants and, as schools "fail" and are closed, to chains of for-profit charter schools.

Those who experienced the decades of vision and hope after World War II still reel from this rejection of equity and human potential, in favor of hierarchical technocracy. Watching the growth of this agenda in the United States in the 1980s, Henry Giroux explained why a society struggling with the complexities of diversity and change would try to retreat to simpler ways of thought, where "authority is given a positive meaning":

> As an ideal that often embodies reactionary interests, this position legitimates a view of culture, pedagogy, and politics that focuses on traditional values and norms. . . . In educational terms, school knowledge is reduced to an unproblematic selection from the dominant traditions of "Western" culture.[371]

Earlier in the century, the Nazi-fleeing psychoanalyst Erich Fromm called such retreats into authoritarianism *Escape from Freedom*. He noted that "modern man still is anxious and tempted to surrender his freedom to dictators of all kinds, or to lose it by transforming himself into a small cog in the machine, well fed, and well-clothed, but an automaton".[372] Wilhelm Reich referred to this impulse as the "emotional plague".[373]

On a local, contemporary level, Barlow and Robertson pointed out:

> Casting schools as the villain and competition as the hero appeals to the human need to keep things simple. . . . Popular movements and political leaders prepared to provide chillingly simple solutions to their particular take on a problem will be assured of some following. When they put words to public anxieties, carefully orchestrated and often repeated, myths become facts and followers become believers.[374]

Barlow and Robertson also noted that gender played a role in the re-casting of education, a project in which teachers were rarely consulted.

> In the public mind, the way women and teachers see the world is entirely too similar. What is required to get things on track is hierarchy, unquestioning discipline and punitive supervision, as imposed by the masculine world of business.[375]

One parent whose family was at ALPHA during the "Harris years" observed that, as much as democracy is theoretically Canada's inspiration, our histories lie within a different paradigm:

> *I remember actually understanding, under the Harris leadership . . . we strive for democracies and cooperatives and sensitivities and sensibilities, but in fact we live in hierarchies. . . . And the leader is the moral head who sets the tone. And I remember understanding the difference between the Trudeau era or other kinds of generous attitudes versus when we encountered Harris and those kinds of persons.*

Under this regime, profit-seeking business was portrayed as *innovative* and *responsible*, while people fighting for their homes, schools and jobs (and even for social initiatives like women's shelters and environmental responsibility) were labeled "special interest groups". Instead of continuing progress being made toward a balance between the needs of living beings and the potentials offered by industrial mass civilization, there would begin decades of fighting once again the same battles for simple human rights, and often losing.

Susan Garrard Retires

At ALPHA, Susan Garrard survived her encounter with cancer and worked for several more years until she retired in June of 1996. Garrard's good-bye letter was lovingly framed with a photo of ALPHA's founding teacher sitting against a backdrop of trees, on a bench built into a large, weathered deck. Knee up, one foot resting on the bench, she is grey-haired but limber and smiling, the picture of health. A cushion beneath her, a glass of wine beside her and a book held in both hands complete the vision of contentment. Her letter contains the following message to the ALPHA Community:

> It was hard to leave you, but it's time for a rest. I started teaching in 1960. Imagine that, if you can. I worked in five different schools in four different communities before coming to ALPHA and learned a lot from all those kids. By the time we moved to Toronto, I needed a school where that learning could be put into practice. Finding ALPHA was a miracle. It has been tough—always unrelentingly tough. But the rewards have been correspondingly great.
>
> The intelligence, compassion, talent and imagination in the ALPHA Community have been consistently abundant throughout the years. Together we have created the unique entity which is ALPHA. We started with a set of ideals and the pressing needs of our children. Together we problem-solved and each discussion contributed to defining what we are. When I think back over the multitude of crises which we endured I am amazed at how often and how thoroughly we were threatened. Yet in almost every instance the outcome was strongly in our favour. I always thought of it as magic and was careful not to say that out loud.
>
> I do think we were rewarded for integrity. We have principles and we stick to them.

So great was the strength that ALPHA parents, teachers and children drew from Susan Garrard that we had often asked one another whether the school could survive without her. But her steady mentoring had ensured that the structure and personnel were adequate for the difficult transition. In the ever-renewing community, she lingered as a legendary figure to those who had known her.

Save Us!

A year after Garrard's retirement, ALPHA held a 25th Anniversary reunion. Facilitated by the artistic family of the teacher hired in Garrard's place, students performed a pageant in which a giant puppet representing Conservative Education Minister John Snobelin threatened to close the school. A herd of little children stampeded, screaming, "Susan, save us!" and up rose another giant puppet of a grey-haired, smiling lady. With children dancing around her, ALPHA's hero frightened the bad guy away.

This is not an example of excessively politicized alternative school kids. Such was the controversy and division fostered by this regime that these politicians' names were household words. A news item from November 14, 1998 would report that about 40,000 public school students who "packed Toronto's Skydome to greet Nelson Mandela" spontaneously booed when premier Mike Harris approached the stage.[376]

The Conservative government that was elected in 1995 had started literally with a bang—the police shooting of Chippewa activist Dudley George during the reclamation of Stoney Point, Ontario. George was shot a few hours after Premier Harris blurted to a high-level meeting that he wanted the "Indians out of the park". Soon afterwards, Minister of Education John Snobelin also managed to shock a roomful of civil servants when he suggested they help him in "creating a useful crisis" that would soften up the province for "core change, transformational change" in schooling.[377]

A high school drop-out who had made his money in haulage and moved on to management consulting, Snobelin personified the Harris government's practice of assigning people with no expertise in their portfolio, in order "not to allow 'insiders' to be co-opted by their bureaucracies".[378] Experience and commitment, in this ascendant world-view, were synonymous with "special interests".

Gidney pointed out:

> Between June, 1995 and the spring of 1998, the "Mike Harris government" imposed changes on Ontario schools that were remarkable in scope, in the sheer speed of execution, and in the turmoil they engendered.[379]

The Harris Tories rejected the culture of consultation and deliberation that Ontario citizens had been accustomed to, from all political parties, in favor of directly wielding provincial power.

A New Level of Centralization: Amalgamation

On January 1, 1998, in an amalgamation of seven municipalities into one "megacity", the Toronto Board of Education (TBE) was absorbed into the Toronto District School Board (TDSB). This was a direct enforcement of provincial power, carried out despite fierce opposition by politicians of all of the municipalities and a citizenry that voted it down in a referendum.

Amalgamation wasn't good news for alternative schools, for a locally based, responsive, argumentative school board had been vital to their formation in the 1970s. In 1982, the policy statement *Alternative Schools: A General Policy* had recognized that

> alternative schools and their communities are fearful of any move towards centralization. The success of Toronto's alternatives has been largely based on the idea that each is unique and exists in order to meet the special needs of particular students.[380]

This time was very traumatic for the people who had been working for years on issues ranging from Indigenous rights to education, from women's shelters to the arts. Opposition was massive, including numerous demonstrations, a teachers' strike, many legal battles, and several Days of Action, in which 250,000 people from unions and social justice organizations mobilized together to protest what Premier Harris and his allies in business and media called the "Common Sense Revolution".

Some ALPHA community members were participants in this resistance:

> ***1980-1991***: [The Days of Action were] *exciting. It didn't do anything, besides give people a lot of good memories.*
> ***1992-2002***: *Well, he was a force, right?*
> ***1980-1991***: *We had to do it to save our souls, but he was unstoppable.*

Powerlessness was a hallmark of this time in Ontario.

Doublespeak

Under the influence of the *Hall-Dennis Report*, Ontario in the 1970s had a complex view of educational equity that included diverse initiatives like heritage language classes, integrated special needs education, and alternative schools. In contrast, under the new/old education regime that has gripped schools since the 1990s, equity was to be expressed by sameness and standardization. Alternative schools became convenient scapegoats, even for formerly progressive political interests that submitted to the neo-conservative agenda.

> ***Parent 1974-1990***: *I think it was the NDP who accused us of being elitist. It shocked me to the core, because we were offering something different that wasn't available to every child in the system. I suppose that's their rationale. It seemed very twisted to me.*

In this classic divide and rule scenario, officials let citizens on the ground do some of the dirty work of enforcing standardization agendas. In the words of one parent informant from those years:

> *I remember really seeing that what happens is, the heavier it comes down, we begin to fight amongst each other. And I remember my awareness of that time being about: "Let's not let that happen." Because the pressures become so intense that you begin taking from each other. The more that they push and take away, we don't go for them and stop that. We start fighting here.*

As a charge leveled against alternative schools, the use of terms like *elitist* and *elitism* is a classic example of Orwellian doublespeak, in which a term means its opposite. According to my handy Encarta® World English Dictionary, *elitism* is not just a feeling of superiority to others, but the "belief" or "active promotion" of a system in which "government or control should be in the hands of a small group of privileged, wealthy, or intelligent people". This is the opposite of the successful experiments in local control that have been worked on in alternative schools. On the other hand, those who promoted agendas of standardization in education did not only feel superior; critics pointed out that they belonged to actual economic elites, and worked to consolidate the power of wealthy interests.

Hair of the Dog

If the kinds of measures instituted during what Michael Apple called the *conservative restoration* did, in fact, "ensure results" and "success for all", we might all be willing to entrust our children to the experts in the public school. We could retire from education activism to focus on our careers, see more of family and friends, work on other vital issues, and enjoy our children's successes.

John Taylor Gatto's publisher David Albert described what he saw happen instead:

> And so, the latest iteration of "education reform" (the fifth such set of reforms in my brief lifespan) comes with new (actually old) testing strategies where it can be ensured that large majorities of children will regularly "fail", either in comparison with each other, with those in another school, or with children living in the much more productive economies of Tunisia or Slovenia. The answer to those deficits and the perpetual dissatisfaction they engender is simply more of the same, rather like "the hair of the dog that bit you".[381]

Gatto challenged:

> There is no life-and-death international competition threatening our national existence, difficult as that idea is to think about, let alone believe, in the face of a continual media barrage of myth to the contrary.[382]

In 1994, Maude Barlow and Heather-Jane Robertson looked into the information sources that "business lobby groups such as the Conference Board of Canada, which comprises the one hundred largest corporations doing business in Canada" used to make their arguments: that Canada was over-funding education, while it fell behind in literacy, mathematics and dropout rates. They found that the problems were non-existent, and argued that statistics had been profoundly distorted:

> The arguments that smear schools have been manufactured in the absence or in spite of the evidence. Under these circumstances, what possible explanations are there for what is taking place? One is that we are witnessing a number of coincidental and mutually reinforcing errors, based inadvertently on hastily conducted and misinterpreted research, linked by muddled but well-intentioned reasoning. This model could be called the "collusion of incompetence." The other possibility is that we are watching a consciously orchestrated campaign, a strategy with well-articulated goals, an agenda with a purpose.[383]

York University professor Alison Griffith contended that this campaign included "the (at-times deliberate) political misreading of educational research and evaluation".[384]

Whether a "collusion of incompetence" or a politically driven agenda, these arguments were used in Ontario to institute a system in which every teacher's daily work could be policed against a detailed curriculum, and every student's daily life controlled by strangers at the Ministry of Education.

Wien and Dudley-Marling pointed out that a curriculum can have value if used as a guide and inspiration, a "map to a terrain that can never be exhaustively described".

> If teachers and school boards were able to use *The Ontario Curriculum* more as a reference document . . . it would then provide outsiders to education with a partial explication of what those implementing education are trying to do. . . . However, to treat the documents as moral codes prescribing what shall be done is to prevent the integrative, holistic, enquiry-orientation from ever being possible, because the finite energies of teachers are dominated by documenting lists of discrete (and often trivial) outcomes.[385]

Common goals stated in curricula provide starting points and guidelines to provoke inquiry and keep educators' eyes focused on literacy and numeracy. But an outcomes-based curriculum, imposed grade-by-grade throughout the system and policed by mass testing, succeeds mainly in enforcing lines of authority. Judging by their effects, the underlying purpose behind ratings and mass testing may be, rather than evaluation, social control and discipline—of students and of the workers in the schools.

Joel Spring pointed out contradictions in neoconservative concepts of freedom:

> While neoconservatives advocate a free market for schools, they retain the traditional conservative view that the government should regulate social behavior. . . . The regulation of schools, neoconservatives argue, should be through the creation of state educational curriculum standards and the measurement of student progress through standardized tests.[386]

The liberties defended by these interests don't include freedom of thought or action beyond a parent's theoretical option to shop for a higher-scoring school, within a regime that has predetermined what will happen and when, in every school.

A standardized curriculum is a good example of the kind of "text-mediated relations" identified by sociologist Dorothy Smith as the *relations of ruling* "in which power is generated and held in contemporary societies". Ontario's Curriculum was designed for what Smith called *replicability*.[387] Its TV promo was a cheerful fantasy of scrubbed suburban children starting at a new school, confident that they could pick up the curriculum where their former school left off.

This is truly a fantasy. Yet, as documents and software enter diverse local settings, from downtown Toronto to Moosonee, they stimulate identical behaviors in the people. Diverse schools come to resemble one another more and more, whether or not this works for the students and their communities.

Under a regime of enforced standardization, the bureaucratic reflex to sweep away the small eccentricities gathered in the corners of the education system becomes a bureaucratic imperative. As Dorothy Smith's term implies, the *ruling relations* are all related—the exams and report cards are necessitated by the drive to enforce the curriculum. A prime example of ALPHA's struggle with these ruling relations is the "report-card fight of 1995-98."

16:

THE REPORT CARD FIGHT

Report cards are so entwined with schooling that it's hard to think of one without the other. Many parents and teachers want them. But for three decades after the 1968 *Hall-Dennis Report*, provincial evaluation requirements were flexible enough so that no one cared that ALPHA didn't participate in this all-consuming educational ritual. However, since 1996 ALPHA teachers have had to spend many hours preparing report cards. Then they file them in a drawer. Anyone can ask to see their child's report, but few do. While the teachers must fill them out, the parent body refuses to participate in or condone this form of evaluation.

The public school report card ritual makes some families proud, while consuming a great deal of the system's energy. It also causes anxiety in many families, who see their kids slotted into levels in school that they fear will reflect their class level in life. Pitting children against one another and giving them a constant feeling of being judged, the report card process conforms to Henry Giroux's description of "domination [that] works against the notion of authentic community through forms of authority that actively produce and sustain relations of oppression and suffering".[388]

When Ontario chose to enforce this ritual, in the exact same form in every school in the province, it was certainly an act of domination, the triumph of Ministry supremacy over local Board of Education and local school control. Alison Griffith pointed out, "Standardized tests, standardized report cards, standardized staffing formulas are constructed to exert central office control over most aspects of local school life."[389]

Deborah Meier is one of many contemporary educators to note that rigid evaluation systems undermine the trust that is necessary for learning:

> Learning happens fastest when the novices trust the setting so much that they aren't afraid to take risks, make mistakes or do something dumb. Learning works best, in fact, when the very idea that it's risky hasn't even occurred to kids. . . . No one is sorting or ranking us, and we are not confronted with much that is out of our family's control, stuff that is arbitrary and could hurt us.[390]

Ivan Illich saw educational record-keeping as a human rights issue:

> Inquiries into a man's learning history must be made taboo, like inquiries into his political affiliation, church attendance, lineage, sex habits, or racial background.[391]

In other words, it isn't anyone's business whether literacy happened at four, eight or twelve, or when a student began to understand fractions, or whether they fell asleep in science class. There is evidence that these records affect the way that a young person is treated:

> Professor Robert Rosenthal of Harvard University recently reported in the New York Times on a study which clearly indicated that the expectations of teachers in many instances affected the achievement level of children. . . . One cannot help but suspect that some children are victims of self-fulfilling prophecies made by teachers prejudiced by their stereotyped judgments of children.[392]

If we had not lived with such human rating systems all our lives, we might experience them as dehumanizing and downright strange, as New Zealander Sylvia Ashton-Warner did when she arrived in America in 1974: "We grade fruit, meat, wool and eggs in my country, inanimate products without a mind, without the capacity to change."[393]

ALPHA's charter stood firmly against "formal evaluation of a child's performance," and favoured "encouraging children and adults to define, pursue and achieve their own educational goals".[394] ALPHA correspondence from the late 1990s states that when the school was informed late in 1995 that its teachers would have to fill out the Ministry-approved report card, there was 100 percent agreement to argue and resist.

One parent reported difficulty joining the consensus—not from principle but from fear:

> *I remember some actual parent meetings with that one, and I can actually sort of hear myself in that context: one of the few times when I felt myself out of step with what the teachers wanted. I remember arguing for some tactical response rather than some opposition to it, because I was very afraid, I remember at the time that they were looking for an excuse to close ALPHA.*
>
> *I just remember one of the teachers saying: "You just don't understand what this is going to do to us, if we have to do this." And I remember not pushing it, because I said, "I don't understand. I don't know."*

The teachers' resistance placed their jobs in jeopardy. Levin and Gladstone had pointed out that parents "often have more political clout when dealing with the Board and administration".[395] At ALPHA, such issues are a signal to strike an action committee, to establish a dialogue with administrators and to negotiate toward outcomes agreed on by the Parent Meeting.

On December 15, 1995, ALPHA parents conveyed to the Board of Education their decision to keep ALPHA exempt from "any form of report card that requires written evaluations of individual student performance, and/or compares one student's performance with another".

After quoting ALPHA's charter, the parents "cut to the chase":

> The recent return to detailed, performance comparing report cards was prompted to a large degree by parents who felt schools were not giving them a clear, useful picture of how their children were doing.

> If the ultimate purpose of the Board's new report card is to bring parents, students and teachers together to develop effective communication and optimize the educational experience, then we at ALPHA have already cut to the chase.
>
> We have formalized parent-student-teacher conferences at least once each semester, lasting up to an hour or for however long it takes.
>
> But even more than that, any parent at ALPHA has clear access to any teacher at virtually any time. That's one of the natural aspects of co-operative education.

Having committed themselves to "non-competitive" education and a direct, supportive method of evaluation, the "logical conclusion" for these parents was "there is nothing that a report card can do to enhance the ALPHA educational experience, and a great deal a report could do to damage that experience".

A follow-up letter from an ALPHA parent representative to the Director of Education on January 18, 1996, courteously recognized that the Director "has been handed a Gordian knot to unravel". It didn't ask for an immediate resolution, but requested that the teachers, who "have been informed, under threat of discipline, that they must accept the new report card and fill it out in the prescribed manner" be exempted until all the arguments have been made. It noted that the teachers "are being forced to go against the will of 100 percent of the parent body, not to mention a 25-year tradition of non-competitive education." To use Dorothy Smith's terminology, the teachers were caught between opposing sets of ruling relations: ALPHA's charter and custom plus the explicit will of the parents as expressed at Parent Meetings, versus a directive from the Ministry of Education through Toronto District School Board administrators.

This scenario constituted a particularly stark example of the kinds of risk and struggle faced by those who teach in public alternative schools. The imposition of arbitrary outside control also undermined the democracy at the community level.

> ***Parent 1992-2004****: I remember that as being one of the times where I really didn't come away from a meeting feeling like we had arrived at a consensus—that in fact, without it ever being a vote, that there had been one opinion within the group, not one person's opinion, but one cluster of opinion within the group that had carried the day and that I felt like "Hmm; I don't think we've arrived at a magic thing here."*
> ***Parent 1980-1991****: You weren't in control. The government was overwhelming.*
> ***Parent 1992-2004****: We were out of control. That's what I remember about that one.*

Eighty-six adults, representing every ALPHA family of this era, signed a petition that presented a thoughtful argument in support of ALPHA's non-judgmental methods:

> At ALPHA the child's individuality is the foundation for learning. Teaching focuses on the child's progress relative to themselves, rather than assessments according to a group level or standardized norm. A non-competitive atmosphere is the core of our philosophy. We believe that young children should explore, make mistakes, take risks, and challenge themselves. Comparative grading and standardized testing undermine this learning process and for this reason we firmly oppose these strictures.

A parent from this period recalled visiting the Board of Education as a member of an action committee that was struck to deal with this problem:

> ***Parent 1992-2002****: I remember* [another parent] *kicking me under the table, up at the school board. I have to say I remember being really adamant. . . . I was very opposed, and knew what it would mean. And I felt, no. You say no and you defend your position and you do not let yourself be bullied. Because that was basically the strategy: fear and bullying.*

Parents are in the best position to help administrators to see their alternative school as more than a bureaucratic annoyance. Even if the students remain numbers to the administrators, their parents are encountered as the kind of caring, involved families that the public system claims to want. Sometimes this works: administrators see the aims of education being conscientiously addressed, and the eccentricity is permitted to carry on until the next challenge. In this case, while Toronto administrators seemed sympathetic, their provincial masters had no interest in permitting exceptions to their edict. Administrators often are not in control, but are forced to pass their own coercion further down the line.

This particular struggle would last for about two years. In a letter to ALPHA dated February 7, 1997, the Director of Education recognized that the "board's requirement that a common reporting system be used in all schools puts the parents and teachers of ALPHA in a difficult position in terms of the school's original mandate and philosophy". Based on the requirement of the Ministry of Education, the director pointed out the school's "obligation to report to parents on achievement of outcomes in the Ministry's Common Curriculum", adding "it is our expectation that reports will be prepared for all students".

The Director, however, offered a possible solution to ALPHA's dilemma:

> Whether or not some parents choose to receive these reports is, of course, left to their parents' discretion and I hope that within this aspect of choice there might be a resolution to this issue that, at least in part, honours the concerns that you have expressed.

The drawbacks of this suggestion are obvious: the teachers are still required to spend many hours each term on a job that, at worst, undermined the alternative, and at best, was irrelevant and would be ignored. The Director of Education—perhaps regretfully—confirmed that the wishes of 100 percent of the parent community for exemption from report cards could not be respected because the Provincial Ministry had an "obligation to report to"—to whom?—the parents.

As the school community considered taking legal action, the lines of authority were explained in a memorandum from a lawyer within the parent community. The lawyer concluded that the law does not require the Ministry of Education to enforce a single vision on the organization of schooling in Ontario, but gives it the power to do so if it chooses. The parent body concluded that legal action would not work out.

Where the school loses the argument, the administrator may also feel the pain, as can be seen in this careful but regretful letter from a senior TDSB administrator dated May 4, 1998, and addressed to "Parents of ALPHA Children":

> While we have full understanding of why your group has made this request, we must acknowledge that the provincial government, through the Ministry of Education and Training, has decided that our students should no longer be evaluated on the basis of their individual progress but against a set of predetermined criteria or standards.
>
> As you are aware, this was not an approach that was traditionally supported by the former Toronto Board of Education and alternative methods of teaching and learning have been a hallmark of our educational philosophy. Unfortunately, we are no longer in the position to provide such latitude.

Every year, ALPHA teachers spend dozens of hours demonstrating their submission to the provincial authority. However, subsequent parent communities have kept their commitment to ignore the report cards. Discussions between parent, teacher and student remain centered around the actual child, rather than a piece of paper. A few years later, in 2005, Windsor House in British Columbia reached a similar compromise in a battle that threatened to close the school.

This can only be seen as a defeat because, in an era of diminishing resources for public education, it cuts into teacher time that would otherwise benefit the students. Whether or not a school wins its arguments, there's always loss in such struggles.

Weeks or years of parent volunteer time go towards defense and argument instead of student/teacher support and programming.

A routine (if regretted) chore for administrators causes distress and distraction for everyone associated with the school:

> ***Parent 1992-2004****: I do remember times of looking at other parents and looking at my child, whichever child it was, and looking at the other children and they're all anxious and worried about what it was that the parents were so upset about.*
> ***Parent 1992-2002****: Yeah, I remember too.*

Yet, from ALPHA's point of view, the battle had to be engaged, and the strategy— suggested by sympathetic administrators—of ensuring the report cards don't directly affect the students has been surprisingly successful.

Resistance for Cultural Survival

Education officials likely expected that, over time, parents wouldn't be able to resist looking at the reports ALPHA teachers now spend so much time preparing. Administrative pressure had succeeded in eroding the identities of a number of alternatives, so the bureaucracy had every reason to expect that within a few years, students at alternative schools would be vying for marks like every other student.

In ALPHA's case, however, this hasn't happened. For twenty-five years, the parents' authentic lack of interest in the report cards has been passed on to their children. The act of resistance passed on affirms the school's identity with each generation, so that when the opportunity arrives, the school can still reclaim its wholeness. Two decades after the defeat, the periodic teacher stress and scurrying at ALPHA are identical to every other school in Ontario. But since teachers engage in the activity critically and the parents and students abstain, the ruling relation hasn't managed to "replicate", to make the school like all others.

But the loss still weighs on the school. Back in 1982, Levin and Gladstone found that ten of the twenty-three alternative school teachers they interviewed "reported that their workload was currently much heavier than anything they had experienced in the regular schools". Additional responsibilities included "many more meetings" in the collaborative environment and "individualizing their programs. . . . They had to be much more aware of what each child's needs were and to adapt their program to meet these needs". Alternative school teachers could meet these responsibilities because the workload was balanced somewhat by not having to engage in marking and reporting.[396] The cost is, ultimately, the well-being of teachers, which impacts their students.

A parent from the Harris years recalled that parents and teachers worked to mend social relations damaged by authoritarian imposition.

> *I just remember sort of all the destruction, of all of it, all over the place, all of the schools, all of the community centers and actually ALPHA planted trees and built a garden. I remember at that point that we were much more savvy about the conditions we were under, and how you wouldn't fall into those vicious fightings. . . . But it's very hard to recover from those times, and things have not recovered.*

There is always tension at ALPHA about the next project that might be on the drawing boards of the School Board and the Provincial Ministry. ALPHA's *Report Card Fight* demonstrated that administrators and officials also get caught in situations where they cannot simultaneously satisfy their employers, themselves and the school communities they work with. During ALPHA's existence, good faith on both sides has been vital, often between parties who might not agree on some substantive educational matters. People with different views and interests have been able to maintain dialogue in a democratic context, both at community and bureaucratic levels.

17:

EQUITY AND COMMUNITY

After the Hall-Dennis Report, Ontario's education system had been slowly moving toward child-focused education methods and social supports like nutrition and family literacy programs. A social goal was to make school a place of support and succor that could help to balance what might be, for many children, a hard life outside of school. Under this general approach, whereby groups of teachers and parents were empowered to try out solutions, alternative schools grew in number and kind, despite administrative resistance.

There really wasn't much wrong with alternative schools. They didn't draw extra resources, their students liked them, parents liked them, they brought different ideas into the school system without imposing them on the unwilling, they were self-sufficient yet accountable to parents and students. Yet, their very existence was a challenge to those who wanted to keep power concentrated, and administrative models simple.

Divide and Rule

In the 1990s, as the glittering new "reform" imposed educational standardization and system-wide tests, school was to be a place where the kids had to measure up. Alternative schools became increasingly vulnerable.

One ALPHA parent from this time told this story:

> *The biggest change that happened was when the school boards were amalgamated. Then all of a sudden, the philosophy of the supportive Toronto School Board got caught up in this whole thing of "equalization". I remember going to a meeting at an alternative school in York at some time as an ALPHA parent going to support this alternative school. That was a meeting where there was this huge drama being played out—and for me it was a really difficult one in terms of different issues of political morality—where the parents who were opposed to the alternative school in this school were saying: "Why is it right that you White Canadians who can afford to go sit in your school with your children should be able to give them a different education from we parents who have to go to work?" And there was a hugely powerful dynamic, and that was the point at which ALPHA became one of very very few remaining alternative schools at that level.*

To "sit with your children" is hardly an accurate description of community participation at alternative schools, but the bureaucracies had rarely been inclined to understand or to explain how it really works. Instead, the enforcers of the new regime in education applied the principle "divide and rule" against those who had been attempting community-generated reforms, using their most deeply held values against them. To direct public support away from alternative schools, one tactic has been easy and reliable—and inflicted deep damage: tagging them with the vague but distasteful epithet, *elitist*.

Accusations of Elitism

The term *elitist* was seldom used to describe private or public schools in wealthy neighborhoods. It was most often applied to alternative schools that were using non-mainstream pedagogy. It was used from the beginning, even by the very people who might have been expected to explain and support the alternatives.

In a 1975 interview in Maclean's Magazine, the Toronto Board of Education Director managed to express the whole spectrum of administrative ambivalence. He referred to SEED as "sophisticated and elitist", but also called it

> the most successful of the board's attempts at alternative education— "an escape hatch for kids who can't work in the regular system, and for schools that can't cope with those kids." He says alternatives are important to the regular system because they force schools to incorporate ideas they'd never experiment with themselves.[397]

It's difficult to figure out how institutions that offer choice to families, help kids, and relieve their local schools can also be "elitist". But this is typical of the tortured logic often applied to alternative schools. Accusations that alternative schools were elitist hurt people, breaching core values embraced by ALPHA since its founding, when the community declared that "the education of all children can and should be served by a public rather than private system".

The accusations divided people with common problems, and demoralized schools. This tactic also, inaccurately but effectively, announced to families from economically challenged and racialized communities that the opportunities offered in alternative schools were not for them.

Privilege can be a factor in being able to start and sustain alternative schools. Writing about the struggles of the community that created the Africentric School in 2009, James and Samaroo would note the importance of parents in school creation. They analyzed the role of privilege: "It is often middle-class parents who have the knowledge of teaching philosophies and learning, a sense of entitlement, and an understanding of what to expect from the school system."[398]

ALPHA's founding community, significantly, included an architect and professors. But the press identified them as diverse in terms of social class: "people in public housing and in the hip counterculture, as well as middle-class professionals living mainly in the Annex and Rosedale".[399] The founders created a public alternative school so that its liberating pedagogy would be available to all income levels—including their own.

In *Community Schools*, Mark Golden explained how this goal had influenced the location for ALPHA's first home. With the parents deadlocked between a site at the comfortable north end of Toronto and the YMCA in the working class Broadview area, ALPHA's first teachers "strongly favoured the Y".

> The reasons for the decisions were good ones: there was a feeling that exposure to one of the poorer parts of town wouldn't do the kids harm and some parents were eager to provide an alternative to the inner-city schools in the area.[400]

This influence of ALPHA's first teachers was lasting. When ALPHA moved from Broadview, it was to an area with a similar class profile, the garment district south of Kensington Market, Chinatown and Queen Street West. It was a mixed area of light industry and cheap workers' housing that became an arts hub for a while and has since substantially gentrified. Some families found work and housing in the area, and the school attracted many locals and several generations of artists.

ALPHA's diverse class profile may have been a factor in its long-term survival. People who lack privilege aren't just victims—they are survivors. They are creators and transmitters of culture, experts at surviving and even thriving on little material wealth. Some are visionaries, creating solutions directed at the very root of a problem, and visualizing different ways of learning, teaching, building and caring.

In Toronto, uptown, middle class "free schools" didn't survive as such, for long. Throughout ALPHA's struggles, professionals in the community used their status and expertise to carry weight with administrators. But vital in the balance were low-income families and bohemians who were committed to holding their ground, strategizing for survival, and toughing out the gritty consequences of their choices.

The general non-judgmental atmosphere is the only explanation I can figure out for a rare and glorious ALPHA phenomenon. ALPHA has long been a haven for gay parents and for a highly vulnerable population: gender non-conforming children and families. An early ALPHA alumni, recalled:

> The school welcomed my dad, an out gay activist, without a hiccup as far as I know. Even in San Francisco in the public schools in the Castro today, that's not something that consistently happens. What a surprising and rare gift to a parent who didn't have to fight to spend time with the kids helping us do musicals; to a kid who wasn't shamed or stigmatized; and to a family that was already under extra strain from homophobia.[401]

Some students cross-dress for years, and are included in the children's community without comment. All that said, gender expectations hit children hard from the time they are in the womb. In a hundred ways—in princess fixations, macho games, or experiments with forbidden words—our problematic culture penetrates the children's world and at times causes pain, isolation and conflict in the community.

The problem of Whiteness

The parent who opposed the presence of an alternative within their local school made an accurate observation: the families within the elementary alternatives were largely White. ALPHA wouldn't make progress on this problem until after the millennium.

Since their origin in the early 1970s, many observers noted the relative lack of diversity of ALPHA and other elementary alternatives, compared to other downtown Toronto schools. In ALPHA pictures from the first four decades, the few faces of kids of Colour stand out.

Until the early years of this century, it wasn't usually hard to get into ALPHA, once you knew about it. The school often struggled to meet its enrollment. So several generations of mostly

White ALPHA parents wondered why the living and learning community our children enjoyed wasn't being embraced by more families of Colour. Early parents reported that ads placed in community centers and ethnic newspapers had "absolutely no response". I recall such efforts also being made through the 1980s and 1990s.

The problem of Whiteness in the free school movement was named early and passionately by Jonathan Kozol, a White Jewish teacher who had co-founded the New School for Children, with Black parents in the Boston suburb of Roxbury. In his 1972 book *Free Schools*, published the year ALPHA opened, Kozol had pointed out that many Black families wouldn't risk what appeared to be (and sometimes was) a casual attitude towards teaching their children to read.

All urban free schools wrestle with this issue. In Albany, New York, Mary Leue was influenced by Kozol to "locate her experiment in the heart of the inner city. She was determined that the poor of all races would have ready access to a school that would endeavor to meet the multilevel needs of their children".[402] Kids in the largely Black neighbourhood were attracted to the school, and the independent Albany Free School's financial model could accommodate them. Yet, even though the kids weren't thriving in their public school, former Albany co-director Chris Mercogliano observed:

> The working-class parents wanted the Free School to look and function like the local public school. . . . To these doubtful parents, our school represented the fast track to failure and low status.[403]

Most parents find the rituals around mass coercive schooling reassuring, whether or not they benefited from them as children. Enforced deskwork, report cards, tests and homework, what Mercogliano called the "trappings of a real school" seem to show a commitment to literacy and numeracy, despite the fact that many children don't learn well in these conditions.

Though low-income and racialized families have worries in this respect, pressure is exerted by privileged White families also. An early ALPHA student described a common family and community reaction to free schools:

> *There was a lot of almost hostility that I could perceive from the outside world in terms of parents of kids who didn't go to ALPHA who wanted to know how I got any work done. You know: "Do you just sit around and play all day?" The grandparents who ended up sending me to the Christian boarding school were fairly hostile about ALPHA.*

Regardless of pressure from the system and from anxious relatives, an ethical educator works with students in ways that they see actually help them. This is the kind of rigor seen in long-lived democratic schools. Summerhill and Sudbury Valley students thrive with no academic pressure. Staff at the urban independent Albany Free School learned the "hardest operating principle of all: you can't be all things to all people". They support their students' freedom while nurturing relationships with families. Mercogliano noted that many neighbourhood families hung in "long enough to discover that their kids were growing in ways that would ultimately set them free".[404]

Even in its most informal decades, ALPHA prioritized literacy. The school became more formal after Garrard's retirement, but by 2006, staff members were discussing Kozol's and Mercogliano's work on urban free schools. Greater freedom of movement and choice was restored, while teachers also explored ways to proactively engage kids and reassure parents. Thus ALPHA tilted away from Sudbury-Valley-style libertarianism, while supporting student agency and community democracy.

Meanwhile, an Admissions Committee of three mothers, concerned about the experiences of families of Colour in a school "that existed in a framework of Whiteness and was in denial about this" was tackling the problem of ALPHA's Whiteness head on.

ALPHA's Equity Admissions Process

During the decades when ALPHA struggled to meet its enrollment, a first-come, first-served waiting list was sufficient for keeping track of interested families. An Admissions Committee of parents took interested families on school tours, to find out whether ALPHA would be a fit for them. Children who didn't get a place in the first year they applied were often admitted after a year or two.

In 2005, Alternative Primary School (APS), which had been struggling for its life, identity and enrollment, was closed, and ALPHA could have been next on the chopping block. ALPHA may owe its survival to the parents whose pressures would, in a few years, create the Africentric School, the Grove School, da Vinci and Equinox. With a long waiting list at ALPHA, and four activist communities clamouring to open new alternative schools, closing existing schools suddenly became much more difficult.

The situation for alternatives seemed to change overnight. Perhaps the increasing rigidity of public schools was driving families out of them. Perhaps the Internet was giving families the opportunity to research possibilities. Whatever the reason, by 2006, many more families called at ALPHA than it had spaces for. As timing, dating and keeping track of inquiries became more labour-intensive and problematic, administrators at all levels stopped supporting a system they couldn't ensure was fair.

As ALPHA's new coordinator, I became aware that ALPHA was under pressure from the bureaucracy to simply submit all names to a lottery. With no way to ensure incoming families would even be fully aware of how the school operated, this was a threat to the school's identity. ALPHA was facing another crisis.

The three volunteers who formed the Admissions Committee of 2006 were faced with developing a process that would meet Board requirements and would ensure that incoming families were aware of, and committed to, the school's democratic philosophy. They designed a solution that would also, over time, address the oft-stated problem of ALPHA's Whiteness. They would later note that in this era: "54% of the population of the ward where ALPHA was situated was racialized and yet the school had remained overwhelmingly white".

These three volunteers were mothers, artists and academics, from minoritized communities. All had experience in addressing difference and racism within their professional practices. They recalled that they decided together to design a new admissions process that would "move the school towards antiracism".

> *This is a very different goal than a 'diversity' goal. While some support for the plan came from White parents who could see the benefit of diversifying the student body in order to bring the richness of diversity into the community, our intent was not primarily to give the White kids in the school the benefit of diversity, but to actually combat the racism that is integral to White spaces. To make the school a livable space for racialized and Indigenous kids and families who experienced racism there, to make the idea of alternative stretch to include anti-racism, not just freedom and student-led learning.*

The Admissions Committee pooled their expertise to create a fair and informative system. In 2007, the following admissions procedure was instituted: ALPHA holds two Open Houses each winter, then conducts tours of the school in operation. Families still interested after this orientation are chosen by a two-stage lottery. First, 75 percent of all names are drawn on a random basis from all applicants. The remaining 25 percent are selected, on a random basis, only from applications of families who voluntarily self-identify as "families of Colour, Aboriginal and LGBT/queer families".[405] The LGBT/queer category "includes [the] child who is and/or may experience discrimination due to non-gender conforming appearance or behaviour".[406]

After decades of the ALPHA Community's stated good intentions, the proposal of an affirmative action admissions policy was surprisingly contentious. To ensure that all who feel strongly are duly notified and have a chance to participate, consensus at two Parent/Teacher meetings is required to make a policy change to ALPHA. The questions posed at the meetings, and some of the blowback afterward, revealed ALPHA's institutional biases.

It was a naked moment. Reactions ranged from liability concerns to accusations of "rigging" admissions. The vague, bizarre concept "reverse racism" was raised. Though the initial 75 percent draw was to be from a pool of all interested families, a startling number of parents expressed visceral fear that their own child would have been shut out from such a process. The requirement for a lottery process had come from the Administration, but the Admissions Committee bore the anger of community members who defended the original waiting list, arguing that the school's identity needed the presence of families so committed that some even tried to register their children when they were toddlers—in one case, in utero.

Members of the Admissions Committee met the challenges calmly. With the backing of a number of parents whose support they could count on, they faced the often-hostile questions and led two contentious meetings to a hard-won consensus. However, there was more to come, in the form of emails from community members who hadn't attended either meeting. They repeated the suspicions that the committee had successfully calmed at two meetings. Years later, members of the 2006 Admissions Committee recalled this grueling struggle:

> *The few racialized families at the school felt fear, exhaustion, frustration and sadness at having to explain, yet again, the realities of their experiences at the school and in the world.*
> *This was not a community rallying around an anti-racist corrective to problematic admissions policies, although there were many who supported the work, of course. . . .*

This process revealed the ways in which progressive communities replicate existing relationships of power, even when that may not be their intent, or when they are in theory committed to unsettling many aspects of the status quo.

There was an interesting grace note. Jewish students aren't included in this policy, and Jewish families did not challenge this. An Admissions Committee member noted:

I felt very strongly we were fighting for access for racialized and Indigenous students/families. Jews were (for the most part although of course not always) white, and as some of the key founders of the school were Jewish, I don't think there was a sense of us being excluded in the same way racialized kids and families were.

After having overcome community resistance, ALPHA's Equity Admissions Policy faced challenges from the Toronto District School Board. Some executives in the Administration objected to this affirmative action. Other alternative schools that wanted to use it were at first forbidden, and subsequent Admissions Committees had to negotiate with administrators annually about whether it could be carried out.

The effect of this innovation on ALPHA was incremental, and the families who instituted it didn't see significant change in their time. The Committee's self-evaluation is:

As was hoped for, over a number of years, the equity admissions initiative changed the face of ALPHA making it a richer and more inclusive space for LGTBQ+ and racialized families.

It is perhaps, in the end, one of the most effective ways to make this kind of change. You change who is in the school, and bit by bit, the word of mouth reaches the communities you hope to be accessible to. Families see other racialized kids, and may be more likely to see this as a place they could send their children. Far more effective than trying to attract diverse communities through outreach and advertising.

Thus, late in ALPHA's fourth decade, it began its transformation into a diverse downtown Toronto school. Fears that the school's democratic culture could suffer from the new admissions policy, weren't borne out. The careful orientation process instituted by the 2006 Admissions Committee ensured that entering families were informed and committed.

The work that this Admissions Committee accomplished had an impact beyond ALPHA. ALPHA's Equity Admissions Policy is no longer opposed by the TDSB administration, and similar models appear to be in the process of becoming the accepted procedure for admission into alternative schools.

When we think of equity, we usually think in terms of class, ability (addressed in the section on Special Needs), gender, and race—still unresolved in the culture at large. Alternative and community schools aren't oases where such immense issues have been solved. At ALPHA, they are worked on in community, with each generation of children, parents, and staff. The school continues the never-ending work, with school-wide initiatives that respond to students' questions about who and where they are, in a civilization whose ramparts include white supremacy and colonialism. The messy work is ongoing.

18:

DEMOCRACY STILL TO COME

As of ALPHA's fiftieth anniversary, the trees parents planted have matured to make a dappled oasis of the formerly sun-scorched inner city playground.

At the big reunion party for its fortieth anniversary in 2012, school starters rubbed shoulders with ALPHA's newest families. A parent from the seventies revived his traditional "Scary Story Time" for a delightful hour. Alumni in their twenties, thirties and forties met one another's children. Following their tradition, current and former parents fed the community rotis, hot dogs, soup, and baked delicacies. There was a lion dance, a campfire, rock'n'roll, and even a baby lamb. With all the kids dancing, playing, running and partying, there was not a single bruise. Sometimes ALPHA gets lucky. Tension and crises rise as regular as the tides, but so far pluck, synchronicity and hard rowing have borne it through the waves.

Today, in 2022, in the Ontario public school system overall, hours of homework are still the norm, even in elementary grades. With neighborhood schools closed and sold, children are warehoused in large schools. These trends caused huge problems during the 2020/21 pandemic, when there was little extra space—not even libraries, labs or art rooms—to spread the students out into smaller cohorts.

A number of alternative schools were closed over the decades, but those that remained gained strength early in the new millennium, becoming popular enough to have waiting lists, and new ones were created by parents and educators. Toronto parents also started four new primary alternatives: an Africentric school, two holistic alternatives, and one focused on social justice. Home-schooling is no longer rare. Parents are challenging an arduous education system, whose solutions never solve its problems.

It's a good time for citizens, educators, students and parents to ask ourselves what we want from education, and how we want children to feel during their time at school. It's a good time to focus on the well-being of the vulnerable people in our care. As ALPHA's community affirmed over the years, children have good insight about what their real needs are. Time and time again, Susan Garrard would urge nervous parents: "Trust the kids."

Meaningful Lives

Through AERO, the support organization he founded, Jerry Mintz has worked with people from hundreds of alternative schools all over the world. He observes that those who involve themselves with alternative schooling "have a different set of criteria" than those who settle for the mainstream:

> We care how happy [students] are. We care if they know how to get along with other people. And those are not things that they test for with their standards. We care if they're creative: we care if they can take responsibility. We have standards—those are them. Another standard is: Does your kid like this school? How about the most basic thing: is the customer satisfied?

These are not the kind of abstract "standards" that parents anxiously scan their kids' report cards for. These are qualities a regular human being can appreciate and observe in youth they know.

John Dewey was adamant about the importance in education of the "normal processes of life":

> Life is the great thing after all; the life of the child at its time and in its measure no less than the life of the adult. Strange it would be, indeed, if intelligent

> and serious attention to what the child now needs and is capable of in the way of a rich, valuable, and expanded life should somehow conflict with the needs and possibilities of later, adult life.[407]

This may be my favorite concept of Dewey's. We can't control all the good and evil that will come their way. We can't save them from the disappointments and conflicts of living. We can't even shelter them from our own mistakes, or our ignorance. But to challenge ourselves to offer children a "rich, valuable, and expanded life" is inspiring for the mentors as well as for the children.

Dewey pointed out the illogic of sacrificing the present lives of children on the altar of mythical future "success". Neill challenged all educators with his approach to that fraught concept. He deeply respected the caretaking, service, labour and craft that enable a society to function, and resisted class division. He disdained the mediocrity he often saw in leadership classes.

> Of course the philistine can say, "Humph, so you call a truck driver a success in life!" My own criterion of success is the *ability to work joyfully, and to live positively. Under that definition, most pupils in Summerhill turn out to be successes in life.*[408] [Italics Neill's.]

Graduates of Summerhill and ALPHA include professionals and PhDs, but the schools are equally proud of those who live ethical lives in any class context. ALPHA's founding community couldn't agree on education methods, but their 1971 proposal listed values that they all wanted the school to nurture, and that they therefore had to model: cooperation, diversity, freedom of expression, autonomy, social responsibility, and affiliation.

A former student from the early 2000s recalled: "values are woven into everyday life at ALPHA, not tacked on as an extra":

> *The learning system at ALPHA is so humanizing that it is almost inevitable that those values are going to come out of you. At other schools they drown it out of you and then have to assign it back.*

> *ALPHA treats you like a person; elsewhere they just want you to be a piece of the machine.*[409]

It's a simple expectation, to be treated like a person. Yet in practice, it's radical. It challenges the giant institutions of our huge, overpopulated civilization, to make each decision as if every child matters.

> ***Student 1974-1982****: Some of the work that I do is as a tutor with high school kids. I was just working with one kid on an essay and we were looking at Martin Luther King's concept of "somebodiness." I thought wow, that's a great ALPHA concept: the idea that the littlest kid in the kids' meeting has a voice and they might put up their hand and say, "Ummmm" and they might have nothing to say or they might forget. Or it might be completely out of left field. It doesn't really matter, because that kid is a valued member of the community just as anybody else. So that for me is really the essence of ALPHA.*

Democratic schools are meaningful for adult participants, too, and it's not all seriousness and struggle. Daily life at ALPHA is playful, informal, organic, full of stories and mischief and creativity—as well as eye-rolling frustration at times.

Kozol described in free schools an ambiance of "high energy and fun, pupil-irreverence and adult unprotectedness, none of that glaze and lacquer of 'professional behaviour' which is identified with the . . . dehumanized existence of the veteran teacher in the public system".[410]

Free school educators value the deeper relationships with students that occur when one is not constantly prodding and maneuvering them, the complexity that both adult and child can reveal in their characters. One parent said:

> *I just want to add that I felt that I could be who I am there.*

The Democracy and the Bureaucracy

ALPHA's community recognizes that without the Toronto District School Board there would be no beloved public democratic school that their kids actually want to attend (on most days). One former parent summed up:

> *The same way ALPHA was a partnership within a school community, we are in a partnership with the Board of Education. And they have a different philosophy. They have a different belief system. They're tolerant of us; we're tolerant of them. They have bosses above them who they are accountable to and so we need to respect their position. It's kind of like two people of different values sharing or co-habiting.*

In 1968, the *Hall-Dennis Report* challenged Ontario's education bureaucracy:

> Of all public exercises, education can least afford to have its spirit dampened by bureaucracy. By its very nature, learning is the antithesis of the rules and regulations of uniformity. But if administration seems sometimes to curb the right to learn freely, it is also the guardian of that right.[411]

The *Hall-Dennis Report* urged "changes which must be made if Ontario's largely hierarchical system is to become truly a system of service to children".[412] Yet it showed that each level had a positive function and place, arguing,

> the fundamental role of the provincial authority should be to equalize educational opportunity by means of a redistribution of money to the local education authorities, while leaving most of the decisions concerning its expenditure to them.[413]

Re-visioning the roles of the school boards and the provincial ministry, two massive bureaucracies that it saw expending a "great deal of energy . . . on the perpetuation of the organization",[414] it's no wonder that the *Hall-Dennis Report* made so many enemies.

Democracy for Survival

In a generous era, the democratic educator's tendency to fend off well-meaning administrators can be seen as churlish, or even "elitist". But a "benign authority" can shift its priorities at any time. Progressive agendas, relying on decisions made within massive political machines and bureaucracies, rise and fall even within a single decade. School Board trustees lose elections or find their powers drastically reduced; bureaucrats move on, are pushed out, or change their ways when a conservative wind blows.

Though its very existence was criticized by some members of the community schooling movement, ALPHA demonstrates that democratic power can be successfully shared by the families and workers of a school community. Longtime teacher Susan Garrard sees democracy as ALPHA's secret of survival, both to solve the school's internal problems and to defend against external threat.

> *I really put it down to the democratic process, myself. What I recall is just having a parent meeting. You are going to address a problem. We work through that problem and we make a decision. It might not be the right one and you try something, and then on to the next problem. We just kept problem-solving in a democratic way, and gradually things started to have some form—just through problem-solving. But always sticking to the democratic process. It was essential. If ever that broke down, then everything broke down. I think the fact that people were able to stick to that all through those years is why it's still going.*

In 1986, the Ontario Ministry of Education applied Garrard's observation to all the alternative schools, noting: "If the alternative was to survive and thrive, it would be because the community of parents, pupils, and staff made it do so."[415]

Though we have seen that it's not a quiet life, self-governance by its community of students, parents and teachers gives a school the deepest form of accountability.

As Community Schooling activist George Martell explained:

> If power is shared equally in a community—then collectively they will make the best decisions about life in that community, in our case about the quality of education. Certainly, community people are going to make mistakes, lots of them, but they're also going to find ways to correct them, because the mistakes hurt *them*.[416]

An arms-length relationship with the responsible education bureaucracies can enhance rather than undermine democratic local governance, securing funding and resources, and supporting initiatives. Some administrators during the years of ALPHA's creation responded flexibly to support each public school's capacity to fulfill the current, genuine needs of the youth in their communities. I am sure that some still try.

Goodbye to Totalizing Revolutions

If we are to put the needs of youth foremost, public school reforms can't be accomplished through a frantic imposition of one kind of schooling for all, such as was undertaken in response to the Sputnik panic of the 1950s, and under the globalization and austerity agenda that has ruled since the 1990s. These mass agendas didn't succeed in solving the problems they named.

In education systems, I've seen children subjected to vast, failed experiments, from imposed "discovery" methods during progressive eras, to zero tolerance discipline, to—in the current era—the enforcement on younger and younger children of long hours of study and homework, mass testing, and pressure to achieve. How can different ways of schooling be instituted without experimenting on vulnerable children, yet again? Toronto's *schools of choice* show a way: the community school strategy that Dale Shuttleworth described as human rights based—community-initiated and cooperatively governed "in response to local needs".[417]

Alternative and community education proponents argue that family and community, rather than a faraway authority, have the greatest stake in the vitality of their children and, as Deborah Meier contends, should have "sufficient authority to act on its collective knowledge of its children".[418] "The project," writes Matt Hern, is to "give communities and families the opportunity to comprehend what it means to grow up right and to define their ideals of learning".[419]

We can expect critiques of mainstream schooling to continue, hopefully in a more expanded form than we've been accustomed to, entertaining many more kinds of questions and possibility than student "success" and "failure". But I share the stance of the late Roger Simon, who cautioned:

> While I will be putting questions of social transformation on the agenda, I do so with the insistence that there be no more attempts at totalizing revolutions.[420]

This would include the totalizing imposition of democratic or progressive schooling. Indeed, if I were a powerful official who opposed these principles, I would be tempted to impose these universally, welcoming the resulting chaos and calls for a return to the status quo.

I write this after two years of a pandemic strategy in education that was formulated without meaningful consultation. This strategy funded technology upgrades, but resisted hiring staff to reduce class size and help kids with their anxiety and trauma. Ontario's primary commitment was to provide "synchronous delivery of teacher-led learning" online.[421] This policy prioritized school's greatest anxiety-producer, and continues to impose a rigid curriculum that leaves little room for addressing the many urgent questions students have in this time. It persists in the myth that, without this constant mental force-feeding, students will be "left behind".

When I see so many experts in home and alternative learning who are left out of the media and political conversation, I feel frustrated, angry, worried and sorrowful. Only democracy can muster the brainpower and imagination of communities, and facilitate the cooperation essential to ensure the survival and thriving of humanity. Much of the hope that I see lies in grassroots organizations that are re-inventing the human legacy of participatory democracy, while they defend people against climate change, homelessness, food precarity and exploitation. Henry Giroux suggests that schools can be an important part of democratic revival: "Schools are one of the few sites within public life in which students, both young and old, can experience and learn the language of community and democratic public life."[422]

Educational democracy wouldn't result in a proliferation of free schools. The demise by the 1990s of the ideals in Ontario's *Hall-Dennis Report* shows that many parents and teachers feel strongly about the need for the kinds of "standards" represented by report cards. To deny families a traditional method that has their confidence is to set the stage for ongoing cultural conflict and the divisive manipulation of their fears by various power interests.

However, I would argue that, despite having been employed for over a century, mass coercive education still hasn't proven its effectiveness sufficiently to be forced on all families and communities, nor to have its supporting myths go unchallenged. Its excesses must be curtailed. Its most damaging developmental travesties—homework, marks and high-stakes testing—must be eliminated in primary school, so that young children can be cared for, instead of judged. So they can be mentored as they learn the basics, and supported as they mature within the varied challenges they face at home and in society. So they can just be kids again, during and after school hours. And families can be families, not homework enforcers.

A School of Life

With an end to "totalizing revolutions", vulnerable persons like children can stop being victimized by failed social experiments. Public funding with grassroots control of innovative and local schools would ensure that those who care most are in control, and that all social classes can participate, if they wish, while their children need the schools.

Mary Catherine Bateson proposes: "A society of many traditions and cultures can be a school of life".[423] Schools that responsibly explore the limits of democracy promote a wider understanding of democratic possibility, in which society can show itself as generous, expansive and educative.

While free schools are unlikely to become mainstream, such schools should be included in public systems, as part of a diversity of models. In 2000, a powerful attempt to close Summerhill ended with proceedings before the Independent Schools Tribunal, at which A. S. Neill's educational philosophy was explicitly accepted by the Department of Education as "an established strand of modern educational theory".[424]

Their structures honed through constant testing by real children and communities, alternatives show that education need not be carried out in a massive, dehumanizing, coercive way. A former ALPHA student said:

> *I think my ideal world would have a million little ALPHAs in it. Each one small and kind of different.*

Every child should have the right to feel this way about their school, even if ALPHA isn't the school that their family wants and needs. Speaking of his laboratory school in 1900, Dewey warned:

> A working model is not something to be copied; it is to afford a demonstration of the feasibility of the principle, and of the methods which make it feasible.[425]

Neill called Summerhill a "demonstration school"[426] and cautioned: "No school, Summerhill included, is the last word in education".[427] If there's nothing else that educators can reach consensus on, perhaps we could maintain humility on this point at least: no school or method is the last word in education.

Summerhill is a century old. ALPHA, the Albany Free School, and numerous public and independent free schools are now older than Summerhill was when Neill's inspirational book was published in 1960. These alternative schools don't divert energy from mainstream reform; rather, they ground critique in experience, and ally it with hope. They are models of local self-organization and mutual care, and proof that coercive, judgmental schooling is not the only game in town. They can be seen as expressions of what Paulo Freire calls a "pedagogy of hope".[428]

Dale Shuttleworth, the Toronto Board administrator who supported the development of alternative schools in the 1970s, connected the organizational work being carried out in alternative schools with movements toward democratic participation in other aspects of community life, declaring that they provide "new models for service provision, cooperative decision-making, cost-sharing, and problem-solving".[429]

Modernism and empire shatter human communities. Large-scale technocratic systems have efficiencies that award some sectors with astounding affluence, but they grind people and eco-systems into fodder for their markets, while the consumer economy hammers at the planet's limitations. Can we claim, at this point in history, that we don't need to try out different models of schooling, service provision or democratic governance?

The only real certainty is this: positive change can't happen without deep democratic participation. Ontario's *Hall-Dennis Report* declared,

> Democracy does not arise as a result of imposed or structured political practices, but as a dynamic, liberating force, nurtured by the people themselves.[430]

Roger Simon suggested:

> Surely it is time to re-open public discussion about the aims of education and ensure that our current policies and practices are consistent with the core qualities of democracy; democracy not narrowly defined as a form of government, but as Dewey characterized it—as a way of life, as an ethical conception, and hence always about the democracy still to come.[431]

This pandemic teaches us (though Neill knew it well) that all types of people are necessary in society: to keep the water running, the people cared for, the ideas flowing. To support those who struggle with the big questions, to keep room for the creative and the eccentric, to love difference, to honor all whose work helps us to live, to resist bullying, to support courage and vision, to ensure that the vulnerable are not only cared for but helped to live sweet lives, will keep all of us free.

REFERENCES

The ALPHA Community. *The ALPHA Experience*, 1971. https://www.alphaschool.ca/the-founding-document-the-alpha-experience/

The ALPHA Community. *Press Release*, attached letter signed by Roger Simon and discussion paper. From the TDSB Archives and Museum, September 21, 1971.

The ALPHA Community. *Brief for the Management Committee, Toronto Board of Education*, presented by People for an Alternative Elementary School, 1971.

The ALPHA Community. *A Brief to the Policy Committee.*

The ALPHA Community. *alpha 74*. Includes *Operational Guidelines for the ALPHA School Commencing in September, 1973* and *ALPHA Constitution, 1973*, July 30.

The ALPHA Community. *Alpha Centauri*, 1973, September/October.

The ALPHA Community. *The ALPHA First Annual Report*, 1978, October. Included in TBE *Alternative Schools 1978 Annual Reports*, May 1, 1979.

The ALPHA Community. *The ALPHA Parent Handbook,* circa 1988.

The ALPHA Community. *Minutes of ALPHA Parents Meeting, March 12, 2009.*

"The ALPHA Experience". *Educational Courier*, Vol. 42:4, pp. 25-26, 1972, February.

The Alternative Education Research Organization (AERO). *Democratic Schools* (n.d.). Retrieved December 10, 2017 from http://www.educationrevolution.org/store/findaschool/democraticschools/

The Alternative Education Research Organization (AERO). *Nellie Dick and the Modern School Movement* (n.d.). Retrieved March 20, 2021 from https://vimeo.com/82532921/

The Alternative Education Research Organization (AERO). *Annual Meeting of the Modern School at Rutgers University in NJ to Feature Unique Performance This Year!* (n.d.). Retrieved March 20, 2021 from https://www.educationrevolution.org/store/annual-meeting-of-the-modern-school-at-rutgers-university-in-nj-to-feature-unique-performance-this-year/

References

Alternative Schools Advisory Council. "Priority Needs Identified by Discussion Groups" at the Alternative Education Conference May 11, 1985. Attached to Agenda for June 12, 1985.

Apple, Michael W. *Official Knowledge: Democratic Education in a Conservative Age*. New York: Routledge, 1993.

Arthur, James with Richard Bailey. *Schools and Community: The Communitarian Agenda in Education*. London and New York: Palmer Press, 2000.

Ashton-Warner, Silvia. *Spearpoint: "Teacher" in America*. New York: Vintage Books, 1974.

Ashton-Warner, Silvia. *Teacher*. London: Secker and Warburg, 1963.

Avrich, Paul. *The Modern School Movement: Anarchism and Education in the United States*. Edinburgh, Oakland and West Virginia: AK Press, 2006.

Barber, John. "Starting a free school in Ontario". In *This magazine is about schools*, Vol. 3, No. 3, "staple-in" leaflet (Summer, 1969).

Barker, Michael and Ariel Fielding. *Alpha Alternative School 1972/2012. http://michaelbarker.ca/alpha-alternative-school/ (2013).*

Barlow, Maude and Heather-Jane Robertson. *Class warfare: The Assault on Canada's Schools*. Toronto: Key Porter Books Limited, 1994.

Bascia, Nina, Esther Sokolov Fine and Malcolm Levin, ed. *Alternative Schooling and Student Engagement: Canadian Stories of Democracy Within Bureaucracy*. Switzerland: Palgrave MacMillan (2017).

Berg, Sharon with Elder Pauline Shirt. *The Name Unspoken: Wandering Spirit Survival School*. Toronto: Big Pond Rumours Press, 2019.

Brayshaw, A. Neave. *The Quakers*. London: Friends Home Service Committee, 1921/1969.

Bogdan, Robert and Sari Knopp Biklen. *Qualitative Research for Education: An Introduction to Theory and Methods*. Boston: Allyn & Bacon, 1992.

Bull, Richard E. *Summerhill USA*. Penguin Educational Special, 1971.

Burness, Tad. *Monstrous American car spotters guide, 1920-1980*. Osceola, WI, USA: Motorbooks International, 1986.

Canadian Broadcasting Corporation. "Children salute Nelson Mandela". *CBC News,* November 14, *1998*. Retrieved August 28, 2008 from http://www.cbc.ca/news/story/1998/09/25/mandela980925c.html

Chomsky, Noam. *World Orders Old and New*. New York: Columbia University Press, 1996.

Clarke, S. & Linton, M. "A better school for your money". *Toronto Life* (August *1975*): 23-31.

Cohen, Ruth, ed. *Alien Invasion: How the Tories mismanaged Ontario*. Toronto: Insomniac Press, 2001.

Darder, Antonia, Marta P. Baltodano and Rodolfo D. Torres, ed. *The critical pedagogy reader*. New York: Routledge, 2009.

Davis, Robert. Editorial. *This magazine is about schools*, Vol. 1, No. 1, (1966): 1-4.

Deal, Terence E. *An Organizational Explanation of the Failure of Alternative Schools*. Stanford, CA: Stanford Center for Research and Development in Teaching, 1975.

Dennison, George. *The Lives of Children*. New York: Vintage Books, Random House, 1970.

Dewey, John. *The School and Society and The Child and The Curriculum*. Chicago: The University of Chicago Press, 1900, 1902/1990.

Dewey, John. *Democracy and Education*. New York: The Free Press, a division of Simon and Schuster, 1916/1997.

Dewey, John. *Liberalism and Social Action*. New York: Capricorn Books, G.P. Putnam's Sons, 1935/1963.

Durno, Elizabeth and Mang Leslie. *Public Alternative Schools in Metro Toronto*. Toronto: Learnx Press (n.d.), circa 1987.

Edwards, Carolyn, Leila Gandini and George Forman. *The Hundred Languages of Children: The Reggio Emelia Approach—Advanced Reflections*. Santa Barbara: Praeger, ABC/CLIO, 1998.

Fantini, Mario D. *Alternative Education: A Source Book for Parents, Teachers and Administrators*. New York: Doubleday & Company, Inc., 1976.

"Free school averts closing with hiring of two teachers". *The Toronto Star*, August 28, 1973: (n.p)

The Free School Handbook, 1972. Toronto: no publication information.

Freire, Paolo. *Pedagogy of the Oppressed*. New York: Continuum, 1970/2004.

Freire, Paolo. *A Pedagogy of Hope: Reliving Pedagogy of the Oppressed*. New York: Continuum Publishing Company, 1994.

Fromm, Erich. *Escape from freedom*. New York: Avon Books, 1965.

Fromm, Erich. *The Art of Loving*. New York: Harper & Brothers Publishers, 1956.

Gatto, John Taylor. *Dumbing Us Down: The Hidden Curriculum of Compulsory Schooling*. Philadelphia, PA: New Society Publishers, 1992.

Gidney, R. D. *From Hope to Harris: The Reshaping of Ontario's Schools*. Toronto: University of Toronto Press, 1999.

Giroux, Henry. *Schooling and the struggle for public life*. Minneapolis: University of Minnesota Press, 1988.

Gitlin, Todd. *The 1960s: Years of Hope, Days of Rage*. Toronto, New York: Bantam Books, 1987.

The Globe and Mail, "Parents' Group Seeks New Kind of Education". September 24, 1971.

Golden, Mark. "alpha-bits". *Community Schools* (April 1973). The Community Schools Workshop of Toronto.

Grant, Agnes. *No End of Grief: Indian Residential Schools in Canada*. Winnipeg, Canada: Pemmican Publications Inc., 1996.

Graubard, Allen. *Free the Children: Radical Reform and the Free School Movement.* New York: Pantheon Books, Random House, 1972.

Gray, Peter. "Children Educate Themselves IV: Lessons from Sudbury Valley". *Psychology Today* (online), August 13, 2008. Retrieved February 16, 2021, from https://www.psychologytoday.com/ca/blog/freedom-learn/200808/children-educate-themselves-iv-lessons-sudbury-valley/

Gray, Peter. "The decline of play and the rise of psychopathology in children and adolescents". *American Journal of Play*, Vol. 3 No. 4, Spring 2011: 443-463. Retrieved November 28, 2011, from http://www.journalofplay.org/sites/www.journalofplay.org/files/pdf-articles/3-4-article-gray-decline-of-play.pdf/

Gray, Peter. "The special value of children's age-mixed play". *American Journal of Play*, Spring 2011: 500-522. Retrieved November 28, 2011, from http://www.journalofplay.org/sites/www.journalofplay.org/files/pdf-articles/3-4-article-gray-age-mixed-play.pdf/

Gray, Peter. "Kids Learn Math Easily When They Control Their Own Learning". *Psychology Today* (online), April 15, 2010: 4. Retrieved February 17, 2013, from http://www.psychologytoday.com/blog/freedom-learn/201004/kids-learn-math-easily-when-they-control-their-own-learning?page=4/

Greenberg, Daniel. *Free at last: the Sudbury Valley School.* Framingham, Mass: Sudbury Valley Press, 1995.

Griffith, Alison. "Texts, Tyranny and Transformation: Restructuring Ontario Education". In *The Erosion of Democracy in Education*, edited by John Portelli, and Patrick Solomon, 83-98. Calgary: Deselig Enterprises Ltd., 2001.

Hall, Mr. Justice Emmett, Lloyd Dennis et al. *Living and learning: The Report of the Provincial Committee on Aims and Objectives of Education in the Schools of Ontario.* Toronto: Ontario Department of Education, 1968. Retrieved May 26, 2009 from http://www.connexions.org/CxLibrary/Docs/CX5636-HallDennis.htm/

Hern, Matt. *Field Day: Getting Society Out of School.* Vancouver: New Star Books, 2003.

"High School Protest/Toronto". *This magazine is about schools,* Vol. 1, No. 1 (1966): 20-36.

Hill, Christopher. *Reformation to Industrial Revolution.* London: Penguin Books, 1967/1992.

Holt, John. *How Children Fail.* New York: Pitman Publishing Corporation, 1964.

Holt, John. *Freedom and Beyond.* New York: Dell Publishing Company, 1972.

Holt, John. *Instead of Education: Ways to Help People Do Things Better.* New York: E. P. Dutton, 1976.

hooks, bell. *All About Love: New Visions.* New York: HarperCollins, 2001.

hooks, bell. *Teaching Community: A Pedagogy of Hope.* New York and London: Routledge, 2003.

Illich, Ivan. *Deschooling Society*. London, New York: Marion Boyars Publishers, 1970, 2004.

Irving, R., 1989. *The Benefits Possible with an Elementary Free School Education*. Undergraduate research paper.

Johansen, Bruce E. *Debating Democracy: Native American Legacy of Freedom*. Santa Fe, N.M.: Clear Light Publishers, 1998.

Kohl, Herbert. *I Won't Learn from You: And Other Thoughts on Creative Maladjustment*. New York: The New Press, 1994.

Kohn, Alfie. *The Homework Myth: Why Our Kids Get Too Much of a Bad Thing*. New York: Da Capo books, 2006.

Kozol, Jonathan. "Schools for Survival" in *This magazine is about schools*, Vol. 5 No. 4 (Fall/Winter, 1971): 37-43.

Kozol, Jonathan. *Free Schools*. Boston: Houghton Mifflin Company, 1972.

Kozol, Jonathan. *Alternative Schools*. New York: The Continuum Publishing Company, 1982.

Kozol, Jonathan. *Savage Inequalities*. New York: Crown Publishers, 1991.

Krishnamurti, Jiddu. *Education and the Significance of Life*. New York: HarperCollins, 1953/1981.

"Lack of Teachers Threatens to Close City's 'Free' School'", (n.d.) 1973. *The Toronto Star*, n.p.

Lane, Homer. *Talks to Parents and Teachers*. London: Allen & Unwin, 1928/1969.

Lecce, Stephen and Nancy Naylor. *Guidance for Continuity of Learning*: Memo to Chairs of District School Boards, Directors of Education, School Authorities. Ontario: Ministry of Education (May 31, 2020). Accessed January 4, 2020 from https://www.principals.ca/en/who-we-are/resources/Documents/COVID-Resources/GUIDANCE-FOR-CONTINUITY-OF-LEARNING.pdf/

Levin, Malcolm and Frances Gladstone. *Working in Public Alternative Schools: Elementary*. Toronto: University of Toronto, The Ontario Institute for Studies in Education, 1982.

Levin, Malcolm. "And now for something completely different: What's 'alternative' about Toronto's alternative schools?" *Mudpie*, Vol. 5 No. 7 (September, 1984): (n.p.)

LeRoux, Andre. "ALPHA School Tries New Approach to Education". Toronto: *Seven News* (December 14, 1973): 5.

Lind, Loren. "Group Wants 4-year-olds in School All Day". Toronto: *The Globe and Mail* (May 16, 1972): 16.

Lind, Loren. "Experimental Schools: A Motherhood Issue". Toronto: *The Globe and Mail* (May 23, 1972): 5.

Lofland, John and Lyn H. Lofland. *Analyzing Social Settings: A Guide to Qualitative Observation and Analysis. (4th Edition)*. Belmont: Wadsworth/Thomson Learning, 2006.

Martell, George. "Community Control of the Schools—Toronto and New York". *This magazine is about schools*, Vol. 4 No. 3 (Summer, 1970): 7-49.

Martell, George. "Notes to the Blake St. Community Council—the Community Schools Workshop in Toronto: What it is and what it must become". *This magazine is about schools*, Vol. 5 No. 3 (Spring, 1971): pp. 74-84.

Meier, Deborah. *In Schools We Trust: Creating Communities of Learning in an Era of Testing and Standardization*. Boston: Beacon Press, 2002.

Mercogliano, Chris. *Making It Up As We Go Along: The Story of the Albany Free School*. Portsmouth, NH, USA: Heinemann, 1998.

Mercogliano, Chris. *How To Grow a School: Starting and Sustaining Schools that Work*. Oxford, New York: Oxford Village Press, 2006.

Merril, Judith & Emily Pohl-Weary. *Better To Have Loved: The Life of Judith Merril*. Toronto: Between the Lines, 2002.

Miller, J. R. *Shingwauk's Vision: A History of Native Residential Schools*. Toronto: University of Toronto Press, 1997.

Miller, Ron. *Free Schools, Free People: Education and Democracy After the 1960s*. Albany, NY: State University of New York Press, 2002.

Mintz, Jerry. *School's Over: How to Have Freedom and Democracy in Education*. New York: AERO, 2017.

Montessori, Maria. *The Child in the Family*. Translated by Nancy Rockmore Cirillo. New York: Avon Books, 1970.

Murray, Ellen. "At the Board: New School Gets Okay, But Will Others?" *Toronto Citizen* (January 13-27, 1972): 12.

Murray, Ellen. "Report from the Board: Who Makes Decisions?" *Community Schools* (April, 1972): 4-5.

Neill. A.S. *Summerhill: A Radical Approach to Child Rearing*. New York: Hart Publishing Co. Inc., 1960.

Neill. A.S. *Summerhill School: A New View of Childhood*. New York: St. Martin's Griffin, 1995.

Nelson, Fiona. "Community schools in Toronto; a sign of hope". *Canadian Forum* (October/November, 1972): 52-57.

"New School Not Ready Yet But Pupils Busy" *The Toronto Star* (September 15, 1972): n.p.

"Newsletter from the Everdale Place: a school community" *This magazine is about schools*. Vol. 1 No. 3 (1967): 76-106.

Novak, Mark W. *Living and Learning in the Free School*. Toronto: McLelland and Stewart, 1975.

O'Rourke, Debra L. *Defining and Defending a Democratic Public Education Site*. Masters thesis accepted by the Graduate Program in Education, York University, Toronto, 2009.

Ontario Ministry of Education. *Provincial Review Report Number 3: Alternative Schools and Programs in the Public System, 1986*.

Paley, Vivian Gussin. *A child's work.* Chicago: University of Chicago Press, 2004.

"Parents Ask 'Alternative' City-Wide Public School". *The Toronto Star* (November 30, 1971): n.p.

"Parents Lose 4-month Fight Over New Location of School". *The Toronto Star* (June 8, 1977): n.p.

Peck, M. Scott. *The Different Drum: Community Making and Peace.* New York: Simon & Schuster, 1987.

Pelletier, Wilfred. "Childhood in an Indian Village". In *This book is about schools,* edited by Satu Repo, 18-31. New York: Pantheon Books, Random House, 1970.

Pelletier, Wilfred. "Every time a North American Indian begins to disappear, I begin to disappear". *This magazine is about schools,* Vol. 5 No. 2 (1971): 7-22.

Placzek, Beverley R. *Record of a friendship: the correspondence between Wilhelm Reich and A. S. Neill 1936-1957.* New York: Farrar, Straus and Giroux, 1981.

"Radical Private Schools". *This magazine is about schools,* Vol. 1 No. 1. (1966): 5-19.

Ravitch, Diane. *Reign of Error.* New York: Alfred A. Knopf, 2013.

Reich, Wilhelm. *The Mass Psychology of Fascism.* New York: Pocket Books, 1976.

Reimer, Everett. *School is Dead: Alternatives in Education.* New York: Doubleday and Company, 1971.

Sahlberg, Pasi. *Finnish Lessons: What Can The World Learn from Educational Change in Finland?* New York, NY: Teachers College Press, 2011.

Sarnoff, David. "The Fabulous Future". *Fortune* Vol. LI No. 1. (January 1955). New York: Time Inc.

Saul, John Ralston. *A Fair Country: Telling Truths About Canada.* Toronto: Viking Canada, Penguin Group, 2008.

Shukyn, Beverly and Murray Shukyn. *You Can't Take a Bathtub on The Subway: A Personal History of SEED.* Montreal, Toronto: Holt, Rinehart and Winston of Canada Limited, 1973.

Shuttleworth, Dale E. *Schooling for Life: Community Education and Social Enterprise.* Toronto: University of Toronto Press, 2009.

Shuttleworth, Dale E. "How Can Alternative Education Affect the Mainstream? The Toronto Experience". *Orbit* 59 (October, 1981): 12-13

Silberman, Charles E. *Crisis in the Classroom.* New York: Random House, 1970.

Simon, Roger I., 1992. *Teaching Against the Grain: Texts For a Pedagogy of Possibility.* New York: Bergin & Garvey.

Simon, Roger I. "Now's the Time" (foreword). In *The Erosion of Democracy in Education, edited by* John P. Portelli and Patrick Solomon. Calgary: Detselig Enterprises Ltd., 2001.

Smith, C. "The Alpha School of Toronto". *Recess Magazine: A Forum for Canadian Alternative Education* No. 1 (Spring, 1986): 14-16. Comox, B. C., Canada.

Smith, Dorothy. "The Relations of Ruling: A Feminist Inquiry". *Studies in Cultures, Organizations and Societies*, Vol.2 (1996): 171-190.

Smith, Dorothy. *Writing the Social: Critique, Theory, and Investigations.* University of Toronto Press, 1999.

Snitzer, Herb. *Today Is For Children: Numbers Can Wait.* New York: The Macmillan Company, 1972.

Spring, Joel. *A Primer of Libertarian Education.* Montreal: Black Rose Books, 1998.

Spring, Joel. *Political Agendas for Education: From the Religious Right to the Green Party.* Mahwah, New Jersey: Lawrence Erlbaum & Associates, 2005.

Toronto Board of Education (TBE). *Minutes of the Toronto Board of Education*, December 16, 1971. Contains *The ALPHA Experience.*

Toronto Board of Education (TBE), February 9, 1978, "Re: General Policy for Alternative School Programs". Office of the Director of Education: (included in the *Alternative Schools 1978 Annual Reports*).

Toronto Board of Education. (TBE). *Alternative Schools 1978 Annual Reports*, May 1, 1979. Alternative and Community Programs Department, Curriculum and Program Division.

The Board of Education for the City of Toronto. *Alternative Schools, A General Policy* (November, 1982).

The Board of Education for the City of Toronto, 1987. *Issues Paper on Alternative Schools* (marked DRAFT). Included with the Notice of Meeting for the April 7, 1987 meeting of the Alternative and Community Programs Committee.

Toronto District School Board (TDSB), (n.d.). *Alternative Schools*, n. p. Retrieved March 20, 2009 from http://www.tdsb.on.ca/_site/ViewItem.asp?siteid=122&menuid=490&pageid=379

Toronto District School Board (TDSB), (n.d.). *Our Mission Statement.* Retrieved March 20, 2009 from http://www.tdsb.on.ca/_site/ViewItem.asp?siteid=171&menuid=668&pageid=534

The United Nations. *The Universal Declaration of Human Rights, 1948.* Retrieved September 19, 2008 from http://www.un.org/en/documents/udhr/

Valpy, Michael. "12-year-old Unflappable at Campaign Controls". The *Globe and Mail* (December 2, 1972): n.p.

Weatherford, Jack. *Indian Givers: How Native Americans Transformed the World.* New York: Three Rivers Press, 1988/2010.

Wien, Carol Anne and Curt Dudley-Marling. "Limited vision: The Ontario Curriculum and Outcomes-based Learning". In *The Erosion of Democracy in Education*, edited by John P. Portelli and Patrick Solomon, 99-116. Calgary, AB Canada: Detselig Enterprises Ltd., 2001.

Wills, Molly. "Toronto's Alternative Schools". *School Progress* 42 (4) (April, 1973): 30-33, 55.

Yanes, Samuel S., ed. *The no more gym shorts, build-it-yourself, self-discovery, free school talkin' blues*. New York: Harper and Row Publishers Inc. Toronto: Fitzhenry & Whiteside Ltd., 1972.

Zinn, Howard. *A People's History of the United States*. New York: HarperCollins, 1995.

NOTES

ABOUT THE AUTHOR

[1] Kristan Accles Morrison, *Free School Teaching: A Journey into Radical Progressive Education* (State University of New York Press, 2007), vii.

[2] John Taylor Gatto, *Dumbing Us Down: The Hidden Curriculum of Compulsory Schooling* (New Society Publishers, 1992, 2005), 1-10

INTRODUCTION: CHALLENGING MASS COERCIVE EDUCATION

[3] Peter Gray, "The Decline of Play and the Rise of Psychopathology in Children and Adolescents", *American Journal of Play*, Vol. 3 No. 4 (Spring 2011): 458. Retrieved November 28, 2011, from <http://www.journalofplay.org/sites/www.journalofplay.org/files/pdf-articles/3-4-article-gray-decline-of-play.pdf

[4] John Dewey, *The School and Society* (Chicago: University of Chicago Press, 1907), 51.

[5] Ivan Illich, *Deschooling Society* (London, New York: Marion Boyars Publishers, 1970, 2004), 1.

[6] Gatto, *Dumbing Us Down,* 1 - 10.

[7] Maria Montessori, *The child in the family,* trans. Nancy Rockmore Cirillo. (New York: Avon Books, 1970), 13, 14-15.

[8] Dorothy D. Smith, "The Relations of Ruling: A Feminist Inquiry", *Studies in Cultures, Organizations and Societies*, Vol.2, (1996): 171-190.

[9] Carolyn Edwards, Leila Gandini, George Forman, ed. *The Hundred Languages of Children: The Reggio Emelia Approach—Advanced Reflections* (Santa Barbara: Praeger, ABC/CLIO, 1998), 36.

[10] bell hooks, *Teaching Community: A Pedagogy of Hope* (New York and London: Routledge, 2003), xiv.

[11] A.S. Neill, *Summerhill: A Radical Approach to Child Rearing* (New York: Hart Publishing Co. Inc., 1960), 4.

[12] Mario D. Fantini, *Alternative Education: A Source Book for Parents, Teachers and Administrators* (New York: Doubleday & Company, Inc., 1976), 15.

[13] Dale Shuttleworth, "How Can Alternative Education Affect the Mainstream? — The Toronto Experience", *Orbit* 59 (October, 1981), 12-13.

1: A DEMOCRATIC SCHOOL

[14] A.S. Neill, *Summerhill School: A New View of Childhood* (New York: St. Martin's Griffin, 1995), xix.

[15] Emily Chan, "Plenty Love: Sharing Black History Through Student Inquiry and Community Collaboration", *ETFO Voice* (Fall 2018) from https://etfovoice.ca/feature/plenty-love-sharing-black-history-through-student-inquiry-and-community-collaboration/

[16] Crawford (Crocky) Teasdale, interview by Ariel Fielding, *ALPHA Alternative School* 1972/2012, 2013.
Colour Photos by Michael Barker, Text and Interviews by Ariel Fielding, https://michaelbarker.ca/portfolio/crawford-crocky-teasdale/

[17] Lucy Falkner, *ALPHA Alternative School 1972/2012, 2013*. Colour Photos by Michael Barker, Text and Interviews by Ariel Fielding, https://michaelbarker.ca/portfolio/lucy-falkner/

2: EDUCATING DEMOCRATICALLY

[18] Jerry Mintz, *School's Over: How to Have Freedom and Democracy in Education.* (New York: AERO, 2017), 27.

[19] Jerry Mintz, *School's Over*, 34-35.

[20] Wilfred Pelletier, (1971). "Every Time a North American Indian begins to Disappear, I Begin to Disappear" *This magazine is about schools*, Vol. 5 No. 2 (1971): 10.

[21] Pelletier, "Every Time", 11.

[22] Ron Miller, *Free Schools, Free People: Education and Democracy After the 1960s* (Albany, NY: State University of New York Press, 2002), viii.

[23] Wilfred Pelletier, "Childhood in an Indian Village", in *This book is about schools*, ed. Satu Repo (New York: Pantheon Books, Random House, 1970), 21.

[24] Satu Repo, ed. *This Book is About Schools* (New York: Pantheon Books, Random House, 1970), 456

[25] Sharon Berg, with Elder Pauline Shirt , *The Name Unspoken: Wandering Spirit Survival School* (Toronto: Big Pond Rumours Press, 2019) 192.

[26] Sharon Berg with Elder Pauline Shirt, *The Name Unspoken*, 12.

[27] John Dewey, *The School and Society and the Child and the Curriculum* (Chicago: The University of Chicago Press, 1900, 1902/1990), 7.

[28] Dewey, *The School and Society*, 9.

[29] Dewey, *The School and Society*, 32.

[30] Dewey, *The School and Society*, Introduction by Philip W. Jackson, xxxiii.

[31] Dewey, *The School and Society*, 18-19.

[32] Dewey, The School and Society, 13.

[33] Dewey, The School and Society, 14.

[34] Noam Chomsky, *World Orders Old and New* (New York: Columbia University Press, 1996), 86-87.

[35] Beverley R. Placzek, *Record of a Friendship: The Correspondence Between Wilhelm Reich and A.S. Neill 1936-1957* (New York: Farrar, Straus and Giroux, Inc., 1981), vii.

[36] A.S. Neill, *Summerhill School: A New View of Childhood* (New York: St. Martin's Griffin, 1995), 4.

[37] A.S. Neill, *Summerhill School: A New View of Childhood*, xviii.

[38] A.S. Neill, *Summerhill*, 13.

[39] Placzek, *Record of a Friendship*, 19.

[40] Dewey, J. *Liberalism and Social Action* (New York: Capricorn Books, G.P. Putnam's Sons 1935/1963), 2.

[41] Placzek, *Record of a Friendship*, 57.

[42] Placzek, *Record of a Friendship*, 45.

[43] "Summerhill: The Early Days", www.summerhillschool.co.uk.

[44] "Radical Private Schools", *This magazine is about schools*, Vol. 1 No. 1, (1966): 8-9.

[45] Allen Graubard, *Free the Children: Radical Reform and the Free School Movement* (New York: Pantheon Books, Random House, 1972), 14.

[46] Herb Snitzer, *Today is for Children: Numbers Can Wait*, (New York: The Macmillan Company, 1972), 16.

[47] A. S. Neale, "Introduction", *Today is for Children: Numbers Can Wait*, Herb Snitzer, (New York: The Macmillan Company, 1972), 15.

[48] Placzek, *Record of a Friendship*, 139.

[49] A.S. Neill, *Summerhill*, 45-46.

[50] "Summerhill: The Early Days", www.summerhillschool.co.uk.

[51] Graubard, *Free the Children* , 7.

[52] Charles E. Silberman, *Crisis in the Classroom* (New York: Random House, 1970), 9

[53] Robert Bogdan, & Sari Knopp Biklen, *Qualitative Research for Education: An Introduction to Theory and Methods* (Boston: Allyn & Bacon, 1992), 19.

[54] Graubard, *Free the Children*, 4.

[55] Graubard, *Free the Children*, 16.

[56] Gatto, *Dumbing Us Down* , xxiii.

[57] Carl E. James and Julia A Samaroo, "Alternative Schooling and Black Students: Opportunities, Challenges and Limitations", in *Alternative Schooling and Student Engagement: Canadian Stories of Democracy Within Bureaucracy*, ed. Nina Bascia, Esther Sokolov Fine and Malcolm Levin (Switzerland: Palgrave MacMillan, 2017), 42.

[58] James and Samaroo, "Alternative Schooling and Black Students", 45.

3: THE FREE SCHOOL MOVEMENT

[59] Silvia Ashton-Warner, *Teacher (*London: Secker and Warburg, 1963), 29-30.

[60] Paul Avrich, *The Modern School Movement: Anarchism and Education in the United States* (Edinburgh, Oakland and West Virginia: AK Press, 2006), iii.

[61] Samuel S. Yanes, ed., *The no more gym shorts, build-it-yourself, self-discovery, free school talkin' blues* (New York: Harper and Row Publishers Inc. Toronto: Fitzhenry & Whiteside Ltd., 1972), 3.

[62] Todd Gitlin, *The 1960s: Years of Hope, Days of Rage* (Toronto, New York: Bantam Books, 1987), 12.

[63] David D. Sarnoff, "The fabulous future", *Fortune*, Vol. LI No. 1 (January 1955): 114-115.

[64] Justice Emmett M. Hall, Lloyd A. Dennis, et al, *Living and Learning: The Report of the Provincial Committee on Aims and Objectives of Education in the Schools of Ontario* (Toronto: Ontario Department of Education, 1968), para. 1. Retrieved May 26, 2009 from http://www.connexions.org/CxLibrary/Docs/CX5636-HallDennis.htm/

[65] Charles E. Silberman, *Crisis in the Classroom*, 19.

[66] Richard E. Bull, R.E., "Philosophy", *Summerhill USA* (Penguin Educational Special, 1971).

[67] Snitzer, *Today is for Children*, 13.

[68] A.S. Neill, *Summerhill*, 17.

[69] Homer Lane, T*alks to Parents and Teachers* (London: Allen & Unwin, 1928/1969), 2-3.

[70] George Dennison, *The Lives of Children* (New York: Vintage Books, Random House, 1970), 30.

[71] Dennison, *The Lives of Children*, 7.

[72] Dennison, The Lives of Children, 4.

[73] Dennison, *The Lives of Children*, 33.

[74] Jonathan Kozol, *Free Schools* (Boston: Houghton Mifflin Company, 1972), 126.

[75] Dennison, *The Lives of Children*, 33.

[76] Kozol, *Free Schools*, 119.

[77] Kozol, *Free Schools*, 1.

[78] Kozol, *Free Schools*, 4.

[79] Kozol, *Free Schools*, 5,6.

[80] Kozol, *Free Schools*, 7, 16.

[81] Kozol, *Free Schools*, 7, 12.

[82] Kozol, *Free Schools*, 9.

[83] Placzek, *Record of a Friendship*, 57.

[84] Kozol, *Free Schools*, 9.

[85] Ivan Illich, *Deschooling Society*, 36.

[86] Richard E. Bull, R.E., *Summerhill USA*.

[87] Kozol, *Free Schools*, 143.

[88] Graubard, *Free the Children, ix.*

[89] Graubard, *Free the Children*, 40-41.

[90] Graubard, *Free the Children*, 41.

4: TORONTO: A PLACE TO MAKE A DIFFERENCE

[91] Kozol, *Free Schools*, 21, 22.

[92] Kozol, *Free Schools*, 126.

[93] Robert Davis, "Editorial", *This magazine is about schools*, Vol. 1, No. 1, (1966): 1-2.

[94] *This magazine is about schools*, Vol. 1, No. 1, 6.

[95] *This magazine is about schools*, Vol. 1, No. 1, 2.

[96] *This magazine is about schools*, Vol. 1, No. 2, 4

[97] Satu Repo (Ed), *This book is about schools*. New York: Pantheon Books (Random House) (1970), 455-456.

[98] This magazine is about schools, Vol. 2, No. 3, 6.

[99] John Barber, "Starting a free school in Ontario", *This magazine is about schools*, Vol. 3, No. 3, "staple-in" leaflet (Summer, 1969): n.p.

[100] *The Free School Handbook* (1972), 18.

[101] *The Free School Handbook* (1972), 19.

[102] *The Free School Handbook* (1972), 21, 22.

[103] *The Free School Handbook* (1972), 9.

[104] *The Free School Handbook* (1972), 11.

[105] *The Free School Handbook* (1972), 12.

[106] *The Free School Handbook* (1972), 10.

[107] *The Free School Handbook* (1972), 20.

[108] *The Free School Handbook* (1972), 20.

[109] *The Free School Handbook* (1972), 21.

[110] *The Free School Handbook* (1972), 23.

[111] *The Free School Handbook* (1972), 24-25.

[112] *The Free School Handbook* (1972), 25.

[113] Kozol, *Free Schools*, 38.

[114] Loren Lind, "Experimental Schools: A Motherhood Issue", *The Globe and Mail* (May 23, 1972,): 5.

[115] George Martell. "Notes to the Blake St. Community Council—The Community Schools Workshop in Toronto: What It is and What it Must Become", *This magazine is about schools*, Vol. 5 No. 3, (Spring, 1971): 75.

[116] George Martell, "Community control of the schools—Toronto and New York", *This magazine is about schools*, Vol. 4 No. 3 (Summer, 1970): 48.

[117] Martell, "Community control of the schools", 46.

[118] Hall, Dennis et al., 1968, *The Order-in-Council*, para. 4.

[119] Hall, Dennis et al. 1968, *Learning and the School*, para. 1.

[120] Hall, Dennis et al., 1968, *Areas of Emphasis for the Learning Experience*, para. 16.

[121] Hall, Dennis et al., 1968, *Areas of Emphasis for the Learning Experience*, para. 13.

[122] Hall, Dennis et al., 1968, *Areas of Emphasis for the Learning Experience*, para. 5.

[123] Hall, Dennis et al., 1968, *Areas of Emphasis for the Learning Experience*, para. 3.

[124] Hall, Dennis et al., 1968, *The Truth Shall Make You Free*, para. 27,29.

[125] Pasi Sahlberg, *Finnish Lessons: What Can the World Learn from Educational Change in Finland?* (New York, NY: Teachers College Press, 2011), 3.

5: ALTERNATIVES IN THE PUBLIC SYSTEM

[126] Elizabeth Durno & Leslie Mang, *Public Alternative Schools in Metro Toronto* (Toronto: Learnx Press, n.d., circa 1987), 9.

[127] S. Clarke, & M. Linton, "A better school for your money", *Toronto Life*, (August, 1975): 24.

[128] Loren Lind, "Experimental Schools: A Motherhood Issue", 24.

[129] Beverly and Murray Shukyn, *You Can't Take a Bathtub on The Subway: A Personal History of SEED.* (Montreal, Toronto: Holt, Rinehart and Winston of Canada Limited, 1973), 1.

[130] Shukyn, *You Can't Take a Bathtub on The Subway*, 2-3.

[131] Shukyn, *You Can't Take a Bathtub on The Subway*, 12-16.

[132] Shukyn, *You Can't Take a Bathtub on The Subway*, 47.

[133] Fiona Nelson, "Community Schools in Toronto; A Sign of Hope", *Canadian Forum*, (October/November, 1972): 55.

[134] Shukyn, *You Can't Take a Bathtub on The Subway*, 49.

[135] Ellen Murray, "Report from the Board: Who Makes Decisions?" *Community Schools* (April, 1972): 4-5.

[136] Murray, "Who Makes Decisions?", 4.

[137] Murray, "Who Makes Decisions?", 4.

[138] Murray, "Who Makes Decisions?", 4.

[139] Murray, "Who Makes Decisions?", 4.

[140] Shukyn, *You Can't Take a Bathtub on The Subway*, 127.

[141] Shukyn, *You Can't Take a Bathtub on The Subway*, 127.

[142] Murray, "Who Makes Decisions?", 4.

[143] Murray, "Who Makes Decisions?", 4.

[144] Loren Lind, "Experimental Schools: A Motherhood Issue", 5.

[145] Shukyn, *You Can't Take a Bathtub on The Subway*, 127.

[146] Shukyn, *You Can't Take a Bathtub on The Subway*, 131-132.

[147] Shukyn, *You Can't Take a Bathtub on The Subway*, 134.

[148] Shukyn, *You Can't Take a Bathtub on The Subway*, 131.

[149] Loren Lind, "Experimental Schools: A Motherhood Issue", 5.

[150] Shukyn, *You Can't Take a Bathtub on The Subway*, 132.

[151] Shukyn, *You Can't Take a Bathtub on The Subway*, 134.

[152] Shukyn, *You Can't Take a Bathtub on The Subway*, 131.

[153] Graubard, *Free the Children*, ix, x.

[154] Loren Lind, "Experimental Schools: A Motherhood Issue", 5.

6: STARTING ALPHA

[155] Mark Golden, "alpha-bits", *Community Schools*, The Community Schools Workshop of Toronto (April, 1973): 21-24.

[156] Golden, "alpha-bits", 22

[157] "Parents Ask 'Alternative' City-Wide Public School", *The Toronto Star*, (November 30, 1971).

[158] Golden, "alpha-bits", 21.

[159] Dale E. Shuttleworth, *Schooling for Life: Community Education and Social Enterprise* (Toronto: University of Toronto Press, 2009), x.

[160] Shuttleworth, *Schooling for Life,* 154-5.

[161] Toronto Board of Education (TBE) (1971). *Minutes of the Toronto Board of Education.* December 16, 1971. Contains *The ALPHA Experience, 941.*

[162] Toronto Board of Education (TBE) *The ALPHA Experience*, 941-945.

[163] Ron Miller, *Free Schools, Free People: Education and Democracy After the 1960s* (Albany, NY: State University of New York Press, 2002), 130.

[164] Ellen Murray, "At the Board: New School Gets Okay, But Will Others?", *Toronto Citizen* (January 13-27, 1972): 12.

[165] Loren Lind, "Experimental Schools: A Motherhood Issue", 5.

[166] Toronto Board of Education (TBE) *The ALPHA Experience*, 933.

[167] Golden, "alpha-bits", 22.

[168] Loren Lind, "Experimental Schools: A Motherhood Issue", 5.

[169] Toronto Board of Education (TBE) *The ALPHA Experience*, 935.

[170] Murray, "At the Board: New School Gets Okay", 12.

[171] Toronto Board of Education (TBE) *The ALPHA Experience*, 933.

[172] Murray, "At the Board: New School Gets Okay", 12.

[173] Murray, "At the Board: New School Gets Okay", 12.

[174] Murray, "At the Board: New School Gets Okay", 12.

[175] Fantini, *Alternative Education*, 117.

[176] Nelson, Nelson, "Community Schools in Toronto", 54.

[177] Nelson, Nelson, "Community Schools in Toronto", 54.

[178] Toronto Board of Education (TBE) *The ALPHA Experience*, 945.

[179] Loren Lind, "Experimental Schools: A Motherhood Issue", 5.

[180] Loren Lind, "Experimental Schools: A Motherhood Issue", 5.

[181] Toronto Board of Education, *Minutes,* April 13, 1972, 266

[182] Loren Lind, "Experimental Schools: A Motherhood Issue", 5.

7: CHAOS

[183] "New School Not Ready Yet But Pupils Busy", *The Toronto Star*, (September 15, 1972): n.p.

[184] Clarke & Linton, "A Better School for Your Money", 24.

[185] Michael Valpy, "12-year-old Unflappable at Campaign Controls", The *Globe and Mail* (1972, December 2): n.p.

[186] Toronto Board of Education (TBE) *The ALPHA Experience*, 941.

[187] Graubard, *Free the Children*, 48

[188] Shuttleworth, *Schooling for Life,* 156.

[189] Mark W. Novak, *Living and Learning in the Free School* (Toronto: McLelland and Stewart, 1975), 45.

[190] Novak, *Living and Learning*, 44, 45.

[191] Novak, *Living and Learning*, 45.

[192] The ALPHA Community, 1973, "January Committee Recommendations".

[193] Durno & Mang, *Public Alternative Schools in Metro Toronto*, 35.

[194] Chris Mercogliano, *How to Grow a School: Starting and Sustaining Schools that Work* (Oxford, New York: Oxford Village Press, 2006), 78.

[195] bell hooks, *All About Love: New Visions.* (New York: HarperCollins Publishers Inc., 2001), 4.

[196] Peck, *The Different Drum*, 88.

[197] Ellen Murray, "At the Board: New School Gets Okay, But Will Others?", *Toronto Citizen* (1972, January 13-27): 12.

[198] Golden, "alpha-bits", 22.

[199] Golden, "alpha-bits", 21.

[200] Golden, "alpha-bits", 22.

[201] The ALPHA Community, *A Plan for the ALPHA School*, 1973, 2.

[202] Murray, "Who Makes Decisions?", 4.

[203] M. Scott Peck, *The Different Drum: Community Making and Peace* (New York: Simon & Schuster, 1987), 86.

[204] Peck, *The Different Drum*, 88.

[205] Peck, *The Different Drum*, 91.

[206] Peck, *The Different Drum*, 93.

[207] Peck, *The Different Drum*, 95, 97.

[208] The ALPHA Community, *Minutes of General Meeting, March 27, 1973.*

[209] Chris Mercogliano, *Making It Up As We Go Along: The Story of the Albany Free School* (Portsmouth, NH, USA: Heinemann, 1998), 6.

[210] Terence E. Deal, *An Organizational Explanation of The Failure of Alternative Schools.* (Stanford, CA: Stanford Center for Research and Development in Teaching, 1975), 15.

[211] Deal, *An Organizational Explanation*, 2.

[212] Deal, *An Organizational Explanation*, 2.

[213] Deal, *An Organizational Explanation*, 9.

[214] Deal, *An Organizational Explanation*, 10.

[215] Molly Wills, "Toronto's Alternative Schools", *School Progress* 42 (4), (April, 1973): 33.

[216] Golden, "alpha-bits", 22.

[217] "Free School Averts Closing with Hiring of Two Teachers", *The Toronto Star*, (August 28, 1973): n.p.

8: NO CAPTIVE AUDIENCE

[218] The ALPHA Community, *A Brief to the Policy Committee* (1973, April 3).

[219] "Interviews with Alpha Kids", *Alpha Centauri*, (Sept/Oct, 1973).

[220] Dennison, *The Lives of Children*, 4.

[221] Ashton-Warner, *Teacher, 45.*

[222] Dennison, *The Lives of Children*, 21.

[223] A.S. Neill, *Summerhill*, 258.

[224] Golden, "alpha-bits", 21.

[225] *Announcements*, October 2, 1973.

[226] R. Irving, *The Benefits Possible with an Elementary Free School Education.* (Undergraduate research paper, 1989), x.

[227] A.S. Neill, *Summerhill*, 55.

[228] Edwards, Gandini and Forman, *The Hundred Languages of Children,* 64.

[229] Ann Swidler, *Organization Without Authority: A Dilemma of Social Control in Free Schools* (Cambridge, MA: Harvard University Press, 1979), 20.

[230] A.S. Neill, *Summerhill*, 18.

[231] The ALPHA Community, *The ALPHA Parent Handbook*, circa 1986, 9.

[232] Dennison, *The Lives of Children*, 24, 25.

[233] Mercogliano, *Making It Up As We Go Along, 6-7.*

[234] A.S. Neill, *Summerhill*, 55.

[235] Jerry Mintz, *School's Over*, 7.

[236] Snitzer, *Today is for Children*, 14-15.

9: LIVING AND LEARNING

[237] Jerry Mintz, *School's Over*, 2.

[238] Peter Gray, "Social Play and the Genesis of Democracy", Psychology Today, Blog March 4, 2009. https://www.psychologytoday.com/ca/blog/freedom-learn/200903/social-play-and-the-genesis-democracy/

[239] Matt Hern, *Field Day: Getting Society Out of School* (Vancouver: New Star Books, 2003), 8.

[240] Matt Hern, *Field Day,* 60.

[241] Dennison, *The Lives of Children*, 6.

[242] Dennison, *The Lives of Children*, 9.

[243] Dewey, Democracy and Education, 38.

[244] Avrich, *The Modern School Movement*, 10.

[245] Paolo Freire, *Pedagogy of the Oppressed (*New York: Continuum, 1970/2004), 72.

[246] Jerry Mintz, *School's Over*, 3.

[247] A.S. Neill, *Summerhill*, 116.

[248] Toronto Board of Education (TBE), *The ALPHA Experience*, 941-942.

[249] C. Smith, "The ALPHA School of Toronto", *Recess Magazine* (1986): 14.

[250] Vivian Gussin Paley, *A Child's Work* (Chicago: University of Chicago Press, 2004), 7.

[251] A.S. Neill, *Summerhill*, 62-64.

[252] Peter Gray, "Social Play".

[253] Peter Gray, "Social Play".

[254] Holt, *Freedom and Beyond*, 85.

[255] Clarke & Linton, "A Better School for Your Money", 24.

[256] bell hooks, *Teaching Community*, 45.

[257] A.S. Neill, *Summerhill*, 50.

[258] Gatto, *Dumbing Us Down,* 12.

[259] Daniel Greenberg, *Free at last: the Sudbury Valley School* (Framingham, Mass: Sudbury Valley Press, 1995), 17.

[260] Kozol, *Free Schools*, 39-40.

[261] Ivan Illich, *Deschooling Society, 13.*

[262] Kozol, *Free Schools*, 2-3.

[263] Kozol, *Free Schools*, 30-31.

[264] Kozol, *Free Schools*, 50.

[265] Ontario Ministry of Education, *Provincial Review Report Number 3: Alternative Schools and Programs in the Public System,* 1986.

[266] Fantini, *Alternative Education*, 117.

[267] The ALPHA Community, *A Brief to the Policy Committee.*

[268] Deborah Meier, *In Schools We Trust: Creating Communities of Learning in an Era of Testing and Standardization* (Boston: Beacon Press, 2002), 3, 4.

[269] Dennison, *The Lives of Children*, 7-8.

[270] Jerry Mintz, *School's Over*, 42.

[271] The Board of Education for the City of Toronto, *Alternative Schools, A General Policy* (November, 1982), 7

[272] Dennison, *The Lives of Children*, 16.

[273] A. S. Neill, *Summerhill School: A New View of Childhood*, 6.

[274] Holt, *Freedom and Beyond*, 77.

[275] Sharon Berg, Elder Pauline Shirt, *The Name Unspoken*, 335.

[276] Sharon Berg, Elder Pauline Shirt, *The Name Unspoken*, 28.

10: LOCATION, LOCATION, LOCATION

[277] Mercogliano, *Making It Up As We Go Along*, 17.

[278] The ALPHA Community, 1977, *Not to be Removed*, 5

[279] Trustee F.P. Nagle, letter, May 25, 1977, 3.

[280] The ALPHA Community, May 2, 1977, 4.

[281] "Parents Lose 4-month Fight Over New Location of School", *The Toronto Star* (June 8, 1977): n.p.

[282] Toronto Board of Education, *Alternative Schools 1978 Annual Reports* (Alternative and Community Programs Department, Curriculum and Program Division, May 1, 1979), 3.

[283] Toronto Board of Education, *Alternative Schools 1978 Annual Reports*, 4.

[284] Toronto Board of Education, *Alternative Schools 1978 Annual Reports*, 5.

[285] Toronto Board of Education, *Alternative Schools 1978 Annual Reports*, 3.

[286] Toronto Board of Education, *Alternative Schools 1978 Annual Reports*, n.p.

11: STRUCTURING FREEDOM

[287] Toronto Board of Education, *Alternative Schools 1978 Annual Reports*, 52.

[288] Toronto Board of Education, *Alternative Schools 1978 Annual Reports*, 51.

[289] Toronto Board of Education, *Alternative Schools 1978 Annual Reports*, 55-56.

[290] Fritz, *My Encounters with Alternatives (*1975), in Toronto Board of Education, *Alternative Schools 1978 Annual Reports*, 51.

[291] The ALPHA Community, *Brief for the Management Committee*, 1971, 6.

[292] Shuttleworth, "How Can Alternative Education Affect the Mainstream?", 12.

[293] Jonathan Kozol, *Alternative Schools* (New York: The Continuum Publishing Company, 1982), 1.

[294] Toronto Board of Education, *Alternative Schools 1978 Annual Reports*, n.p.

[295] The ALPHA Community, June 1, 1978.

[296] The ALPHA Community, *ALPHA General Meeting*, 1981, 2.

[297] The ALPHA Community, n.d. circa 1983.

[298] Mercogliano, *Making It Up As We Go Along*, 6.

[299] Peck, *The Different Drum*, 93.

[300] Peck, *The Different Drum*, 72.

[301] A. Neave Brayshaw, *The Quakers* (London: Friends Home Service Committee, 1921/1969), 168.

[302] Brayshaw, *The Quakers*, 169.

[303] Pelletier, "Every Time", 12.

12: A BLESSED TIME

[304] *Toronto Star*, June 8, 1977.

[305] The ALPHA Community, *Annual Report 1982-83*, 1.

[306] The ALPHA Community, *The ALPHA Parent Handbook* (1988)*, 1.*

[307] *The ALPHA Parent Handbook, 1-2.*

[308] *The ALPHA Parent Handbook, 2.*

[309] *The ALPHA Parent Handbook, 3.*

[310] *The ALPHA Parent Handbook, 9.*

[311] *The ALPHA Parent Handbook, 3.*

[312] *The ALPHA Parent Handbook, 9.*

[313] *The ALPHA Parent Handbook, 4.*

[314] *The ALPHA Parent Handbook, 6.*

[315] *The ALPHA Parent Handbook, 9*.

[316] The ALPHA Parent Handbook, 15.

[317] The *ALPHA Parent Handbook*, 27.

13: WE WON'T LEARN FROM YOU

[318] Allen Graubard, "The Free School Movement", *Harvard Educational Review*, Vol 42. No. 8 (1972): 364-368.

[319] Board of Education, *Alternative Schools, A General Policy*, 9.

[320] Board of Education, *Alternative Schools, A General Policy*, 17.

[321] Board of Education, *Alternative Schools, A General Policy*, 21, 23.

[322] Board of Education, *Alternative Schools, A General Policy*, 9.

[323] Board of Education, *Alternative Schools, A General Policy*, 21.

[324] Board of Education, *Alternative Schools, A General Policy*, 17.

[325] Board of Education, *Alternative Schools, A General Policy*, 23.

[326] Board of Education, *Alternative Schools, A General Policy*, 18.

[327] Board of Education, *Alternative Schools, A General Policy*, 25.

[328] Malcolm Levin, "And Now for Something Completely Different: What's 'Alternative' About Toronto's Alternative Schools?", *Mudpie*, Vol. 5 No. 7 (September, 1984): n.p.

[329] Michael Apple, *Official Knowledge: Democratic Education in a Conservative Age*. (New York: Routledge, 1993), p. 3.

[330] Levin, "Something Completely Different".

[331] Ontario Ministry of Education, *Provincial Review Report Number 3: Alternative Schools and Programs in the Public System* (1986): 2.

[332] Matt Hern, *Field Day*, 61.

[333] Board of Education for the City of Toronto, *Alternative Schools, A General Policy*, 9.

[334] Ontario Ministry of Education, *Provincial Review Report Number 3*, 25.

[335] Board of Education for the City of Toronto, *Alternative Schools, A General Policy*, 9.

[336] Malcolm Levin & Frances Gladstone, *Working in public alternative schools: elementary* (Toronto: University of Toronto, The Ontario Institute for Studies in Education, 1982), 55.

[337] Board of Education, *Alternative Schools, A General Policy*, 9.

[338] Ontario Ministry of Education, *Provincial Review Report Number 3*, 14.

[339] Ontario Ministry of Education, *Provincial Review Report Number 3*, 3.

[340] The Board of Education for the City of Toronto, 1987, *Issues Paper on Alternative Schools* (marked DRAFT). Included with the Notice of Meeting for the April 7, 1987 meeting of the Alternative and Community Programs Committee, 1

[341] Board of Education, *Issues Paper on Alternative Schools*, 3-4.

[342] Levin, "Something Completely Different".

[343] Toronto District School Board, *Our Mission Statement*, n.p.

[344] Everett Reimer, *School Is Dead: Alternatives in Education* (New York: Doubleday and Company, 1971), 13, 14.

[345] Dorothy Smith, 1996, 172.

[346] Dale Shuttleworth, *Schooling for Life: Community Education and Social Enterprise* (Toronto: University of Toronto Press, 2009), 198-199.

[347] Shuttleworth (2009), *Schooling for Life*, 268-270.

14: DEFENDING ALPHA

[348] Snitzer, *Today is for Children*, 177.

[349] Alternative Schools Advisory Council, April 2, 1992.

[350] Board of Education, *Alternative Schools, A General Policy*, 6.

[351] The ALPHA Community, June 27, 1988, 2-3.

[352] R. D. Gidney, *From Hope to Harris: The Reshaping of Ontario's Schools.* (Toronto: University of Toronto Press, 1999), 205-206.

[353] A.S. Neill, Summerhill, 53.

[354] Graubard, *Free the Children*, 112.

15: THE CONSERVATIVE RESTORATION

[355] Howard Zinn, *A People's History of the United States (*New York: HarperCollins, 1995), 526, 528

[356] Tad Burness, *Monstrous American car spotters guide, 1920-1980 (*Osceola, WI, USA: Motorbooks International, 1986), 113.

[357] Diane Ravitch, *Reign of Error* (New York: Alfred A. Knopf, 2013), 10.

[358] R. D. Gidney, *From Hope to Harris,* 172.

[359] R. D. Gidney, *From Hope to Harris*, 173.

[360] Jonathan Kozol, *Savage inequalities* (New York: Crown Publishers Inc., 1991), 4.

[361] Maude Barlow and Heather-Jane Robertson, *Class warfare: the assault on Canada's schools* (Toronto: Key Porter Books Limited, 1994), viii.

[362] Barlow & Robertson, *Class Warfare*, 11.

[363] Michael Apple, *Official Knowledge*, 33.

[364] Christopher Hill, *Reformation to Industrial Revolution* (London: Penguin Books, 1967/1992), 140.

[365] R. D. Gidney, *From Hope to Harris*, 217-218.

[366] R. D. Gidney, *From Hope to Harris*, 223.

[367] Carol Anne Wien and Curt Dudley-Marling, "Limited vision: The Ontario Curriculum and outcomes-based learning", in *The erosion of democracy in education*, ed. John Portelli, and Patrick Solomon, (Calgary, Detselig Enterprises Ltd., 2001), 100-101.

[368] R. D. Gidney, *From Hope to Harris*, 223.

[369] R. D. Gidney, *From Hope to Harris*, 233.

[370] Diane Ravitch, *Reign of Error*, 11.

[371] Henry Giroux, *Schooling and the struggle for public life* (Minneapolis: University of Minnesota Press, 1988), 74.

[372] Erich Fromm, *Escape from freedom* (New York: Avon Books, 1965), xii.

[373] Wilhelm Reich, *The Mass Psychology of Fascism* (New York: Pocket Books, 1970), 207.

[374] Barlow & Robertson, *Class Warfare*, 20.

[375] Barlow & Robertson, *Class Warfare*, 11.

[376] Canadian Broadcasting Corporation, 1998, n.p.

[377] Ruth Cohen, ed., *Alien Invasion: How the Tories mismanaged Ontario* (Toronto: Insomniac Press, 2001), 142, 148.

[378] R. D. Gidney, *From Hope to Harris*, 236.

[379] R. D. Gidney, *From Hope to Harris*, 234.

[380] Board of Education, *Alternative Schools, A General Policy*, 2.

[381] Gatto, *Dumbing Us Down*, xxiii.

[382] Gatto, *Dumbing Us Down*, 15.

[383] Barlow & Robertson, *Class Warfare*, 41.

[384] Alison Griffith, "Texts, tyranny and transformation: Restructuring Ontario education", in *The erosion of democracy in education*, ed. John Portelli, and Patrick Solomon, (Calgary, Detselig Enterprises Ltd., 2001), 85.

[385] Wien & Dudley-Marling, "Limited vision", 236-237.

[386] Joel Spring, *Political agendas for education: from the religious right to the Green Party* (Mahwah, New Jersey: Lawrence Erlbaum & Associates, Inc., 2005), 28.

[387] Dorothy Smith, "The relations of ruling: a feminist inquiry", in *Studies in Cultures, Organizations and Societies*, Vol.2 (1996): 176.

16: THE REPORT CARD FIGHT

[388] Giroux, *Schooling and the struggle for public life*, 78.

[389] Alison Griffith, "Texts, tyranny and transformation", 90.

[390] Deborah Meier (2002). *In Schools We Trust*, 18.

[391] Ivan Illich, *Deschooling Society, 12.*

[392] Hall, Dennis et al., 1968, "Areas of Emphasis for the Learning Experience", para. 17.

[393] Silvia Ashton-Warner , *Spearpoint: "Teacher" in America* (New York: Vintage Books, 1974), 32.

[394] Toronto Board of Education (TBE), *The ALPHA Experience*, 942.

[395] Malcolm Levin & Frances Gladstone, (1982). *Working in public alternative schools*, 54.

[396] Malcolm Levin & Frances Gladstone, (1982). *Working in public alternative schools*, 38, 41.

17: EQUITY AND COMMUNITY

[397] Maclean's Magazine, September 1975, 9.

[398] James and Samaroo, "Alternative Schooling and Black Students", 40.

[399] *The Globe and Mail*, "Parents' Group Seeks New Kind of Education", September 24, 1971.

[400] Golden, "alpha-bits", 22.

[401] https://michaelbarker.ca/portfolio/stefan-lynch-strassfeld/

[402] Mercogliano, *Making It Up As We Go Along, 103.*

[403] Mercogliano, *Making It Up As We Go Along*, 9.

[404] Mercogliano, *Making It Up As We Go Along, 9.*

[405] The ALPHA Community, "Alpha Admissions Information for Parents For Admissions for Fall 2009".

[406] The ALPHA Community, 2009, "Self-Reflection and Equity Admissions Form".

18: DEMOCRACY STILL TO COME

[407] Dewey, *The School and Society*, 59, 60.

[408] A.S. Neill, *Summerhill*, 30.

[409] The ALPHA Community, 2009.

[410] Jonathan Kozol, "Schools for Survival" in *This magazine is about schools*, Vol. 5 No. 4 (Fall/Winter, 1971): 41.

[411] Hall, Dennis et al., 1968, The Federal Role in Education, para. 8.

[412] Hall, Dennis et al., 1968, Organizing for Learning, para. 3.

[413] Hall, Dennis et al., 1968, School Board Autonomy, para. 1.

[414] Hall, Dennis et al., 1968, The Provincial Department of Education, para 9.

[415] Ontario Ministry of Education, *Provincial Review Report Number 3*, 13.

[416] Martell, "Notes to the Blake St. Community Council", 77-78.

[417] Shuttleworth, "How Can Alternative Education Affect the Mainstream?", 13.

[418] Deborah Meier (2002). *In Schools We Trust*, 4.

[419] Matt Hern, *Field Day, 14.*

[420] Roger I. Simon, "Foreword: Now's the time", in *The erosion of democracy in education*, ed. John Portelli, and Patrick Solomon, (Calgary, Detselig Enterprises Ltd., 2001), 13.

[421] Stephen Lecce and Nancy Naylor, *Guidance for Continuity of Learning*: Memo to Chairs of District School Boards, Directors of Education, School Authorities (Ontario: Ministry of Education, May 31, 2020).

[422] Giroux, Henry. *Schooling and the Struggle for Public Life*, xiii.

[423] D. Jean Clandinin and F. Michael Connelly, *Narrative Inquiry: Experience and Story in Qualitative Research* (San Francisco: Jossey-Bass Inc., 2000), 8.

[424] Summerhill School, n.d. *A. S. Neill*. n.p.

[425] Dewey, *The School and Society*, 94.

[426] A.S. Neill, *Summerhill*, 4.

[427] Snitzer, *Today is for Children*, 13.

[428] Paolo Freire (1994). *A Pedagogy of Hope.*

[429] Shuttleworth, "How Can Alternative Education Affect the Mainstream?", 13.

[430] Hall, Dennis et al, "The Search for Truth in a Democratic Society", para. 2.

[431] Simon, "Foreword: Now's the time", 13.

Made in United States
North Haven, CT
07 May 2023

36348090R00174